A MANUAL OF
MORAL THEOLOGY
FOR ENGLISH-SPEAKING COUNTRIES
BY
REV. THOMAS SLATER, S.J.
VOL II.
FIFTH AND REVISED EDITION

NIHIL OBSTAT:
H. DAVIS, S.J.

IMPRIMI POTEST:
GULIELMUS BODKIN, S.J.

NIHIL OBSTAT:
J. R. McKEE, C.O.,
Censor deputatus.

IMPRIMATUR:
EDM. CAN. SURMONT,
Vicarius generalis.

WESTMONASTERII,
Die 5a Januarii, 1925.

CONTENTS

BOOK I

DUTIES ATTACHED TO PARTICULAR STATES AND OFFICES

PART I. DUTIES OF CERTAIN LAYMEN

	PAGE
Chapter I. Duties of Judges	1
Chapter II. Duties of Advocates	5
Chapter III. Prosecutors, Defendants, and Witnesses	7
Chapter IV. Medical Men	9

PART II. SPECIAL DUTIES OF CLERICS

Chapter I. Holiness of Life	11
Chapter II. Celibacy of the Clergy	13
Chapter III. Clerical Dress	15
Chapter IV. Divine Office	17
Chapter V. Things Forbidden to Clerics	22
Chapter VI. Benefices	25
Chapter VII. Special Duties of Bishops	27
Chapter VIII. Duties of Canons	29
Chapter IX. Duties of Parish Priests	30
Chapter X. Priests without Special Charge	34

PART III. SPECIAL DUTIES OF RELIGIOUS

Chapter I. Nature of the Religious State	37
Chapter II. Entrance into Religion	40
Chapter III. Religious Profession	43
Chapter IV. Religious Poverty	44
Chapter V. Vow of Chastity	49
Chapter VI. Vow of Obedience	51

CONTENTS

BOOK II
THE SACRAMENTS IN GENERAL

		PAGE
Chapter I.	The Nature of a Sacrament	53
Chapter II.	The Matter and Form of the Sacraments	57
Chapter III.	The Minister of the Sacraments	61
Section I.	The Attention and Intention of the Minister	61
Section II.	The Faith and Holiness of the Minister	64
Section III.	The Duty of Administering the Sacraments	66
Section IV.	The Duty of Refusing the Sacraments to the Unworthy	67
Chapter IV.	The Recipient of the Sacraments	71

BOOK III
BAPTISM

Chapter I.	The Nature of Baptism	75
Chapter II.	The Matter and Form of Baptism	77
Chapter III.	The Minister of Baptism	78
Chapter IV.	The Sponsors	81
Chapter V.	Who May be Baptized	83

BOOK IV
CONFIRMATION

Chapter I.	The Matter of Confirmation	87
Chapter II.	The Minister of Confirmation	89
Chapter III.	The Subject of Confirmation	90

BOOK V
THE HOLY EUCHARIST

PART I. THE SACRAMENT OF THE EUCHARIST

Chapter I.	The Nature and Effects of the Eucharist	91
Chapter II.	The Matter and Form of the Eucharist	93
Chapter III.	The Minister of the Eucharist	96
Chapter IV.	The Reservation of the Eucharist	98
Chapter V.	The Subject of the Eucharist	100
Article I.	The Necessity of the Eucharist	100
Article II.	The Dispositions Requisite for the Reception of the Eucharist	102
Section I.	The Dispositions of the Soul	102
Section II.	The Dispositions of the Body	103

CONTENTS

Part II. The Eucharist as a Sacrifice

		PAGE
Chapter I.	The Nature of the Sacrifice of the Mass	106
Chapter II.	The Application of Mass	110
Chapter III.	The Obligation of Applying Mass	112
Chapter IV.	The Time for Saying Mass	117
Chapter V.	Where Mass may be Said	119
Chapter VI.	Requisites for Saying Mass	121
Chapter VII.	The Rubrics of the Missal	122

BOOK VI

THE SACRAMENT OF PENANCE

Chapter I.	The Nature of Penance	125
Chapter II.	The Matter of Penance	128
Chapter III.	On Contrition	132
Section I.	The Nature of Contrition	132
Section II.	The Purpose of Amendment	136
Chapter IV.	Confession	138
Chapter V.	Satisfaction	144
Chapter VI.	The Form of Penance	147
Chapter VII.	The Minister of Penance	149
Chapter VIII.	Jurisdiction of the Minister of Penance	150
Chapter IX.	The Confessors of Religious	153
Chapter X.	Reserved Cases	156
Chapter XI.	De Abusu Sacramenti Poenitentiae	161
Chapter XII.	The Duties of Confessors in the Confessional	165
Section I.	The Confessor as Spiritual Father	165
Section II.	The Confessor as Physician of Souls	166
Section III.	The Confessor as Counsellor	168
Section IV.	The Confessor as Judge	170
Chapter XIII.	Mistakes made in Hearing Confessions	172
Chapter XIV.	The Seal of Confession	174

BOOK VII

EXTREME UNCTION

Chapter I.	The Nature of Extreme Unction	179
Chapter II.	The Minister of Extreme Unction	181
Chapter III.	The Recipient of Extreme Unction	182

CONTENTS

BOOK VIII

THE SACRAMENT OF ORDERS

		PAGE
Chapter I.	The Nature of Orders	183
Chapter II.	The Minister of Orders	185
Chapter III.	The Subject of Orders	186

BOOK IX

MARRIAGE

Chapter I.	Betrothal	189
Chapter II.	The Effects of Betrothal	192
Chapter III.	Dissolution of Betrothal	194
Chapter IV.	Banns of Marriage	197
Chapter V.	The Marriage Contract	200
Chapter VI.	Minister, Matter, and Form of Matrimony	204
Chapter VII.	The Properties of Marriage	206
Chapter VIII.	The Impediments of Marriage in General	210
Chapter IX.	The Prohibitory Impediments	212
Chapter X.	The Diriment Impediments	215
Article I.	Impotence	215
Article II.	Age	216
Article III.	Previous Marriage	216
Article IV.	Consanguinity	218
Article V.	Affinity	220
Article VI.	Spiritual Relationship	221
Article VII.	Adoption	221
Article VIII.	Public Propriety	222
Article IX.	Solemn Vows and Sacred Orders	222
Article X.	Difference of Religion	223
Section I.	Mixed Marriages	224
Section II.	Difference of Religion	225
Article XI.	Crime	226
Section I.	Adultery with Promise of Marriage	226
Section II.	Murder of a Consort	227
Section III.	Adultery and Murder	228
Article XII.	Error, Slavery, Imbecility	228
Article XIII.	Violence and Fear	229
Article XIV.	Abduction	231
Article XV.	Clandestinity	232
Chapter XI.	Doubtful Impediments	236
Chapter XII.	Dispensations from Diriment Impediments	238
Chapter XIII.	Revalidation of Marriage	246
Chapter XIV.	De Debito Conjugali	248

CONTENTS

BOOK X
CENSURES

PART I. CENSURES IN GENERAL

	PAGE
Chapter I. The Nature of an Ecclesiastical Censure	253
Chapter II. Absolution of Censures	257

PART II. DIFFERENT KINDS OF CENSURES

Chapter I. Excommunication	259
Chapter II. Suspension	262
Chapter III. Interdict	264
Chapter IV. Ecclesiastical Penalties	266

PART III. SPECIAL CENSURES

Chapter I. Special Excommunications	268
Chapter II. Special Suspensions	283
Chapter III. Special Interdicts	285

BOOK XI
IRREGULARITIES

Chapter I. Irregularity in General	287
Chapter II. Irregularities from Defect	289
Chapter III Irregularities arising from Crime	291
Chapter IV. Removal of Irregularities	292

BOOK XII
INDULGENCES

Chapter I. The Nature of an Indulgence	293
Chapter II. Conditions Required for Gaining Indulgences	296
Chapter III. The Jubilee	301

APPENDIX

A Short History of Moral Theology	305
Bibliography	339

INDEX

Alphabetical Index to Volumes I and II	343

BOOK I

ON THE DUTIES ATTACHED TO PARTICULAR STATES AND OFFICES

In the preceding volume we have treated of the duties which are incumbent on all men, or at any rate on all Catholics, by the natural, divine, and ecclesiastical law. Some special duties, however, arise from the nature of the state in which one is placed or of the office which one holds. Thus a judge or a doctor has as such certain special obligations as well as the cleric or the religious. The confessor should know all the obligations of his penitents, and so moral theologians usually treat in this place of the special duties of judges, doctors, clerics, and religious. We will follow their example in this Book and treat in the first part of the special obligations of certain laymen, in the second of those of clerics, and finally of those of religious.

Part I

ON THE DUTIES OF CERTAIN LAYMEN

Chapter I

ON THE DUTIES OF JUDGES

1. A JUDGE is defined to be a public person appointed by lawful authority to apply the laws to the settling of disputes between litigants and to the punishment of criminals.

He is said to be a public person because he is appointed by public authority, not chosen like an arbitrator by the litigants themselves, and, moreover, he is guided in his official capacity not by his private knowledge and ideas but by the evidence given in the case and by the laws which he administers. Case law, or judge-made law, in English jurisprudence, is no exception to this rule, for it is but the authentic interpretation and application of the common and statute law to concrete cases made in court by the judges of the superior courts.

A cause in which the private rights of the litigants are to be adjudicated upon is called a civil case or action; if the cause is one in which an offender is tried for the commission of a crime it is called a criminal case or action.

2. By his very position and the nature of his office a judge is bound to pass a just sentence according to law in the cases brought before him, and so he must possess the requisite qualifications for this and set about it in the right manner. He must have a competent knowledge of the law which is to be his guide and which he is called upon to apply, and he must use at least ordinary diligence to get at the merits of the case before him. He must not allow his judgement to be influenced by such improper motives as fear or favour; his sentence must be dictated by a sense of even-handed justice. He must observe the rules of judicial procedure applicable to the case, and he must have the requisite authority or jurisdiction for dealing with it.

If in any of these points the judge is culpably at fault, he sins against justice and is bound to make good the damage which he causes. Moreover, inasmuch as judges ordinarily take an oath of office, he will also sin against the sanctity of his oath. A judge who should allow himself to be bribed to give an unjust sentence would not only be bound in conscience to repair the injustice done, but he would be liable to severe punishment for his offence. Even if he were to take a bribe for delivering a just sentence, he is bound in conscience to restore what he received. For, as his office binds him in justice to give sentence according to the merits of the case, such a service is no ground for special reward or payment, nor a just title for retaining a special reward or payment if he has received any.

3. The judge, as we have seen, must pass sentence according to the evidence before the court, not according to his own private knowledge or views. He may know privately that an accused man is guilty, but he must not condemn him unless his guilt has been proved by the evidence. But what if the judge knows for certain that an accused man is innocent, and yet, according to the evidence available, he has been proved guilty? In such a case as this the judge must, of course, use all the means in his power to bring out the innocence of the accused party, or remit the case to another court. But supposing that he has done all in his power to avoid condemning the innocent man, and nevertheless the jury have found him guilty, and by law it only remains for the judge to pass

sentence according to the verdict. Is he allowed to do so? This question was disputed among theologians. Some, with St Thomas, taught that he might condemn the innocent man, for the witnesses were then guilty of injustice, not the judge, who did his duty in passing sentence according to law. Others denied that this is lawful, for to condemn the innocent, especially if there is question of a death sentence, is intrinsically wrong. Others distinguished, and taught that it is indeed unlawful to condemn an innocent man to death even when, by judicial process, he has been proved to all appearances guilty, but that when there is question of a fine or imprisonment which may be suffered without sin, the judge may pass sentence according to the law, for this is for the public good. Practically, therefore, according to the principles of English jurisprudence the judge may lawfully pass sentence even of death in such a case, but he is bound afterward, by making representations to the proper authority, to do what he can to clear the innocent party.

When the evidence in a criminal trial is not conclusive, the defendant must not be condemned, for a man is presumed to be innocent until he has been proved conclusively to be guilty.

In a civil action, when the rights of the parties are not certain, but only probable, the judge is bound to adjudicate in favour of him who has the more probable right, taking into account possession and all the other circumstances in the case. If there is equal probability on either side, the parties should come to a compromise, or, as some hold, the judge may decide in favour of either party.

4. The judge is bound to pass sentence according to law, for this is presumed to be just. It may, however, happen that particular laws are unjust, as when the seal of confession is not respected or divorce is permitted. May a Catholic judge pass sentence in accordance with such laws as these?

The judge may sometimes obtain permission to pass sentence according to a law which is unjust merely because it is against the laws and rights of the Church. In order to make the position of Catholic judges tenable the Church will sometimes cede her rights in such cases or grant jurisdiction to try a case which of itself belongs to the ecclesiastical courts. Thus Cardinal Gasparri deduces from a decree of the Holy Office, December 19, 1860, that jurisdiction has been granted to judges in England to try cases where there is question of judicial separation of married people.[1]

[1] Gasparri, *De Matrim.* 2, n. 1165.

If the law commands what is contrary to the natural or divine law—as, for example, to give evidence as to what has been declared in confession—it is intrinsically wrong to obey such a law, and no Catholic judge may apply it.

If the unjust law only imposes a fine or imprisonment, some theologians maintain that even then it may not be applied by a Catholic judge. Others, however, hold that for grave reason—as, for example, if no Catholic could otherwise accept the office of judge—sentence may be passed according to such a law. The person unjustly condemned must patiently submit for the public good, especially as he would not escape even if Catholic judges refused to execute the law.

The unjust sentence of a judge imposes no obligation in conscience, and of course the aggrieved party may have recourse to all available remedies which the law allows for redress. If none is available the public good will usually require patient submission to the wrong. If there is a doubt about the justice of a sentence, presumption favours the judge, and obedience must be yielded, as in the case of a just sentence, which has the force of the law which it applies.

5. What has been said concerning the moral obligations of judges is applicable in due proportion to those who have similar functions, such as arbitrators, referees, and jurymen. An arbitrator differs from a judge in that he is chosen by the parties to the dispute to settle their claims. If the submission to arbitration and the decision of the arbitrator be in writing, the sentence is final, and will be upheld by English courts unless it is evidently corrupt or obtained by unlawful means.[1]

Referees are officials or experts to whom the court entrusts some special question for inquiry or decision, and sometimes the cause itself, if it be complicated and not suitable for trial in the ordinary way. They are bound to act according to the terms of their commission and the rules drawn up for their guidance. The report or award of a referee, unless set aside by the court, has the force of a jury's verdict.

A jury is a body of men selected and sworn to inquire into certain matters of fact, and to declare the truth upon evidence to be laid before them. They are therefore bound to form the best judgement in their power as to the facts of the case laid before them, and truthfully and fearlessly to give their verdict. If any one of them has any private knowledge of the facts of the case, he is not precluded from communicating it to the others, and he should do this if justice or charity require it.

[1] *Cf.* Can. 1930.

CHAPTER II
ON THE DUTIES OF ADVOCATES

1. AN advocate is one who undertakes to assist litigants by his advice and help and by pleading their case before the judge. For the purposes of moral theology we may neglect the technical differences between barristers and solicitors in English law.

As the advocate acts in the name of his client he may in general do what his client is allowed to do, and he must not do what it would be wrong for his client to do. He may not undertake a cause which is manifestly unjust; otherwise he will be guilty of sin, and bound to make restitution for all the damage that he causes. If in the course of the trial it becomes manifest that his client's cause is a bad one, he must inform his client of the fact and refuse to proceed with the case. However, it is not necessary that the advocate should be certain that his client is right; it will be sufficient if his cause is probably just, for it may be expected that the doubtful rights of the parties will become clear in the course of the trial. In a criminal action the advocate may always defend the accused by lawful means whether he be guilty or not. If he is guilty, the defence of his advocate cannot do any serious harm, and will at least help toward the merciful administration of justice. The prosecution of an accused person may not be undertaken unless his guilt is practically certain, for otherwise there will be danger of injuring the character of an innocent person and of exposing him to vexation without just cause.

From the decree of the Holy Office, December 19, 1860, in answer to the Bishop of Southwark, it is clear that in England an advocate may undertake a case where there is question of judicial separation between husband and wife. Even in an action for divorce in a civil court he may defend the action against the plaintiff. If the marriage has already been pronounced null and void by competent ecclesiastical authority, a Catholic advocate may impugn its validity in the civil courts. Moreover, for just reason, as, for example, to obtain a variation in the marriage settlement, or to prevent the necessity of having to maintain a bastard child, a Catholic lawyer may petition for a divorce in the civil court, not with the intention of enabling his client to marry again while his spouse is still living, but with a view to obtaining the civil effects of divorce in the civil tribunal. This opinion at any rate is defended as probable by many good theologians. The reason is because marriage is neither contracted nor dissolved before the civil authority; in the formalities prescribed for marriage by civil law there is only question of the civil authority taking cognizance of who are married, and of the civil effects which flow therefrom.

2. With reference to the duties of the advocate toward his client, he must, of course, have the requisite knowledge and skill to undertake the case according to the reasonable expectations of his client, and he must exercise due care and diligence in the execution of the duty which he has undertaken. If in these respects he is culpably negligent, he will be guilty of injustice and bound to make restitution for the harm he does. Furthermore, if his client has no case, and no chance of success in the suit, the advocate must make this known to him; he must avoid useless delays, keep the strictest faith with his client, and use only just means to gain his cause.

English law will not enable a barrister to institute legal proceedings for the recovery of his honorarium if it is withheld. This, however, does not prevent the obligations of a contract existing between an advocate and his client, so that as the former is bound in justice to do his part for the latter, so is the client bound in justice to recompense his lawyer according to the terms which were explicitly or implicitly agreed upon. With regard to solicitors the law sufficiently provides against extortion in the matter of fees.

By the general law of charity a lawyer should be prepared to give his assistance for the love of God to the poor who cannot pay the usual fees. Indeed, if an accused person has no one to defend him, the judge will usually request someone to undertake the office.

English solicitors frequently fulfil the functions of notaries public, and as such receive all acts and contracts which must or are wished to be clothed with an authentic form, confer on such acts the required authenticity, establish their date, and prepare and attest instruments going abroad.

CHAPTER III

ON PROSECUTORS, DEFENDANTS, AND WITNESSES

1. THERE are other persons connected with the administration of justice besides judges and lawyers, and they have special moral obligations of their own. A word must be said about the moral duties of prosecutors, defendants, and witnesses. By canon law the accusation of delinquents in an ecclesiastical criminal trial is reserved to the Promotor of Justice, but as a general rule anyone who has full use of his senses may prosecute according to English law. Nobody should undertake a prosecution when greater evil than good would follow from it, or when there is not moral certainty as to the guilt of the accused. Otherwise it may be done for the sake of the public good, and there may be an obligation to do it, as when one's office compels one to undertake the task, or the defence of the innocent or the public good require it, or a precept of obedience command it. Thus by ecclesiastical law heretics and priests guilty of solicitation in the sacred tribunal are to be denounced to the Ordinary.

2. The defendant in a criminal trial is not himself subjected to examination according to English law, unless he offers himself voluntarily to give evidence, and then he may be examined like a witness. In canon law the accused is examined, and the question arises whether he is bound to tell the truth. According to Canon 1743: " The parties are bound to answer the judge when he interrogates them legitimately, and to tell the truth unless there is question of a crime committed by themselves."

The defendant may in self-defence make known the secret crime of a witness against him, if it really conduces to his defence; but of course he may never impute false crimes to anybody. A criminal may not defend himself against lawful arrest, for that would be to resist lawful authority, but he is not compelled to deliver himself up to justice, and it is not a sin to escape from justice if he can do so without violence. The law prescribes that he shall be kept in durance, not that he shall voluntarily remain in custody. A criminal lawfully condemned to death is not obliged to save his life by escape or other means if he can do so; he should submit to the execution of the sentence passed upon him, and may do so meritoriously.

3. Charity or obedience may impose an obligation to give evidence in a court of justice. If serious harm can be prevented by offering one's self as a witness, there will as a rule be an obligation to do so, and obedience imposes the obligation when one is summoned by lawful authority.

A witness is bound by his oath and by obedience due to lawful authority to tell the truth in answer to the questions lawfully put to him. How far he is privileged when examined concerning what he knows under secret, we saw when treating of the Eighth Commandment of the Decalogue. He is not bound to incriminate himself, nor, of course, may the seal of confession ever be broken (*cf.* Can. 1755).

The canon law laid it down that two witnesses of unsuspected character were necessary and sufficient evidence of any fact alleged in a court of justice. A solitary witness was not usually sufficient or admissible evidence of a crime, and in keeping with this the theologians decided that a solitary witness should not declare what he knew of a crime, inasmuch as he was not lawfully interrogated. English law, however, with most modern systems, admits one witness, if credible, as sufficient evidence of a fact, and so as a rule there will be an obligation on such a one of answering according to his knowledge when questioned lawfully in a court of justice (*cf.* Can. 1791).

CHAPTER IV

ON THE DUTIES OF MEDICAL MEN

1. A DOCTOR who holds himself out as ready to undertake the care of the sick must have competent knowledge of his profession and must exercise his office at least with ordinary care and diligence; otherwise he will sin against justice and charity in exposing himself to the risk of seriously injuring his neighbour. Unless he is bound by some special agreement he is not ordinarily obliged to undertake any particular case, for there are usually others who are willing and able to give the necessary assistance to the sick. Even in time of pestilence he will not commit sin if he leave the neighbourhood, unless he is bound to remain by some special contract. Of course, one who acted thus would show a mean spirit, and would be justly reprobated.

2. He should not make exorbitant charges for his services, nor multiply visits uselessly and thus increase his fees, nor call in other doctors without necessity. On the other hand, even at his own serious inconvenience, he should visit a patient whose case he has undertaken when called as far as is reasonable, and he should be ready to call in other doctors for consultation when necessary or when he is asked to do so. He is sometimes bound by the general law of charity to give his assistance gratis to the poor who cannot afford to pay the usual fees.

3. He may not neglect safer remedies in order to try those which are less safe, but there is nothing to prevent him from prescribing what will probably do good if it is certain that it will not do harm. In a desperate case, with the consent of the sick person and of his relations, he may make use of what will probably do good though it may also probably do harm, provided that there is nothing better to be done in the circumstances. It is altogether wrong to make experiments with doubtful remedies or operations on living human beings, *fiat experimentum in corpore vili.*

What has been said of craniotomy and other similar operations, the use of morphia, hypnotism, and other dangerous remedies, are questions which have been treated elsewhere.

4. When the patient is in danger of death, the doctor is bound out of charity to warn him or those who attend on him of his danger, in order that he may make all necessary preparations for death if it should come about.

A medical man should know how to administer baptism in case of necessity (Can. 743).

Part II

ON THE SPECIAL DUTIES OF CLERICS

CHAPTER I

ON HOLINESS OF LIFE

1. THE sacredness of the duties which a cleric has to perform, and especially the service of the altar, require in him an internal holiness so that he may perform his duties worthily. " Let them therefore be holy, because I also am holy, the Lord, who sanctify them."[1] This holiness must show itself in the exercise of all Christian virtues so that the cleric may be an example to those whom he is called upon to instruct and guide on the way to heaven. As the Council of Trent said: " There is nothing which is so constant a lesson in piety and the worship of God as the life and example of those who have dedicated themselves to the divine service. For since they have been taken from worldly affairs and placed in a higher position, the faithful look upon them as models for their imitation. And so it becomes the clergy who have been set aside for the service of God so to order their lives and morals that in their dress, demeanour, walk, speech, and everything about them, nothing may be seen but what is serious, modest, and breathes the religious spirit. Let them avoid even slight defects, which in them would not be slight, so that their actions may win the veneration of all."[2] This holiness of life is very frequently inculcated on the clergy in the councils and synods.[3]

Their occupations, if worthily performed, are means of sanctifying them and uniting them with God, and, moreover, the Church does what she can to secure the same end by prescribing the daily recitation of the divine office, and spiritual retreats at stated times (Can. 125, 126).

2. Great personal sanctity becomes the cleric, and is required if he is to perform his duties worthily. It is a disputed question among theologians whether the inferior clergy are as such in a state of perfection. It is allowed by all that bishops

---

[1] Lev. xxi 8.   [2] Sess. 22, c. 1, de Ref. *Cf.* Can. 124.
[3] 1 West., d. 24; 4 West., d. 12.

are in the state of practising perfection, inasmuch as they are in a permanent condition of life which is devoted to procuring the sanctification of those committed to their charge. Religious, too, by their vows assume the obligation of aiming at perfection, and in religious life find the means of acquiring it. Both bishops and religious, then, are in the state of perfection. St Thomas and many other theologians deny that the secular clergy inferior to bishops are in the state of perfection, properly so called. The chief reason is because their condition of life has not the permanence required for a state in the technical sense, and although they are occupied in labouring for the sanctification of others, like bishops, yet they do this rather as officials and helpers of bishops, not entirely in their own name and of their own authority. As the learned Suarez admits, the controversy is rather about words than things, and we may accept his conclusion that because the higher secular clergy are bound by vow to continence, and partake also in the duties of bishops, they may be said to be in an inchoate state of acquiring and practising perfection.[1]

[1] Suarez, *De Rel.* 3, lib. 1, c. 17.

CHAPTER II

THE CELIBACY OF THE CLERGY

1. THE celibacy of the clergy rests on a positive enactment of ecclesiastical law which, nevertheless, supposes the doctrine of Christ and his Apostles about the excellence of virginity and its superiority to marriage. From the first ages of the Church it was felt that there was an incongruity between the Christian priesthood, with its duties of offering up the eucharistic sacrifice, and of whole-hearted devotion to the service of God, and the use of marriage. The example of our Lord and the counsels of St Paul told powerfully in the same direction. Already in the fourth century the law of celibacy existed which was formulated by Leo the Great in his letter to Anastasius written about the middle of the fourth century: " Although," he says, " those who are not clerics may freely give themselves to marriage and the procreation of children, yet for the exhibiting of perfect chastity marriage is not allowed even to subdeacons, so that those who have wives should be as those who have them not, and those who have them not should remain single." All the more stringently, he goes on to say, does the same law bind the higher clergy, deacons, priests, and bishops. This law was frequently inculcated by subsequent Popes, re-enacted in many ecclesiastical synods, and at latest in the Second Council of the Lateran (1139) marriage of the higher clergy was prohibited under pain of nullity. By ecclesiastical law, then, clerics in sacred orders are bound to observe perfect chastity, and marriage attempted by them is null and void.[1] This law is known to all who aspire to sacred orders, and so those who choose the clerical state voluntarily embrace the law of continence. Indeed, a vow of perfect chastity is by ecclesiastical usage annexed to the reception of sacred orders, so that all who are ordained subdeacons, by the very fact of receiving ordination, take a solemn vow of chastity. The discipline of the Eastern Church is somewhat milder. Clerics belonging thereto may marry before the reception of sacred orders, and if they have already done this

[1] Can. 132, 1072.

they may keep their wives, except bishops. Even in the East clerics in sacred orders cannot contract a valid marriage.

2. There is a dispute among theologians as to whether the obligation of celibacy, which binds clerics in sacred orders, should be ascribed immediately to ecclesiastical law or immediately to a vow of chastity tacitly taken when sacred orders are received according to the precept of the Church. The question is not of great practical importance, for in any case the obligation of celibacy is derived ultimately from ecclesiastical law, which binds all clerics in sacred orders to the observance of perfect chastity. The violation of such a law, at any rate by external act, is not morally different from a violation of a vow of chastity. The more common and more probable opinion is that the obligation of celibacy is derived immediately from a vow of chastity which every subdeacon takes tacitly according to the precept of the Church when he receives the first of the sacred orders. Tacit profession even of the essential vows of religion was admitted in certain cases until it was altogether abrogated by a decree of Pius IX dated June 12, 1858. Boniface VIII decided that the vow of chastity thus tacitly taken by subdeacons is solemn, and that it annuls subsequent marriage if attempted.

A man who was married but whose wife is dead may be promoted to sacred orders. "Men who have a wife" are prohibited from receiving orders according to Canon 987, 2; and Canon 132, sec. 3, lays down that a married man who, without a dispensation from the Holy See has received holy orders even in good faith is prohibited from the exercise of the same.

CHAPTER III

THE CLERICAL DRESS

1. EVER since about the sixth century clerics have had a special dress of their own to distinguish them from laymen. It is their uniform, like that of soldiers or sailors, and is a perpetual reminder to them that they should always conduct themselves as becomes their profession. At first the clerical dress was introduced by custom, and then sanctioned by positive law. On this point the Council of Trent (sess. 14, c. 6, de Ref.), after saying that although the habit does not make the monk, yet clerics must always wear the dress suited to their order, so that by the decency of their dress they may make manifest the goodness of their moral character, goes on to prescribe under pain of suspension that all in sacred orders and beneficed clerics should wear the clerical dress suited to their order and dignity, according to the ordinance and command of their bishop. " Let all clerics wear a decent ecclesiastical dress according to the lawful customs of the place and the precepts of the local Ordinary " (Can. 136).

The common law of the Church therefore imposes on all the clergy the obligation of wearing the clerical dress, and it leaves to bishops the task of making further regulations on the point suitable to the circumstances of the country. In England, the Fourth Synod of Westminster (d. 11, nn. 12-14) decreed that the Roman collar was always to be worn, that the dress must be of black or dark material, and that in the house or church the cassock should be worn. The Third Plenary Council of Baltimore (n. 77) made the same regulations for the United States, except that the wearing of the cassock in the house or in the church is prescribed, not merely declared to be especially becoming.

2. The clerical tonsure is also prescribed by the common law of the Church, but it has not been reintroduced into England since the Reformation, nor is it in use in the United States. However, the obligation of not wearing hair on the face is laid down in the Fourth Synod of Westminster (*loc. cit.*). On this point Canon 136 prescribes:

" Let them wear the tonsure or clerical crown, unless this

be against the received manners of the people, and let them use a simple and ordinary care of the hair."

All religious are bound by these and similar obligations of clerics according to Canon 592.

3. These laws of themselves bind under pain of mortal sin which, however, would not be committed if there were good cause for doing what they forbid, nor if they were neglected without contempt or grave scandal for a short time. Theologians consider that the clerical dress would have to be neglected for more than three or four days in order to sin grievously, and a much longer time would be required for a grave violation of the law concerning tonsure. Venial sin, of course, is committed by breaking the law without legitimate excuse even for a short time.

CHAPTER IV

THE DIVINE OFFICE

1. ALL who are in sacred orders, all beneficed clergy, and all religious orders which have solemn vows and keep choir, are bound every day to recite the divine office, otherwise called the canonical Hours, or the breviary. This obligation is now enforced by positive ecclesiastical law in Canons 135, 1475 (sec. 1), 610, 413.

The obligation of saying the office begins for secular clerics with the reception of the subdiaconate, or the lawful and full possession of their benefice. The obligation as it affects religious is primarily incumbent on the superior, whose duty it is to provide for the saying or singing of the divine office under pain of grave sin. Each religious is bound to assist in choir unless lawfully excused, and if one who is solemnly professed is absent he must recite the office in private. Religious under simple vows should be present in choir, but if they failed to be present they are not obliged to say the office in private, unless, of course, they be in sacred orders.

2. The obligation of saying the divine office for all who are bound by it is grave, so that a mortal sin is committed by wilfully and without lawful excuse omitting it or any considerable portion of it. According to theologians, one of the little Hours or any portion of the same length is to be reckoned considerable, so that its culpable omission will be a grave sin. Anything less than this will be only venial. A beneficed cleric not only sins by neglecting his office, but he loses his right to a proportional amount of the fruits of his benefice, and if he has already received that amount he must restore it to the fabric of the church or to the diocesan seminary, or give it to the poor (Can. 1475, sec. 2).

When two or more say the office together, the psalms may be said in alternate verses, one side listening while the other is reciting its verse. The rest listen while the lessons are said or sung by those appointed to the task.

3. Although the canonical Hours as said at different periods and in different churches have always been much the same in substance, yet in many details there has been considerable

variety. Pope Pius V desired to introduce greater uniformity in the method of saying the divine office, and for this purpose he issued the Roman Breviary, and made its use obligatory on all who were bound to the office under pain of not satisfying their obligation. He abolished the use of other breviaries with the exception of such as dated back more than two hundred years. The divine office, therefore, must be recited according to the form of the Roman Breviary, and in Latin, the liturgical language of the Church.

Offices proper to particular countries, dioceses, and religious orders, are allowed to be inserted in the breviary and said only by the authority of the Apostolic See, and when a proper office has been thus granted it becomes obligatory on the grantees unless it was expressly conceded as permissive.

Pius V took away the obligation, which existed according to the rubrics of the breviary, of reciting the Little Office of the Blessed Virgin, the penitential and gradual psalms, and the Office of the Dead; but though he took away the obligation, still he exhorted those bound to the divine office to recite them, and granted indulgences to such as followed his exhortation. The recitation of the Litany of the Saints on the feast of St Mark, and on the Rogation Days, forms part of the office.

4. The office to be said on any particular day is indicated in the calendar drawn up and approved by the proper authority. It is a matter of obligation under pain of venial sin to adhere to the calendar, even if it seem to be wrong, unless it is manifestly against the rubrics or decrees of the Sacred Congregation of Rites. A reasonable cause, however, even though it be not a very grave one, will suffice to excuse the substitution of one office for another. If a wrong office has been said by mistake or inadvertence, there is no obligation to say the correct one; but if this is notably longer, some portion should be said to make up the difference.

The calendar to be followed is that of the church, diocese, or religious order to which one belongs. If absent from one's place of domicile for a time, the general rule is that one's own calendar should be followed; but in the case of regulars who recite the office in choir, a regular living for a time in another monastery should conform to the calendar of the place where he resides.

5. In each day's office the order of the Hours should be observed at any rate under pain of venial sin. But here also any reasonable cause of some weight will excuse the saying of the Hours out of their proper order. If the time has arrived

for anticipating Matins and Lauds for the next day, these may be said without any special reason even though the office of the day has not yet been finished, for each day's office is independent of any other.

6. The divine office is a vocal prayer imposed on the clergy by the Church. It is not sufficient to run over it with the eyes or mentally; the words must be uttered and formed without mutilation by the lips, though it is not necessary to produce an audible sound. The different Hours must be said without interruption as one continuous prayer under pain of venial sin, from which any reasonable cause will excuse. The recitation may be interrupted between the several Hours, between Matins and Lauds, and for the space of a few hours even between the Nocturns of Matins. Provided that the whole office be said within the natural or ecclesiastical day, whatever interruptions may have taken place, the obligation will be substantially fulfilled, and when an interruption has been made within an Hour, or even in the middle of a psalm or lesson, there is no obligation to repeat what has already been said.

7. As was said above, the divine office is the task of the day, and provided that the whole of it is said within the day, reckoning from midnight to midnight, the cleric will have fulfilled his duty substantially so as to be excused at least from mortal sin. The rubrics, however, which in this matter bind under venial sin, assign certain times of the day for the saying of the Office. Matins and Lauds should be said before Mass, Prime and Terce should be said before midday, Sext and None are said in the interval between midday and Vespers, Vespers and Compline are said when the sun is midway between the zenith and sunset. All the little Hours may be said before midday, and during Lent, beginning with the first Sunday, Vespers are also said before midday.

Matins and Lauds of the following day may be anticipated on the previous evening. The normal time for anticipating begins with the hour of Vespers, but a special privilege is often granted by which Matins and Lauds of the following day may be begun at 2 p.m. throughout the year. Indeed, there does not seem to be any necessity for a special grant, for a custom has been introduced, by the very common practice of good priests, of anticipating throughout the year after two o'clock. A cleric may safely follow this custom.

Permission to anticipate is a privilege which no one is bound to use; the obligation of the day's office only begins at twelve o'clock.

The breviary contains rubrics directing that certain prayers be said on bended knee; these rubrics, however, do not bind when office is said privately out of choir. In private the office may be said in any place or in any position that is compatible with the due reverence to God which should be shown in prayer.

8. The obligation of saying the breviary is imposed by ecclesiastical precept, and the question arises what internal dispositions are necessary while reciting the office in order to satisfy the positive precept of the Church. Does one who is voluntarily distracted while saying the office satisfy his obligation, or must he repeat what he said with voluntary distractions? It is not a question of what is required that prayer may be pleasing to God—voluntary distractions while praying are certainly venial sins—but the question is, what sort of attention is required by the law of the Church under pain of not fulfilling the obligation imposed by the law?

Attention, which is an act of the mind adverting to what is being done, must be distinguished from intention, which is the will to do something. At least, a virtual intention to say the office is required that the act may be voluntary, such as the law prescribes. Theologians distinguish between internal and external attention. The former consists in directing the mind to God, or in thinking of the sense of the words uttered, or in being careful to pronounce them correctly, and it is certain that any of these forms of internal attention is sufficient to satisfy the precept. External attention means the abstaining while engaged in prayer from any external occupation which is incompatible with internal attention. Thus one who curiously examines a painting while praying, or intently listens to what someone is saying, has not external attention.

It is a disputed point among theologians whether this external attention is sufficient in order to satisfy the precept of saying the office, or whether there must be in addition internal attention. In other words, they dispute whether one who is voluntarily distracted but apparently devout while saying the breviary satisfies the law, or whether he must repeat what he has said with wilful distractions.

Although, of course, all should strive after internal attention, and sin is committed if voluntary distractions are admitted while praying, yet it is probable that external attention is sufficient to satisfy the positive law of the Church. For the Church does indeed prescribe prayer, but there is prayer in a real sense when one says the breviary with the intention of fulfilling his obligation, and with decorum and a devout demeanour, even though he is thinking of something else the while. If voluntary distractions destroy the essence of prayer, involuntary distractions will do so likewise, and yet it is impossible to avoid involuntary distractions altogether. This milder opinion is especially of use in order to calm scrupulous and anxious souls.[1]

9. As the obligation of saying the divine office arises from positive law, it does not bind when it would entail serious inconvenience. On this ground one who is sick, or who cannot say his office without causing a serious headache, is excused. Moreover, other occupations, undertaken for the good of our neighbour and such as cannot be neglected without his loss, will be a sufficient excuse for omitting the office, when both duties cannot be fulfilled. And so missionaries, who are all day long occupied in hearing confessions and preaching, are excused from the office which would interfere with their work. Even when there is not a sufficient cause to excuse of itself from the law, a dispensation may be lawfully obtained from the competent authority, if there be good cause for it. The Pope can grant a dispensation to any cleric, a bishop can dispense in particular cases with those of his diocese, and a regular prelate has similar powers for his own subjects. Wider powers are also granted as a special privilege by the Holy See. The faculty of saying fifteen decades of the rosary instead of the office is frequently granted to missioners who are lawfully prevented from saying the office. The meaning of which is that there must be some difficulty in getting in the office, but it need not be so great as would of itself excuse altogether from the obligation. Inasmuch as the office is composed of several portions which are usually said separately, there will be an obligation to say any such portion if it can be done without serious inconvenience, even though it be impossible to say the whole.

[1] Lugo, *De Eucharist.* 22, n. 25.

CHAPTER V
ON THINGS FORBIDDEN TO CLERICS

1. IN general, clerics are forbidden to do anything which is unbecoming their state of life or which interferes with the due discharge of their duties—" No man being a soldier to God entangleth himself with secular businesses," says St Paul (2 Tim. ii 4). They are expressly forbidden to indulge in games of chance for money, to carry arms unless there is good reason to fear attack, to hunt with hounds, to enter inns and similar places without necessity or some good reason approved of by the Ordinary of the place (Can. 138).

Similarly, they are forbidden to practise medicine or surgery without leave of the Holy See, to act as public notaries, except in the ecclesiastical court, to hold public offices which involve the exercise of lay jurisdiction or administration.

2. Without leave of their own Ordinary they should not undertake the agency for property belonging to laymen, nor secular offices which entail the duty of rendering accounts; they should not exercise the office of procurator or advocate except in the ecclesiastical court, or when a cause of their own or of their church is being tried in the civil court; they should take no part, not even as witnesses, without necessity in a lay criminal trial.

Clerics are forbidden to go surety even with their own property without consulting the local Ordinary.

3. They are forbidden to offer themselves for the post of Members of Parliament or to accept it without leave of their own Ordinary and of the Ordinary of the place where the election is held (Can. 137, 139).

4. Clerics are forbidden to retain in their houses or in any way to be familiar with women about whom any suspicion can arise.

They may live under the same roof only with those women of whom natural ties allow no suspicion to be entertained, such as mother, sister, aunt, and so forth, or whose good character and mature age make them free from all suspicion.

The judgement as to whether the retaining or being intimate with women, even with those on whom suspicion does not usually fall, can in any particular case create scandal or be a danger to morals, belongs to the Ordinary of the place, whose duty it is to forbid such retaining or intimacy to clerics (Can. 133; 4 West., d. 11, n. 3).

5. Canon 140 forbids clerics to be present at spectacles, dances, and pageants which do not become them, or when their presence would cause scandal, especially in public theatres.

"The word *spectacula*," says Fr. Ayrinhac, "comprises all theatrical representations and likewise such exhibitions as horse-races, bull-fights, prize-fights, etc., at least if it be taken in its most general sense." Dom Augustine gives a similar definition of the term.

Provincial legislation often makes this general law more precise. Thus 4 West., d. 11, n. 9 is as follows: "We strictly prohibit ecclesiastics who have received sacred orders from being present at stage representations in public theatres or in places temporarily made use of as public theatres, under the penalty to transgressors of suspension to be incurred *ipso facto*, as has hitherto been the rule in all parts of England, with reservation to the respective Ordinaries."

Clerics, therefore, are forbidden to be present at public not at private theatricals by this law. Custom in England makes an exception with regard to those exhibitions which are given by mere children.

6. Clerics are forbidden to enter military service, unless they do so with the leave of their own Ordinary in order that they may be free the sooner, and to aid in any way civil war and disturbances of public order (Can. 141).

Clerics are forbidden to trade in person or through another, whether in their own interest or in that of others (Can. 142).

The trading which is forbidden to clerics and all religious is trading in the strict sense of the term. In this sense to trade is to buy commodities, not for consumption, but with the intention of selling them again at a higher price without changing their nature. So that it is not trading in the strict sense to sell the produce of one's own land, nor to sell what was bought for consumption but was found to be unsuitable, nor to sell without profit to the poor, nor to sell a picture painted by one's self with colours bought in the market. However, certain transactions which have the appearance of trading are sometimes forbidden on account of the danger and scandal which they are apt to cause.

It is not illicit trading to invest money in Government stock or other bonds which bear interest, though it would be unlawful speculation to invest money with the intention of selling out at a profit if the price rises. Although it is forbidden to clerics to act as directors or to take part in the management of industrial and commercial companies, yet it is probable that a cleric may lawfully invest money in such enterprises as are honest merely with a view of getting interest on his investment. He only buys the right to receive interest on his money, much in the same way as if he invested it in Government stock.

The prohibition against trading binds under pain of grave sin if the matter be considerable. However, trading implies a habit, and so in the opinion of many divines to trade once in a way, even in a considerable quantity, would not be a mortal sin.

Canon 2380 prescribes that clerics and religious who violate the law against trading be punished by the Ordinary according to the gravity of the fault.

CHAPTER VI

ON BENEFICES

MENTION has several times been made already of benefices, and in this place moral theologians usually treat of the special obligations in conscience of beneficed clergy.

An ecclesiastical benefice is a juridical entity founded or erected in perpetuity by competent ecclesiastical authority, and it consists of a sacred office and the right to receive the income from the dowry annexed to the office (Can. 1409).

The dowry of a benefice consists either of property whose ownership belongs to the juridical entity itself, or of certain and due payments made by some family or moral person, or of certain and voluntary offerings of the faithful, which belong to the rector of the benefice, or stole fees, as they are called, within the amounts fixed by the diocesan tax or lawful custom, or of choral distributions with the exception of a third part of them, if the whole income of the benefice consists of choral distributions (Can. 1410).

When he has lawfully taken possession of his benefice, every beneficiary enjoys all the rights both temporal and spiritual which are annexed to the benefice (Can. 1472).

Although the beneficiary may have other property besides what is derived from his benefice, he can freely use and enjoy the fruits of his benefice which are necessary for his decent support; but he is bound by the obligation of spending what remains over on the poor or on pious causes, but a Cardinal can dispose even by will of all the fruits of his benefice (Can. 1473).

If a cleric violates this precept and disposes of what remains over in other ways, he sins against obedience but probably not against justice, so that there is no obligation to restore what has been disposed of against ecclesiastical law.

The beneficiary is bound faithfully to fulfil the special duties annexed to his benefice, and, moreover, daily to recite the canonical Hours (Can. 1475, sec. 1).

If, without any legitimate excuse, he has failed to satisfy his obligation of reciting the canonical Hours, in proportion to his omission he does not make the fruits of the benefice his own, and must hand them over to the church fabric or to the diocesan seminary, or must give them to the poor (Can. 1475, sec. 2).

The beneficiary, as the guardian of his benefice, ought to administer the property belonging to his benefice according to law (Can. 1476, sec. 1).

If he is negligent or in any other way in fault, he ought to make good the damage done to the benefice, and he should be compelled to make compensation for it by the local Ordinary, and if he be a parish priest he can be removed from his parish in accordance with Canon 2147 ff.

The Code of Canon Law and the canonists should be referred to for fuller treatment of this matter.

CHAPTER VII

ON THE SPECIAL DUTIES OF BISHOPS

1. THE duties of bishops of the Catholic Church are treated of at length in canon law; here we will touch upon the chief of them in so far as they affect conscience.

In order to be able to fulfil his various duties a bishop must habitually reside within the limits of his diocese. It is a disputed point among theologians whether this obligation is derived immediately from the divine law or from the positive law of the Church. We may say that at least remotely and in substance it belongs to the divine law, for in detail it is determined by the positive law of the Church. The bishop need not always live in the episcopal city, but he should be there to pontificate in the cathedral on the more solemn festivals of the year. Notwithstanding the obligation of residence the Code of Canon Law allows a bishop to absent himself from his diocese for good cause for a period of two or three months every year provided that he can do so without injury to his flock.[1] His own conscience must decide what cause is sufficient to justify his absence. Besides these two or three months a bishop may further absent himself if Christian charity, urgent necessity, due obedience, or the evident advantage of Church or State require it. But besides these reasons, in countries subject to the Sacred Congregation of Propaganda, the leave of the Sacred Congregation is also required for longer absence than the two or three months mentioned above.

2. At stated times bishops are bound to visit their dioceses in order to promote sound religious teaching and to correct errors in doctrine, to protect the good and punish the wicked, and to exhort the people to lead religious, peaceful, and good lives.[2] They are specially bound to watch over the morals and discipline of the clergy, and that there may be a constant supply of zealous priests for the needs of the diocese they should have a seminary for the education of those whom God calls to the clerical state. By the authority of the Holy See several dioceses may have a seminary in common if they are too small and poor to support a separate one for themselves.[3]

[1] Can. 338.   [2] Can. 343.   [3] Can. 1354.

28   DUTIES ATTACHED TO STATES AND OFFICES

The care of sound Christian doctrine is specially entrusted to bishops, and in the exercise of this charge they may visit public and private institutions, except such as are exempted from their jurisdiction, and they may condemn bad books not only by their ordinary authority, but as delegates of the Holy See in this important matter. They are bound at times to preach the word of God; every Sunday and day of obligation, even on the feast days that have been suppressed, they are bound to offer up Mass for the people committed to their charge; they should hold a diocesan synod every ten years, and make their visit *ad limina* at the fixed times, in order to render an account of the state of their dioceses to the Holy See.

CHAPTER VIII
ON THE DUTIES OF CANONS

. The canons attached to a cathedral church form the council or senate by whose advice and help the bishop is assisted in the government of the diocese. Collegiate churches were also served by a body of canons. By the common law, besides helping the bishop in the government of the diocese, canons were bound to residence near the church which they served; they were bound to sing the divine office every day in choir, and in turn to celebrate the conventual Mass. When a bishopric becomes vacant the government of the diocese devolves on the chapter of canons, who must elect within eight days after the vacancy occurs a vicar capitular to administer the affairs of the diocese until the appointment of a new bishop.

2. As there are either no prebends for the support of the canons in this country, or their income is too small for the purpose, our canons have been dispensed by the Holy See from the obligation of residence near the cathedral and from the daily celebration therein of Mass and divine office. They are, however, still bound to assemble at the cathedral on some one day in every month to be designated by the bishop, and on that day to sing office, say a conventual Mass, and hold a chapter. Similar provisions have been made in other countries. In the United States the place of canons is to some extent taken by the diocesan consulters.

In diocesan matters of importance the bishop is bound to ask the advice of his canons, and sometimes it is specially provided that he must obtain their consent to what he proposes to do.

Canons in England do not indeed elect a new bishop, but the Holy See has granted them the right of commendation, which is exercised by electing three clerics whose names they send in alphabetical order to the archbishop or to the senior bishop if the vacancy occurs in the archbishopric. The bishops then hold a meeting and after deliberation send the names with their remarks and opinions concerning the merits of each to the Holy See. The Holy See selects one of the three or someone else as it is judged more expedient.

CHAPTER IX

ON THE DUTIES OF PARISH PRIESTS

1. THE parochial system is not an institution of the primitive Church, much less of divine origin. For some centuries it was usual for the bishop to reside in some city with his body of clergy around him, some of whom were despatched as occasion required to minister to the faithful in outlying districts. In the fifth and sixth centuries parishes began to make their appearance in some places in the country districts, and in the eleventh, parish churches began to be instituted in the cities. Even at the period of the Council of Trent the parochial system had by no means become universal, but this council commanded that where churches had no fixed limits nor the pastors their own flock, and the sacraments were administered promiscuously to any who asked for them, the bishops should divide the people into fixed and proper parishes and assign to each its perpetual and separate parish priest, who might know them, and from whom alone they might lawfully receive the sacraments.[1] It added, indeed, that they might provide in some better way as circumstances of place demanded.

The Code of Canon Law prescribes that the territory of each diocese be divided into distinct parts called parishes, and that to each parish be assigned its own parish church with separate parishioners, and over it is to be placed its own parish priest for the necessary cure of souls (Can. 216).

The bishop should also divide his diocese into separate districts consisting of several parishes and called *vicariates forane,* or *deaneries.*

In the same way, where it can be done conveniently, vicariates apostolic and prefectures apostolic are to be divided.

The parts into which vicariates and prefectures apostolic are divided are called quasi-parishes, and the priests placed over them are called quasi-parish priests.

A parish priest is a priest or moral person or corporation who is collated to a parish in title with the cure of souls to be exercised under the authority of the local Ordinary (Can. 451).

A monastery or a cathedral chapter may have the habitual

[1] Sess. 24, de Ref., c. 13.

cure of souls as parish priest, but in accordance with Canon 471 such corporation must constitute a vicar to exercise the actual cure of souls, and allow him his decent support according to the judgement of the bishop.

When the parish priest has obtained possession of his parish, it is his lawful title for the exercise of all the duties and rights belonging to the office, and for the receiving of all the emoluments connected with it.

Quasi-parish priests and vicars of parish priests have in general all the rights and duties of parish priests (Can. 451, sec. 2).

2. In order that a parish priest may be able to fulfil his duties and be ready to help his parishioners in their spiritual needs, he should reside in the presbytery near the church.

The parish priest is allowed to be absent for two or three months, either continuous or interrupted, in the year, unless a grave reason in the judgement of the Ordinary himself requires a longer absence or permits only a shorter.

The days during which a parish priest is engaged in spiritual exercises, in accordance with Canon 126, once a year, are not reckoned in the two months of vacation.

Whether the time of vacation be continuous or interrupted, when the absence is to last beyond a week, the parish priest, besides a legitimate cause, ought to have the leave of the Ordinary in writing, and leave a vicar as substitute in his place to be approved by the same Ordinary; and if the parish priest is a religious he requires, in addition, the consent of his superior, and his substitute ought to be approved both by the Ordinary and by his superior.

If a parish priest is compelled by some sudden and grave reason to depart and to be absent beyond a week, let him inform the Ordinary by letter as soon as possible, telling him the reason of his departure and the priest who supplies for him, and let him abide by his commands. Even for a period of shorter absence a parish priest ought to provide for the needs of the faithful, especially if special circumstances demand it (Can. 465).

The Westminster Synods require that curates give notice to the parish priest if they wish to absent themselves even for a day.

3. On Sundays and on the other days of obligation throughout the year it is the peculiar duty of the parish priest to preach the word of God to the people in the usual homily, especially in the Mass, which is more frequented by the people.

The parish priest cannot habitually satisfy this obligation by employing another to do it, except for a good reason approved by the Ordinary.

The Ordinary may allow the sermon to be omitted on certain more solemn festivals, or even on some Sundays for a good reason (Can. 1344).

The kind and manner of instruction should be accommodated to the people, teaching them what is necessary for salvation, inveighing against vice and inculcating virtue, so that the people may be able to avoid hell and gain heaven, as the Council of Trent teaches.

The parish priest should prepare the children of his parish for the reception of the sacraments of Penance and Confirmation, and more specially for their first Communion. Moreover, after their first Communion he should take the opportunity to give them fuller instruction. On Sundays and days of obligation at some suitable time he should give catechetical instruction to the grown-up people of his parish (Can. 1330-1332).

4. To be able to fulfil his duties towards the members of his flock, a parish priest must know them, and he should not wait till they come to him; he should visit them and seek out those who have wandered from the fold. He is bound to correct the erring and to strive to recover them. He should also be able to devote some time to inquiring souls outside the fold. He should keep a book in which to enter particulars concerning the *status animarum*. He must be ready to administer the sacraments at the reasonable request of his parishioners, and he must say Mass in order that they may be able to fulfil their obligation of hearing it on the appointed days. Indeed, the provincial synods express a desire that there should be Mass daily in the parish church, and it will be the duty of the priest to provide this wherever the faithful have been led to expect it and frequent the church for the purpose.

On all Sundays and holidays of obligation, even on those that have been suppressed, parish priests are bound to apply Mass for their people (Can. 466).

Quasi-parish priests are bound to apply Mass for their people at least on the more solemn feasts mentioned in Canon 306.

The parish priest should say the Mass to be applied for the people in the parish church unless circumstances require or suggest otherwise. If he is lawfully absent he can apply the Mass for the people either himself in the place where he is staying, or through the priest who supplies for him in the parish (Can. 466, secs. 4, 5).

The Code mentions five kinds of parochial vicars: Vicarius curatus, Vicarius oeconomus, Vicarius substitutus, Vicarius adjutor, and Vicarius co-operator.

It will be sufficient for our purpose to say something on the duties of Vicarii co-operatores, or curates, as they are frequently called in this country.

If, on account of the number of people or for some other good reason, the Ordinary judges that one priest cannot look after a parish, he should appoint one or more curates and assign them a decent support.

The rights and duties of a curate are to be learnt from the diocesan statutes, from the letters and faculties of the Ordinary, and from the commission of the parish priest, but unless his sphere of activity is expressly limited, he should, from the nature of his office, take the place of the parish priest and help him in the whole care of the parish, except that he is not bound to apply Mass for the people. He is subject to the authority of the parish priest, who ought in a fatherly manner to instruct and guide him in the cure of souls, watch over him, and at least once a year send a report concerning him to the Bishop (Can. 476).

CHAPTER X

ON PRIESTS WITHOUT SPECIAL CHARGE

1. THE Council of Trent declared[1] that no one should receive ordination who was not, in the judgement of his bishop, necessary or useful to the diocese, and it decreed that nobody should in future be ordained without being *incardinated* in the diocese for whose necessity or advantage he was taken, so that all priests may have occupation and may not wander about without fixed abode.

The new Code of Canon Law prescribes that all clerics must belong either to some diocese or to some religious order, so that unattached clerics are nowise tolerated. A cleric is incardinated in the diocese for whose service he was promoted by the reception of the clerical tonsure (Can. 111).

All clerics, but more especially priests, are bound by a special obligation to show reverence and obedience to their respective Ordinaries. As often and for so long as the necessity of the Church requires it, in the judgement of the Ordinary, and unless excused by some lawful impediment, clerics must accept and fulfil the duties of the office which is assigned them by the bishop (Can. 127, 128).

Although they have not a benefice or a residential office, clerics may not depart for any considerable time from their diocese without at least the presumed leave of their own Ordinary. One who with the leave of his own Ordinary has gone to another diocese while remaining incardinated in his own, can be recalled if there is a good reason and natural equity is observed, and the Ordinary of the other diocese also can for a good reason refuse him leave to stay any longer in his diocese, unless he has conferred a benefice on him (Can. 143, 144).

2. Before ordaining a cleric the bishop should satisfy himself that the candidate is worthy and fit for the work of the sacred ministry. He must have the requisite holiness of life, without which the receiving of orders will only add to his greater condemnation. He must possess the knowledge necessary for the exercise of his duties, and he must be called

---

[1] Sess. 23, c. 15, de Ref.

by God. There is some apparent difference of opinion as to what precisely is implied by the necessity which all admit of a vocation from God to the clerical state. It is certain that no one may lawfully intrude himself into the ministry of his own accord. He must be duly approved and chosen for the work by the bishop. According to the catechism of the Council of Trent the words of the epistle to the Hebrews are to be understood of this external vocation through the lawful ministers of the Church. " Neither," we there read, " doth any man take the honour to himself, but he that is called by God as Aaron was."[1]

It is commonly admitted that besides this external vocation by the lawful prelates of the Church in the name of God, an internal call is also necessary. To be consecrated to the service of God a man must have the requisite gifts of body, mind, and soul, and, moreover, he must be satisfied that it is the will of God that he should devote himself to the sacred ministry, and that he will be able to perform its duties worthily, and thereby save his soul. The will of God in such matters is made known in various ways. Sometimes it is as plain and evident as was the call of St Paul on the road to Damascus. As a rule it becomes known by internal inspirations by which one is brought to think highly of the ministry, and by motions of the will by which one is drawn to desire it for the glory of God, the good of one's fellow-men, and the salvation of one's own soul. To embrace the priesthood without the consciousness of any such divine call would be hazardous and rash, and it would be grievously sinful if there were no wish or no prospect of being able to fulfil the duties of the clerical state. On the other hand, if the motive for embracing the clerical life were not seriously wrong, and if there were the firm resolve to fulfil the duties of the priesthood faithfully, and a reasonable prospect of being able to do so, many approved divines consider that a person choosing the priesthood without a divine vocation would not sin grievously.

Divines discuss the question as to whether a cleric who has contracted a bad habit of secret sin would sin grievously by receiving sacred orders before he had overcome his bad habit. Some defend the view that he would do so, because he would violate the law of the Church which requires holiness of life in one who is admitted to sacred orders. Even if we admit with others that it is difficult to sustain this view, that the Pontifical seems not to countenance it, yet in ordinary

[1] Heb. v 4

cases it expresses the correct opinion in practice, for commonly there will be little chance of a cleric living up to his profession who before ordination had contracted a vicious habit. Such a one undertakes more than he can fulfil and sins grievously against the natural, if not against the positive law. His confessor then would be justified in bidding him defer ordination till he has corrected himself, and enforcing his command with a threat of refusing absolution, except in some extraordinary case of sudden and complete conversion.

Canon 1363 forbids the Ordinary to receive into his seminary any but legitimate boys whose disposition and will give hope that they will always devote themselves to the ministry of the Church with fruit. Before reception they must show certificates of legitimate birth, of baptism and confirmation, and testimonies of being of good character. Special provisions are made with regard to those who have been dismissed from another seminary or from a religious order (Can. 1363).

There used to be a controversy as to whether a priest as such was bound to say Mass. This question is settled by Canon 805: "All priests are bound to say Mass several times a year; moreover, let the Bishop or the religious superior take care that they say Mass at least on all Sundays and holidays of obligation."

Part III

ON THE SPECIAL DUTIES OF RELIGIOUS

CHAPTER I

ON THE NATURE OF THE RELIGIOUS STATE

1. WE learn from the Gospels that, besides the ordinary way of the Commandments to be followed by all who wish to save their souls, our Lord proposed the way of perfection to the select few who wished to follow him more closely.[1] This way of perfection consists in renouncing the goods of this world and the cares of family life, and following our Lord's example of perfect obedience to the will of our heavenly Father. From the first ages of the Christian Church there were many who accepted our Lord's invitation and lived in voluntary poverty and chastity. Comparatively few historical documents of the earliest centuries of the Christian era have survived, but we find traces of a body of ascetics and virgins to whom a place of special honour was assigned in the Church. At first they seem to have lived in the bosom of their families, but soon they fled to the deserts of Egypt, Syria, and Palestine, and for guidance and encouragement put themselves under the rule of some experienced hermit. Nothing was then wanting to the essence of the religious state except vows and a rule. When the counsels of perfection began to be practised under vow cannot be determined exactly; the first formal religious rules are the work of St Basil and St Benedict. Thus in its essence the religious state has been instituted by Jesus Christ, and, as historically evolved under the guidance of his Church, it may be defined as a fixed and stable way of life approved by the Church for the faithful who, under a certain rule and a common way of living, wish to aim at perfection by the observance of the three vows of poverty, chastity, and obedience, with the entire surrender of one's self to God. Thus those who devote themselves to works of piety and charity without vows, or with only private vows, are not in the religious state, nor are they technically called religious. They want the necessary

[1] Matt. xix.

stability. This stability is given by the profession of public vows of poverty, chastity, and obedience, the chief of the counsels of the Gospel, by which a person renounces the attractions of this world which draw so many away from God, in order to give himself wholly and entirely without let or hindrance to the love and service of God. The Church has always watched over and fostered the practice of religious life. In the thirteenth century there was danger of the great variety of religious orders causing confusion, and the Fourth Council of the Lateran forbade any new orders to be founded. The practical effect of this law was to prohibit new orders without the approbation of the Holy See. It is still in force as regards orders with solemn vows, which cannot be founded without the special approbation of the Pope. According to the new Code, bishops, but not Vicars Capitular or Vicars General, can found religious congregations with simple vows, but they are forbidden to found them or allow them to be founded without consulting the Holy See. If there is question of founding tertiaries living in common, the leave is also required of the General of the first order to which the tertiaries are to be affiliated (Can. 492).

A religious congregation founded by a bishop may in process of time acquire houses in other dioceses, but it remains diocesan and is wholly subject to the local Ordinaries, according to law, until it obtains a decree of the Holy See in praise of its end and scope, or one of formal approbation.

The end of religious life is perfect union with God, in which man's perfection consists, and this union the religious disposes himself for by the constant practice of works of sublime charity and of renunciation of all that could be an obstacle to charity. Thus the religious state is the state of perfection; not that religious are supposed to be already perfect, but because perfection of Christian charity is the end aimed at, and suitable means are furnished therein for obtaining that end.

2. The special obligations under which a religious lies follow from the nature of the religious state which we have described. Inasmuch as he devotes himself to the service of God in religion, he must do nothing that would endanger his perseverance or cause him to be dismissed from the order. He is especially bound to observe his vows of poverty, chastity, and obedience. which he has voluntarily made to God, and in which the essence of religious life and the chief means of practising perfection consist. He is bound to keep the rule which he takes for his guide in life by the very fact of entering into the order which

he has chosen as well as by ecclesiastical law (Can. 593). The obligation imposed by the rule is not the same in all religious orders. In some it binds under sin like the precepts of the superior. The rules of the Dominicans, Jesuits, and of most of the modern congregations, of themselves, speaking generally, do not bind under sin. Particular precepts are sometimes inserted in the rule, and these of course are to be observed under sin like any other precepts of obedience. Apart from these the rule is rather a guide of conduct in religious life, and an indication as to how the superior should govern his subjects, than a rigid code of law binding under pain of sin. However, divines point out that frequently violations of such a rule will be sinful, not precisely because they are infractions of the rule, but because there will frequently be something defective in them as moral acts. If the silence which the rule prescribes is broken without just cause, the act will be sinful on account of the motive which led to it, the scandal which it causes, and its tendency to loosen the bonds of religious discipline. Formal contempt of the rule, by which a religious refuses to be guided by it, and wishes to show his independence, is mortally sinful, because it is directly contrary to his religious profession.

CHAPTER II

ON ENTRANCE INTO RELIGION

1. Our Lord Jesus Christ proposed the counsels of perfection to all his followers in general: " He who can take, let him take it "; " If thou wilt be perfect." When, however, we consider particular cases, we see that many are debarred as a matter of fact from embracing the religious state. Many find themselves in a fixed position in life with duties to be performed towards parents, relations, and others, which will not allow of their abandoning the world. Many more are unsuitable by character and temperament for the religious life. None of these can properly be said to have a divine call to the religious state, for when God gives a call he provides the necessary means for following it. There are others whom God calls in wonderful and different ways, making known his will to them sometimes in an extraordinary manner, more often by slowly developed inclinations and desires to forsake all and give themselves to him. The question arises whether such a divine vocation is a necessary condition for lawfully entering into religion, and whether one who felt himself called would sin if he neglected to follow the call.

Anyone who is free and who wishes to enter religion to be able to do more good, or to save his soul with greater security, is in fact called by God, for such desires are special graces given by God, and so they are signs of a divine vocation. So that all who have the aptitude, are free, and are led to religion by supernatural motives of some sort, are divinely called by God. One who entered religion from merely natural motives would probably soon find that he had made a mistake, and would return to the world. However, if such a one chose to rectify his intention and remained in religion to do good and to save his soul, he would not commit sin. He embraces a more perfect state of life, and if he does what in him lies, God will give him abundant grace to live a good religious life. Of course, sin is committed by one who enters religion from merely natural motives, and does not intend to fulfil the obligations of the state into which he has intruded himself. One who is called to religion and prefers to remain in the world acts very foolishly, throws away a great grace, and may expose his salvation to great danger. If such a one is persuaded that he cannot save his soul in the world, he commits grave sin by not taking the necessary means to secure his eternal salvation. If, however, he hopes with God's grace (which will not be wanting to him) to lead a good life in the world, he will not commit sin by not following the divine call; for this is a counsel, not a command, and counsels do not bind under sin. Some divines disagree with the foregoing doctrine, but it is supported by the authority of St Thomas and many approved authors (*cf.* Can. 538).

2. As, therefore, the observance of the counsels is not only lawful but a more perfect state of life, anyone may enter into religion who is not prevented by some obstacle. Those who have not possession of their faculties, and children who have not arrived at the age of puberty, and are still subject to their parents, cannot enter into religion. In former times parents used occasionally to present their children to be brought up in monasteries with the intention of their becoming religious when they reached the proper age. This custom, however, has long been abandoned.

Besides safeguarding what the constitutions of each institute prescribe on the point, the Code declares that the following cannot be validly admitted to the novitiate:

Those who have formally belonged to a non-Catholic sect.

Those who have not the age required for the novitiate.

Those who enter religion induced thereto by violence, grave fear, or deceit, or whom the superior receives from the same motives.

A spouse while the marriage lasts.

Those who are bound or who have been bound by the bond of religious profession.

Those over whom hangs a penalty on account of committing some grave crime of which they have been or can be accused.

A Bishop, whether residential or titular, although only designated by the Roman Pontiff.

Clerics who, by an arrangement of the Holy See, are bound by an oath to work for the benefit of their diocese or mission, for the time during which the obligation of the oath lasts.

The following are admitted unlawfully but validly:

Clerics in sacred orders without the local Ordinary being consulted, or against his will, because their departure would be to the great loss of souls, and this loss cannot otherwise be avoided.

Those in debt who are not solvent.

Those who are liable to render accounts or who are implicated in other secular business from which religion may have to fear lawsuits and troubles.

Children who ought to assist parents—that is, father, mother, grandfather, or grandmother—placed in grave necessity, and parents whose care is necessary for the support and education of children.

Those destined for the priesthood in religion, but who are debarred from it by irregularity or other canonical impediment (Can. 542).

3. Girls may not be admitted to the novitiate or be professed before they have completed their fifteenth year, and before doing so they must be examined by the bishop or by someone deputed by him as to whether they know the grave character of the step they are about to take, and whether they are acting of their own free and unfettered will (Can. 552).

4. Boys cannot be lawfully admitted into any order or congregation before the superiors thereof have received from the Ordinaries of their place of birth and of any place where they have lived for more than a year after attaining their fifteenth year testimonial letters bearing witness to their having the qualifications necessary for entering religion.[1] By the common law a full uninterrupted year of probation must be spent by the candidate for religion in the house of the novitiate. Although the novice has not yet taken the vows of religion, he is subject to the authority of the superiors of the order and is bound to obey them.

---

[1] S.C. super Stat. Reg., January 25, 1848; can. 544.

CHAPTER III

ON RELIGIOUS PROFESSION

1. PROFESSION is the promise lawfully made and accepted by which a religious binds himself to observe the vows of poverty, chastity, and obedience, according to the constitutions of his order.

For the validity of any religious profession whatever it is required:

(1) That he who makes it be of the legitimate age, so that he must have completed for the temporary profession, his sixteenth year, and for the perpetual profession whether solemn or simple, his twenty-first year.

(2) That the legitimate superior according to the constitutions admit him to profession.

(3) That it be preceded by a valid novitiate according to the terms of Canon 555.

(4) That the profession be free from violence, grave fear, or fraud.

(5) That it be expressed in formal terms.

(6) That it be received by the legitimate superior according to the constitutions, either personally or by delegate.

(7) For the validity of the perpetual profession, whether solemn or simple, it is required besides that it be preceded by a temporary simple profession. Except in the case of a professed religious who joins another institute, in every order with solemn vows both of men and of women, and in every congregation with perpetual vows, the perpetual vows, whether solemn or simple, must be preceded by the profession of simple vows, which the novice on the completion of his novitiate shall make in the novitiate house itself, this profession is valid for three years, or for a longer period if the subject requires more than three years to attain the age prescribed for perpetual profession, unless the constitutions require annual profession (Can. 572-574).

Simple profession, whether temporary or perpetual, renders acts contrary to the vows illicit, but not invalid, unless it be otherwise formally expressed; while solemn profession renders such acts also invalid if they can be nullified (Can. 579).

CHAPTER IV

ON RELIGIOUS POVERTY

1. POVERTY in general is the want of temporal goods that have a money value. It is not a virtue of itself, but rather a physical defect, for a suitable provision of temporal goods is very useful and necessary for men to lead a decent life. Poor human nature, however, is inclined to attach itself too much to wealth, and for the sake of wealth to forget why man was created by God and placed in this world. Jesus Christ taught that detachment from worldly possessions was a necessary condition for being his disciple: " Every one of you that doth not renounce all that he possesseth, cannot be my disciple."[1] And for such as were not content to follow him in the ordinary way of the observance of the Commandments, but aimed at perfection, he proposed not only detachment from wealth or spiritual poverty, but actual poverty, the actual renunciation of wealth for his sake in order to imitate him more closely: " If thou wilt be perfect, go, sell what thou hast, and give to the poor, and thou shalt have treasure in heaven; and come, follow me."[2] Hence voluntary poverty in imitation of Jesus Christ is the foundation of the religious state. Voluntary poverty, however, does not constitute the essence of religious perfection; all Christian perfection consists in charity, to which poverty is but a means. Hence there is not an absolute and uniform standard of religious poverty, but it varies with the different ends which religious orders propose to themselves. Indeed, religious poverty is personal; it is the voluntary renunciation of personal and individual wealth, so that the love of wealth may not be an obstacle to the perfect following of Christ. Its essence consists in the renunciation of personal and independent ownership and use of property, for this it is which constitutes a snare for men's affections and a hindrance to perfection. So that religious poverty does not of itself prevent property being owned in common by religious, and if the end for which an order was founded requires it, there is nothing to prevent it having large possessions in common, provided that the individual religious practises poverty and is imbued with its spirit.

[1] Luke xiv 33. [2] Matt. xix 21.

The effects of the vow of poverty depend to a great extent on the rules and constitutions of the various religious orders and on the positive law of the Church. The chief distinction is that between solemn and simple vows of poverty, due to positive ecclesiastical law. The legal effects of a solemn vow of poverty are to render the religious incapable of individual and personal ownership of any property that has money value. So that after taking a solemn vow of poverty the religious cannot own any property in his own personal right. As a member of a religious community he may be a joint owner of vast possessions, but individually he is incapable of having anything as his own.

Ownership may be absolute or qualified. Absolute ownership is the moral right to dispose of property and of all its uses for one's own advantage. Qualified ownership is the right to dispose of the property or of its uses for one's own advantage. Divines call the qualified ownership of the thing itself direct ownership, and the qualified ownership of its uses they call indirect ownership. A religious, even though solemnly professed, retains his personal rights to life, good name, and honour; he can still dispose of his personal actions, such as the celebration of Mass, and such personal rights as that of presenting to a benefice; he may own a relic and dispose of it by gift, for it has no money value. As a solemnly professed religious is incapable of owning property in his own right, so he cannot acquire it for himself; whatever he gains by his labour, or whatever comes to him by gift or inheritance, becomes the property of the community to which he belongs; "whatever a monk acquires he acquires not for himself, but for his monastery," as the old adage had it. By the special constitutions of their respective orders, Capuchins, Observantines, and professed Jesuits cannot take property, even in the name and for the benefit of the community to which they belong, if it come to them by any hereditary title or by operation of law. They may, however, take gifts and legacies, and these become the property of their communities (Can. 582).

The simple vow of poverty does not deprive the religious of the direct, but of the indirect, ownership of property; so that he cannot lawfully use or dispose of anything that has a money value without the leave of his superior. Notwithstanding, then, the simple vow of poverty, religious retain the direct ownership of all the property that they had before profession, and of all that comes to them afterwards by any legal title or gift.

Several Canons of the new Code affect the matter of religious poverty. By Canon 568, if during the novitiate a novice in any way whatever renounces his benefices or his property or encumbers them, such a renunciation or encumbrance is not only illicit but also null and void.

Canon 569 prescribes: Sec. i. Before the profession of simple vows, whether temporary or perpetual, the novice must cede, for the whole period during which he will be bound by simple vows, the administration of his property to whomsoever he wishes, and dispose freely of its use and usufruct, unless the constitutions determine otherwise.

Sec. ii. If the novice, because he possessed no property, omitted to make this cession, and if subsequently property come into his possession, or if, after making the provision, he becomes under whatever title the possessor of other property, he must make provision, according to the regulations of Sec. i, for the newly acquired property, even if he has already made simple profession.

Sec. iii. In every religious congregation the novice, before making profession of temporary vows, shall freely make a will of all the property he actually possesses or may subsequently possess.

While safeguarding this latter canon, Canon 580 prescribes that all those who have made profession of simple vows, whether perpetual or temporary, unless the constitutions declare otherwise, retain the ownership of their property and the capacity to acquire other property. But whatever the religious acquires by his own industry or in respect of his institute, belongs to the institute.

As regards the cession or disposition of property treated of in Canon 569, sec. 2, the professed religious can modify the arrangement, not, however, of his own free choice unless the constitutions allow it, but with the permission of the Superior General, or, in the case of nuns, of the local Ordinary, as well as with that of the Regular Superior if the monastery be subject to regulars; the modification, however, must not be made, at least for any considerable part of the property, in favour of the institute; in the case of withdrawal from the institute this cession and disposition ceases to have effect.

Except within sixty days preceding the solemn profession, the professed of simple vows cannot validly renounce his property, but within this time, he must, saving special indults from the Holy See, renounce in favour of whomsoever he wishes all the property which he actually possesses on condition of his profession subsequently taking place. The profession having been made, the necessary measures must be immediately taken to insure that the renunciation be effective also according to the civil law (Can. 581).

After profession of solemn vows, likewise without prejudice to special indults of the Apostolic See, all the property which comes in whatever manner to a regular—

(1) In an order capable of ownership, goes to the order, to the province, or to the house, according to the constitutions:

(2) In an order incapable of ownership, such as the Capuchins, it becomes the property of the Holy See (Can. 582).

Those who have made profession of simple vows in any religious congregation:

(1) May not abdicate gratuitously the dominion over their property *per actum inter vivos*. This phrase is technical, and signifies any way of disposing of property except by will. So that after profession of simple vows the professed cannot lawfully make a gift of his property to anyone.

(2) May not alter the will made according to the terms of Canon 569, sec. 3, without the permission of the Holy See, or if the case be urgent and time does not admit of recourse to the Holy See, without the permission of the higher superior, or, if recourse cannot be had to him either, without the permission of the local superior (Can. 583).

Within the limits indicated above, a religious, with the leave of his superior, may lawfully use and dispose of property. In order to justify such use and to excuse it from sin against the vow, the presumed leave of the superior is sufficient, which consists in a reasonably founded judgement that the act contemplated is not against the superior's wish. Much more will the actual, virtual, or tacit leave of the superior excuse an act of ownership on the part of a religious and prevent it from being a violation of the vow.

2. Sins against poverty are grievous if the matter be considerable. The measure as to what matter is considerable is the same here as in theft, for just as the sin of theft consists in taking away the property of another against his reasonable wish, so a sin against religious poverty consists in the use, disposal, or acceptance of property contrary to one's promise to God and the wish of religious superiors. The absolute sum which is necessary and sufficient for a mortal sin against the vow in all cases will be one pound sterling, and less will be sufficient if the community whose property is used or disposed of without leave is poor. Divines, however, allow that a moder-

ately rich monastery may be considered in this matter as equivalent to an absolutely rich individual proprietor.

3. In some orders it was customary for the religious to have money, books, eatables, for their own use, and such allowance was called the *peculium* of the religious. Such a practice is against the purity of religious poverty, and it was forbidden by the Council of Trent, as well as by several Roman Pontiffs. Indeed, if it was understood that subjects had the right to use and dispose of the peculium as they pleased, in perfect independence of the will of their superior, it would be against the very essence of religious poverty. In many orders the custom is still sanctioned of having a peculium in more or less dependence on the will of the superior.

It is not against poverty to administer money in the name of another, for such administration is not an act of ownership. A religious may, then, act as the almoner of another, but he must not distribute alms in his own name as if the money were his own. To keep a deposit of money with the obligation in justice of accounting for it is against religious poverty.

CHAPTER V
THE VOW OF CHASTITY

1. THE Catholic Church, following the teaching and example of our Lord and of St Paul, esteems very highly the beautiful virtue of chastity. According to her teaching, the state of marriage is indeed good, and Jesus Christ raised marriage to the dignity of a sacrament, but the state of virginity is better. For such as wish to follow Jesus Christ more closely and to dedicate themselves wholly to God, celibacy and absolute chastity are proposed as a counsel of perfection. There is no fear that the number who embrace this counsel will ever be so great as seriously to interfere with the proper increase of the population. There will always be a sufficient number left in the world to enter upon the married state. Nor is the heroic renunciation of the pleasures of married life made by religious lost upon the world. As long as there are numbers of men and women to be seen who for love of God and chastity lead solitary lives, it should be more easy for people in the world to curb their fleshly appetites so as to keep within the bounds of reason and virtue.

By the vow of chastity the religious promises Almighty God that he will altogether abstain from all venereal pleasure, whether of thought or deed. In consequence he is bound to observe perfect chastity of body and mind, so that any act which he commits contrary thereto will be a double sin, against the virtue and against his vow. We saw, when treating of the Sixth Commandment, that sins by which venereal pleasure is directly sought or consented to are always grave, and so, when such sins are committed by religious, their grievous malice will be twofold.

2. One who has taken a solemn vow of chastity is incapable of contracting a valid marriage by the law of the Church, and *a fortiori* he cannot enter on valid espousals. A marriage contracted and consummated before the taking of a solemn vow of chastity remains valid, but by ecclesiastical law a marriage which has not been consummated is dissolved by solemn vows taken in a religious order (Can. 1119). A simple vow of chastity never annuls a previous marriage, but it makes

the use of marital rights unlawful. It is a disputed point as to whether a simple vow annuls previous espousals. A simple vow of chastity certainly makes subsequent espousals invalid, as being an unlawful promise, and it renders subsequent marriage unlawful though not invalid, except the simple vow made in the Society of Jesus, which is a diriment impediment to marriage by a special privilege of the Holy See.

3. In order to safeguard the chastity of religious, and to enable them to lead more quiet and tranquil lives, the law of enclosure has been introduced. The enclosure in a religious house is all the space within which the religious may move freely, but which they may not leave without the required permission, and to which others are denied access.

The law of enclosure is laid down in detail in the new Code of Canon Law, Can. 597 *ff*.

Papal enclosure should be kept in the houses of regulars, whether of men or women, if they are canonically erected, even though less than six professed religious live there.

Enclosure should also be kept in the houses of religious congregations whether of pontifical or diocesan law. The bishop has authority in this matter, and can enforce his regulations by censure.

Even societies of men or women who live together under a superior like religious, but without vows, are subject to the law of enclosure according to Canon 679, sec. 2.

CHAPTER VI

THE VOW OF OBEDIENCE

1. MEN of the world find it difficult to understand how one man can surrender his liberty and bind himself by vow to obey another. And yet this counsel of perfection, too, is contained in the life and teaching of the divine Founder of the Church. He did not intend that all the members of his Church should be equal; he placed some in authority over the others, and he gave them power to teach, instruct, correct, and guide those who were subject to them. He therefore laid a duty of obedience to spiritual rulers on all the faithful. Those who were content to observe the Commandments were bound only to obey such positive precepts as the rulers of the Church judged it expedient to impose on all Christians; but those who aimed at perfection became as a consequence subject to the teaching and authoritative guidance of their rulers in matters which pertain to perfection as well. Those who were content with observing the Commandments reserved some liberty for themselves; those who aimed at Christian perfection gave themselves wholly to obedience after the example of him who was obedient even unto death. The prelates of the Church are therefore the superiors of religious men and women, and even if some are exempt in some matters from the jurisdiction of the ordinaries, all are subject to the Pope, not only as the Supreme Head of the Church on earth, but as their highest religious superior.[1] In approving of a religious order or congregation the Pope and the bishops delegate the necessary authority to the lawful superiors of the order, and give them power to command their subjects in all that pertains to the observance of the rule.

A religious, therefore, who takes a vow of obedience binds himself thereby to obey all the precepts which his superiors lay upon him according to the rule of the order.

In order, then, that the obligation of the vow may become operative, a precept must be given by the superior. And here we must distinguish between the vow and the virtue of obedience. The virtue of obedience inclines to the most per-

---

[1] St Thomas, 2-2, q. 186, a. 5; can. 499, sec. 1.

fect conformity of will and judgement of the subject with the will and judgement of the superior. A subject who has the virtue of obedience will strive to execute the known will of his superior without waiting for a strict command. The obligation of the vow is not so extensive as the virtue of obedience. The vow will be saved if precepts are externally executed, for, according to the more common opinion, the vow of obedience does not extend to merely internal acts.

The superior's authority is limited and defined by the rule, and so the subject is only bound to obey such commands of the superior as are sanctioned by the rule directly or indirectly. It is not, however, necessary that the precept should be expressly sanctioned by the rule in order to enable a superior to impose it with authority: it is sufficient if it be implicitly and indirectly sanctioned, as it will be if its imposition conduces to the better and more perfect observance of the rule.

2. Violations of the vow of obedience are grave sins of themselves. However, in practice, sins of religious against obedience are seldom mortal, for want of sufficiently grave matter, or because the superior does not intend to impose a grave precept. Such sins will be mortal when in grave matter the superior commands anything to be done in virtue of obedience, or when serious harm follows from disobedience, or when a subject refuses to obey from formal contempt of authority, wishing to exercise and display his independence.

When the vow of obedience is violated, there is a double malice in the sin. Such a violation is a sin against the vow, and thus it is a sacrilege; and it is also a sin against the Fourth Commandment of the Decalogue, which prescribes obedience to be rendered to all lawful superiors. Such lawful superiors are armed with spiritual jurisdiction delegated to them by ecclesiastical authority, or at least they have the natural authority which belongs to all rulers of a community, great or small. Superioresses of nuns have this natural authority, and so they can impose even grave precepts of obedience on their subjects, although as women they cannot have ecclesiastical jurisdiction.

BOOK II

THE SACRAMENTS IN GENERAL

CHAPTER I

THE NATURE OF A SACRAMENT

1. MERELY external religion, without devotion of mind and heart to the service of God, is hypocrisy, but though we should serve God in spirit and in truth, external rites and ceremonies are not excluded from religion. On the contrary, they form an essential part of it. Man is composed of body and soul; both come from God, and both should share in the worship due to their Creator. Besides, internal religion will be faint and likely to evaporate altogether, unless it sometimes finds expression in outward acts. God has provided for these wants of human nature by instituting the sacred rites, which we call sacraments, as essential parts of true religion. They serve also as signs by which the faithful are known to and united among themselves and distinguished from those outside the fold. They serve, too, as an external profession of faith, and as a means of practising the very salutary virtue of humility, inasmuch as we are compelled to seek in external rites the spiritual help of which we stand in need, whereby intellectual pride is humbled.

There were sacraments under the Old Law as there are under the New, although the latter are far more efficacious than the former. As expressing what is common to the sacraments of Judaism and Christianity, a sacrament may be defined to be an outward sign of inward grace. A sacrament, then, is some outward rite or ceremony instituted by God, to show forth and make known the grace which he thereby bestows on the soul of the recipient. Thus circumcision signified separation from the idolatrous world, incorporation among the people of God, and the infusion of grace into the soul for the remission of original sin. The sacraments of the Old Law produced their effects by exciting the faith of the ministers and recipients of them and by the profession of faith in the coming Redeemer which their use contained.

The sacraments of the New Law were instituted by Christ

our Lord, and they confer the grace which they signify, not on account of the meritorious dispositions with which they are ministered or received, but on account of their dignity and intrinsic excellence. They were instituted by Christ, they are administered in his name and by his authority, and thus they are in a true sense the actions of Christ our Lord executed by his ministers. Divines express this by saying that the sacraments of the Christian Church confer grace *ex opere operato*, while those of the Old Law produced it *ex opere operantis*. A sacrament, then, of the New Law may be defined to be an outward sign of invisible grace instituted by Christ to confer the grace which it signifies.

There are certain rites and ceremonies in use in the Church which are called sacramentals. Of these we may mention the consecration of abbots, the first tonsure of clerics, the sacring of kings, the blessing of chalices and bells, holy water, *Agnus Dei*, scapulars, and many more. They are called sacramentals because they are sacred rites which, if properly used according to the mind of the Church, confer spiritual graces on the soul of him who uses them. They do this through the approbation and blessing of the Church, the Spouse of Christ, whose prayers and desires Christ always listens to, and through the good dispositions of those who use them. They thus differ from sacraments, as also in the grace which they produce. They confer actual graces, special helps to do good and avoid evil, given by God in answer to the prayers of the Church and the pious desires of those who use them properly (Can. 1144).

2. The Council of Trent defined as of faith that there are seven sacraments instituted by Christ our Lord: Baptism, Confirmation, the Eucharist, Penance, Extreme Unction, Orders, and Matrimony; that these sacraments contain the grace which they signify, and that they always confer grace on all those who receive them and put no obstacle to their effect. The sacraments, then, require certain dispositions on the part of the recipient in order that they may produce their effect. They will be validly received if nothing that is essential be wanting to them, but in order to produce their effect when they are received the recipient must have the required dispositions. I may apply a match to a faggot of wood, but this will not take fire if it is sodden with water. Similarly, if an adult asks for Baptism and is rightly baptized the sacrament will be validly received, but if the recipient has no faith or no sorrow for his sins the Baptism will indeed imprint a character, but it will not infuse sanctifying grace in the soul. In such a case as this

the sacrament is validly but not licitly received; it is said by divines to be unformed, not formed.

3. The Council of Trent also defined it to be of faith that the three sacraments, Baptism, Confirmation, and Orders, whenever they are validly received, imprint on the soul a certain spiritual mark which is called a character. This character serves to distinguish in the eyes of God and of his saints those who have received the sacrament in question; it is indelible, and prevents the sacrament from being received a second time. It is, however, compatible with the presence of mortal sin in the soul, so that, as was said above, a valid sacrament imprints its proper character even when on account of some obstacle in the recipient it is unformed and does not convey sanctifying grace to the soul.

The question here occurs whether a valid but unformed sacrament will afterward produce grace in the soul, if and when the obstacle be removed. The common opinion of Doctors and divines is that it will do so in the case of the three sacraments which impress a character on the soul. This opinion is founded on the tradition of the Church and on what is to be expected from the goodness of God and the nature of the sacraments. A cause which is in existence, but which was hitherto prevented from producing its full effect on account of some obstacle in the way, will produce that effect when the obstacle is removed. Many divines hold the same doctrine of reviviscence concerning the sacraments of Matrimony and Extreme Unction, which may not be repeated at the will of the recipient. Whether it is also applicable to Penance is a much disputed point, while it is commonly denied that the sacrament of the holy Eucharist can afterward produce its effect if it was unformed when received.

4. The sacramental grace which is conferred by the sacraments is habitual or sanctifying grace as directed toward the particular end for which the sacrament from which it flows has been instituted. Together, then, with the grace which justifies the sinner, or which increases the sanctifying grace of the soul in friendship with God, a sacrament gives a title to receive from God special help or actual graces when they are required by the recipient of the sacrament. Thus, the sacrament of Penance, if worthily received, infuses sanctifying grace into the soul by which the sins confessed are blotted out, and, moreover, it gives the sinner a title to receive actual graces in time of temptation, so as to enable him not to yield. In the same way the holy Eucharist increases sanctifying grace

within the soul, making it more holy and more pleasing in the sight of God, and fresh help is given to enable it to remain steadfast in the friendship of God.

The sacraments of Baptism and Penance, which remit sin and give sanctifying grace to souls that were deprived of it, are called sacraments which give the first grace, or sacraments of the dead, inasmuch as they give spiritual life to those who were spiritually dead; while the sacraments which should only be received by such as are already in the state of grace are said to confer the second grace, and are called sacraments of the living. If the soul is already justified and in the state of grace, sacraments of the dead confer second grace; while Extreme Unction may, as we shall see, confer the first grace, although it is primarily a sacrament of the living; and it is a probable opinion that the other sacraments may *per accidens* confer the first grace when received in good faith by the sinner. Inasmuch as a sacrament confers grace in virtue of the worth and dignity of the sacred rite itself, the quantity of grace given will *per se* be the same for all who receive it. However, *per accidens*, since a cause acts with greater or less efficacy in proportion to the dispositions of the subject on which it works, so a sacrament will give more grace to such as receive it in better dispositions. It may, then, very well be that more grace will be obtained from Holy Communion received two or three times a week with better dispositions than from daily Communion made without fervour.

5. The Council of Trent anathematizes anyone who shall say that the sacraments of the New Law are not necessary for salvation, though it also teaches that not all the sacraments are necessary for every individual. Under each sacrament it will be explained how far it is necessary and in what sense.

CHAPTER II

THE MATTER AND FORM OF THE SACRAMENTS

1. THE decree of Eugenius IV, for the instruction of the Armenians, lays down that all the sacraments consist essentially of three things: the matter, the form, and the minister who makes the sacrament with the intention of doing what the Church does. And, it adds, if any one of these elements be wanting the sacrament is not made. The sacraments, then, are not simple, but composite signs, which consist of two distinct elements. One of these in technical language is called the matter, because it is that portion of the sacramental sign which is the most indeterminate with respect to conveying the meaning which the sacrament signifies. This matter is called remote when considered by itself; it is called proximate when it is taken and applied by the minister to the making of the sacrament. The second element consists of words, and this part is called the form of the sacrament, because the words determine the matter to the more complete signification expressed by the whole sacramental sign. Thus in Baptism the water, considered by itself, is the remote matter of the sacrament and does not necessarily signify washing; water may be used to slake the thirst, and for many other purposes. The application of the water to the person to be baptized is the proximate matter, and when this is done with the form of words, " I baptize thee in the name of the Father, and of the Son, and of the Holy Ghost," the whole composite rite assumes a religious aspect, and signifies, according to the intention of the minister, the washing away of sin from the soul.

2. The minister of a sacrament must necessarily use the matter and form which were instituted by Christ, for he alone as God-Man has the power to cause grace to be conveyed to the soul by means of sacred rites.

There must be no change made in the matter and form of the sacraments; not even the Church's authority suffices for that. If a substantial change be made either in the matter or in the form, the sacrament is destroyed. The matter will be substantially changed if in the estimation of ordinary men it is no longer the same, but something else. Thus, if the wine has become vinegar, it cannot be used as the matter of the Eucharist. The form will be substantially changed if the sense is no longer the same, but different. Thus, " I baptize thee in the name of the Father, and of the Son, and of the Holy Ghost " is the divinely instituted form for Baptism, and if the minister baptize with the words, " I baptize thee in the name of the Trinity " it is no sacrament, because of the substantial change. It is not lawful to make any change in the matter and form of the sacraments, but if an accidental and not a substantial change be made, so that the matter and the sense of the form remain the same, the sacrament will not be rendered invalid, as a general rule. However, a change which in itself is slight and accidental may be made substantial by the perverse intention of the minister. For the sense may then be quite different, and that different sense is expressed in the form. Thus Pope Zacharias wrote to St Boniface that Baptism administered with the form, *Baptizo te in nomine Patria, et Filia, et Spiritus Sancta*, is valid when the mistakes are made through ignorance of Latin, and not through heresy or a perverse intention.[1] If, then, such changes were introduced to give expression to heresy, the sense would be substantially changed and the form would be invalidated. Similarly, if Baptism were given with the form " I baptize thee in the name of the Father, and of the Son, and of the Holy Ghost, and of the Blessed Virgin Mary," the sacrament would be invalid if the minister intended to baptize in the name of the Blessed Virgin as of one of the Persons in the Godhead; if the addition was made through mistaken devotion to the Mother of God the sacrament would not be invalid. On the principles just stated Leo XIII decided that Anglican ordinations are invalid.

3. Except in case of necessity it is not lawful in the administration of the sacraments to use only probable matter or a probably valid form. An opinion contrary to this doctrine was condemned by Innocent XI, March 2, 1679. Justice and charity, which demand that the minister confer a sacrament validly, and do nothing to imperil its validity, require that he should use only certain matter and the certainly valid form as far as possible. Reverence also for the sacrament and for Christ, who instituted it, makes it necessary to take all due care that when a sacrament is administered it should be properly and validly administered. If, however, in a particular case only doubtful matter is at hand, and unless the sacrament is at once administered, the subject may be

[1] C. 86, d. iv, de Consec.

altogether deprived of it, then such doubtful matter may be used, since the reasons to the contrary then cease to be valid, because the sacraments were made for the benefit of man, not man for the sacraments.

4. As the matter and the form of a sacrament constitute together one composite sign of grace, there must not be such an interval between them as to destroy their unity. In the holy Eucharist the form requires that the matter should be physically present at the time when the words of consecration are uttered. In the other sacraments it is not necessary that the matter and form should be put at the same time in order that the sacrament may be valid; it is sufficient for the validity if there be a moral union between them so that according to a moral estimate they form one whole. Thus in Baptism, although the rubrics prescribe that the words should be said while the water is poured on the head, yet if a brief interval, say the space of a *Pater* or of an *Ave*, separate the matter and the form, the sacrament will still be valid.

The matter and the form should be applied by one and the same minister. Baptism would not be valid if one poured the water while another pronounced the words. In the Eucharist, however, and in Extreme Unction there are more than one form, each with its separate matter, and the sacrament would be valid if one minister consecrated one species or anointed one sense and another finished the rite. This, however, is only lawful in case of necessity, nor is it lawful for many ministers to make one sacrament at the same time, except when newly ordained priests celebrate Mass with the Bishop who has ordained them.

5. The sacraments should ordinarily be administered absolutely according to the manner in which they were instituted by Christ. If, however, in any particular case it is doubtful whether a sacrament was validly administered and there will be danger of grave spiritual loss to the subject unless it is repeated, it may and should be repeated conditionally. The condition should be expressed when the rubrics require it, as in the case of Baptism and Extreme Unction. Otherwise the condition may be implicit, and it will be sufficient if the minister intend to do his duty according to the institution of Christ and the laws of Holy Mother Church.

The Ritual expressly warns the minister that the conditional form for administering Baptism is not to be used at random or lightly, but with prudence, when after diligent inquiry there is a probable doubt whether the sacrament was validly conferred before. The same principle is to be applied to the conditional administration of the other sacraments.[1]

Except in the case of Matrimony, which is a contract and follows in this the rules affecting other contracts, a sacrament cannot be validly administered under a condition which regards a future and uncertain event. The reason is because such a condition would of its nature suspend the effect of the sacrament, and when the condition is verified the matter and form no longer exist and cannot now produce their effect. Thus Baptism conferred on a child under the condition, "If you attain the age of reason," would be null and void. On the other hand, a sacrament conferred under a past or present condition will be valid if the condition be verified; it will be invalid if the condition be not verified. We have already seen when it is lawful to administer a sacrament conditionally. There will be an obligation to do so whenever justice and charity due to our neighbour require it in order to prevent his spiritual loss, or when reverence for the sacraments and for Christ, who instituted them, makes it necessary in order to avoid their invalid administration.

[1] Can. 732, sec. 2.

CHAPTER III
THE MINISTER OF THE SACRAMENTS

THE sacraments were instituted by Christ as so many channels or conduits by which he might convey to the souls of men the fruits of his passion and death. They are administered in his name and by his authority, and so Christ himself is the principal minister of the sacraments. However, he deigns to make use of men as his instruments for administering them, and it is of these secondary ministers who make the sacraments in the name of Christ that we have here to treat. In Matrimony, as we shall see, the parties to the contract themselves are the ministers to each other of the sacrament, and anyone who has the use of reason may confer Baptism validly. The minister of the other sacraments, at least for their lawful administration, must have the twofold spiritual power of order and jurisdiction which was given by Christ to his Church. We shall see, when treating of the several sacraments, how far order and jurisdiction are also required for their valid ministration. In the following sections we will lay down the conditions and dispositions which a minister of the sacraments should have to perform his office worthily.

SECTION I
The Attention and Intention of the Minister

1. While administering a sacrament the minister should attend to what he is doing and remember that he is engaged in a religious function. If he voluntarily allows his mind to wander on other and profane matters, he is guilty of irreverence toward God for whose worship the sacraments were instituted and should be administered. This irreverence, however, is not grave in itself, probably not even if a priest is voluntarily distracted during the consecration in Mass, so that voluntary distractions while administering the sacraments are only venial sins. Attention, then, or advertence of the mind to what is being done, is not necessary for the validity of a sacrament; only three things are necessary for its validity, as we saw above

—the matter, the form, and the intention of the minister to do what the Church does.

2. Intention is an act of the will directing an action to a certain end. Divines distinguish between an actual, a virtual, an habitual, and an interpretative intention. When a minister wishes here and now to administer a sacrament, he has an actual intention to perform the rite. If he had such a wish and in consequence set about his task, but became distracted while administering the sacrament, he has a virtual intention. An habitual intention is a wish to do something, which wish has not been retracted but which does not issue in action. An interpretative intention is a wish which would be conceived if one thought of it, but for want of thinking of it is not elicited.

An intention of some sort in the minister is necessary for the validity of a sacrament; the Council of Trent anathematized anyone who should say that there is not required in ministers while they make and confer the sacraments at least an intention to do what the Church does.[1] Now the Church by her ministers and through the sacraments baptizes, confirms, absolves from sin, and so forth; so that the minister while making a sacrament must intend to baptize, confirm, absolve. However, it is not necessary to have an actual intention of doing this; distractions cannot always be avoided, and always to have an actual intention while engaged in conferring the sacraments would be an impossible requirement. Nor would an habitual intention suffice, for it does not exist while the action is put, nor has it any effect upon the action. Much less would an interpretative intention be sufficient. It remains, then, that a virtual intention is necessary and sufficient in the minister while he makes a sacrament.

3. Ambrosius Catharinus, Salmeron, Contenson, and other theologians thought that an intention to perform the external rite of a sacrament, even if the minister internally expressly withheld his intention to do what the Church does, would be sufficient for the validity of a sacrament. Such an intention to perform the merely external rite while internally withholding the intention to baptize, absolve, and so forth, is called an external intention. The common opinion is that such a merely external intention is not sufficient, but that an internal intention or a positive wish to baptize, absolve, and so forth, is necessary for the validity of the sacrament. On December 7, 1690, Alexander VIII condemned the proposition that Baptism is

---

[1] Sess. vii, c. 11.

valid when it is conferred by a minister who observes all the external rite and form of Baptism but inwardly in his heart makes this resolution, " I do not intend to do what the Church does." This decree would seem to settle the matter, for it seems to have been directed against Fr. Farvacques, O.S.A., who, in a little book published ten years earlier, had defended the opinion of Catharinus and Salmeron. A few theologians even subsequently to the decree of Alexander VIII have defended the same view, on the ground that the decree was aimed at the Lutheran error which asserted the validity of the sacraments even when administered in joke. No Catholic, however, defended the Lutheran doctrine at the time, and it had already been condemned by the Council of Trent. We must, then, at least say with Benedict XIV that the condemnation of the above proposition inflicted a serious blow on the opinion of Catharinus, and no theologian of note now defends it. The Church does not merely apply the matter and form when ministering the sacraments, but by means of those external rites she intends to do what Christ instituted the sacraments to effect—that is, to baptize, to absolve, and so forth. An intention, then, to do this—to baptize, to absolve, or an internal intention—is necessary for the validity of a sacrament.

4. It is not sufficient for the minister while making a sacrament to have a vague intention of conferring it on somebody or other, or of taking and applying some matter in general for the making of the sacrament. The intention must be definite in its scope and object, otherwise there is no reason why this matter should be taken rather than that, or why one person should be benefited rather than another. An intention, therefore, to absolve anyone in a crowd who may need it, or to consecrate five hosts out of a larger number on the altar would not be effective.

Neither ignorance nor mistake on the part of the minister about the nature or effect of a sacrament makes it invalid. Baptism conferred by one who knows nothing of its nature, or by one who denies baptismal regeneration, is valid, provided that the three essential elements of the sacrament are not wanting.

Difficulties may arise from the fact that a minister while making a sacrament had mutually contradictory intentions. Thus an heretical priest while saying Mass may have the intention to do what Christ instituted but not to offer sacrifice, as he denies that Mass is a sacrifice. In this and in similar cases divines give the following rules for discovering whether the sacrament is effected or not. When the contradictory intentions are present in the mind at the time of making the sacrament, that will prevail which is the stronger, and that is the stronger which would be chosen by the minister if he realized the contradiction. So that, in the example given, the heretical minister will actually say Mass if the intention to do what Christ instituted be the prevailing and stronger one; he will not say Mass if his intention not to offer sacrifice is the stronger. When the contradictory intentions follow one another, the last will ordinarily prevail, unless the former revoked all subsequent intentions.

5. Except in case of necessity the minister of a sacrament may not use probable opinions with reference to what belongs to the validity of the sacrament. As we saw when treating of the matter and form, it would be against the reverence due to the sacraments, against justice, and against charity, if the minister exposed the sacraments to the danger of nullity through following a merely probable opinion. He is bound to follow the safer opinion when he can do so in what relates to the validity of the sacraments. In questions, however, which only touch the lawfulness or the integrity of the sacraments, and when the Church supplies what is wanting in order that the sacrament may be valid, which she sometimes does, as we shall see later, there is no reason why the minister should not use probable opinions. The same doctrine applies also to the recipient of the sacraments.

Section II

The Faith and Holiness of the Minister

1. Neither faith nor the state of holiness and friendship with God is necessary in the minister for the validity of the sacraments which he confers. This is of faith, and it was defined by the Council of Trent. The sacraments do not depend for their effect on the good or bad dispositions of the minister, as they derive their efficacy from the institution and the merits of Christ. They produce their effect *ex opere operato*, not *ex opere operantis*. However, one who has been consecrated and deputed to be a dispenser of the mysteries of God is bound to fulfil his office in a worthy manner. Holy things must be treated holily. The minister acts in the name of Christ; he becomes the instrument of Christ for the sanctification of the souls of others by means of the sacraments; he would be greatly wanting in reverence and decency if, while

engaged in so holy a task, his own conscience were stained with grievous sin. An enemy of God himself, he is guilty of great presumption in undertaking such holy functions. A consecrated minister who solemnly administers a sacrament while conscious of being in a state of mortal sin certainly sins grievously. The question whether a lay person who in case of necessity baptizes another or contracts marriage in the state of sin himself sins grievously, as being an unworthy minister of the sacrament, is much disputed among divines. Many weighty authorities excuse such a minister from grave sin because he is not under so strict an obligation to put himself in the state of grace before administering a sacrament as is one who has been set aside and consecrated to that office. All citizens are bound to defend their country when threatened, but there is a special obligation to do so incumbent on those who, like soldiers, have undertaken that duty. Similarly, all should indeed treat the sacraments with proper respect, but consecrated ministers are specially bound to do so while fulfilling their office. So that it is a probable opinion that a lay person who baptizes in sin in a case of necessity, or one who marries and so ministers the sacrament in sin to the other party, does not thereby sin grievously. For the same reasons it is also probable that even a consecrated minister who while in sin administers Baptism privately in case of necessity does not sin mortally, for he then acts as a private person, not as a consecrated minister.

2. A priest who says Mass in the state of mortal sin is thereby guilty of several grievous sins. He celebrates Mass unworthily, he receives Holy Communion unworthily, and he gives himself the sacrament though he knows that he is unworthy to receive it. Some add a fourth sin, which is committed precisely by handling and administering the Blessed Sacrament in a state of sin. It is probable, however, that this last act, though wanting in due reverence, does not amount to a grievous sin. All the more is it a safe opinion that deacons and subdeacons who exercise their functions in a state of sin do not sin grievously by so doing, nor do Bishops and priests who in sin consecrate or bless pious objects, or preach the word of God.

Divines are not agreed whether a priest would commit one sin or as many sins as he administered sacraments unworthily who in a state of sin should hear many confessions or administer many Baptisms or other sacraments at the same time. If there were moral interruptions between the several sacraments, there would at least be as many sins as interruptions. But if there were no such moral interruption, it is a probable opinion that a priest who at one time administers a sacrament to many only commits one big mortal sin. The sin takes its unity from the fact that he exercises his office on one occasion unworthily, an office which he was consecrated to perform in a worthy manner. It is not, then, necessary for a priest who has sinned by hearing confessions in sin to say how many persons he has absolved; it will be sufficient if he states how often he has heard confessions in mortal sin.

It will be sufficient for a priest who is in sin to make an act of contrition before administering any of the other sacraments, but before saying Mass and receiving Holy Communion it is necessary for such a one to go to confession. The Council of Trent, commenting on the precept of St Paul, " Let a man prove himself, and so let him eat of that bread," says that the custom of the Church has always interpreted these words as implying that no one who is conscious of mortal sin ought to approach Holy Communion without sacramental confession, however contrite he may feel. It is, of course, advisable that this should be done before a minister who is in sin administers any of the sacraments, though it is only of strict obligation before saying Mass and receiving Holy Communion.

SECTION III

The Duty of Administering the Sacraments

1. All who have the cure of souls are bound in justice and in charity to administer the sacraments to the members of their flock when these need them or ask for them reasonably. The obligation is principally one of justice, and it arises from the implicit contract which those who have the cure of souls enter into on assumption of office. The obligation is a grave one if the subject is in extreme or grave necessity, and even when there is no grave necessity one who has the cure of souls would commit serious sin if he frequently refused the sacraments to those who ask for them reasonably. An occasional refusal in such cases would not be a grievous sin, as although the spiritual good of which they are unjustly deprived is considerable, yet the loss can without much inconvenience be made good at another time.

The obligation of justice is so strict that those who have the cure of souls are bound even at the risk of life to administer the sacraments to their flock in extreme or in grave necessity. This obligation, however, only extends to those sacraments which are necessary for salvation, such as Baptism and Penance; it does not extend to those which are not necessary, not even to the holy Eucharist, according to a very probable opinion. Mortal sin will be committed not only by frequent refusal of the sacraments to those who ask for them in a reasonable manner, but also by making one's self difficult to approach and by an ungracious manner of yielding to reasonable requests, inasmuch as such methods deter the faithful from exercising their just rights.

2. Ministers of the sacraments who have not the cure of souls are bound in charity to administer the sacraments to such as are in extreme or grave spiritual necessity. This obligation is less strict than that which lies on those who have the cure of souls, so that those who have no such cure will only be bound at the risk of life to administer the sacraments which are necessary for salvation to those who are in extreme necessity. But in order that this grave obligation of charity may exist there must be moral certainty that the person in question is in extreme spiritual necessity, or in other words, that he is in proximate danger of damnation unless the sacraments be administered. There must also be a reasonable certainty that the attempt to administer the sacraments will be successful; it would be hard if a minister of the sacraments were bound to imperil his life for a mere probability of being able to help another in spiritual distress. Furthermore, before so grave an obligation can be imposed on anyone it must be morally certain that he who is in spiritual necessity is unable to help himself by making an act of contrition for his sins or of perfect love of God, and that there is no one else who is able and willing to succour him in his necessity. As all these conditions are seldom verified in any concrete case, it is apparent that those who have not the cure of souls will seldom be under a grave obligation of administering the sacraments to those who are in extreme necessity at the risk of life.

Section IV

The Duty of Refusing the Sacraments to the Unworthy

1. "Let a man so account of us," says St Paul, "as of the ministers of Christ, and the dispensers of the mysteries of God. Here now it is required among the dispensers, that a man be found faithful."[1] As, then, the administration of the sacra-

[1] 1 Cor. iv 1, 2.

ments is entrusted to the ministers of the Church, they must be faithful to their charge and administer them according to the intention of Christ and the rules of the Church. These rules are chiefly contained in the Ritual and in other liturgical books. The prescribed rites are of grave obligation in serious matters, for the Council of Trent anathematized those who should assert, " That the received and approved rites of the Catholic Church, wont to be used in the solemn administration of the sacraments, may be contemned, or without sin be omitted at pleasure by the ministers, or be changed by every pastor of the churches into other new ones."[1]

Ministers are specially required to refuse the sacraments to such as are unworthy: " Give not that which is holy to dogs," said our blessed Lord.[2] The minister should have positive reasons for judging that those who ask for the sacraments of Penance and Orders are worthy to receive them. For the dispositions of the subject enter into the substance and validity of Penance, and the duty of seeing that everything is present which is required for the validity of the sacraments belongs to the minister of them. Public officials of the Church are constituted by Orders, and the public good requires that only those who are worthy should be chosen. All lawful subjects who ask for the other sacraments are presumed to be worthy unless it is certain that they are unworthy.

With special reference to the holy Eucharist the Ritual lays down that, " All the faithful are to be admitted to Holy Communion except those who are forbidden for just cause. Those who are notoriously unworthy are to be refused, such as the excommunicated, interdicted, and openly infamous, as are strumpets, those living in concubinage, usurers, wizards, sorcerers, blasphemers, and other public sinners of that kind, unless it is certain that they have repented and amended, and have made satisfaction for the public scandal which they have given " (Can. 855). However, in the judgement of theologians, it will be sufficient if such public sinners openly go to confession; in this way, according to modern discipline, they will show their amendment and make satisfaction for the scandal which they have caused, unless more is required in special cases by the bishop or by other competent authority.

The Ritual proceeds: " Let the minister also repel secret sinners when they ask in secret unless he knows that they have amended; but not when they ask publicly, and cannot be passed by without scandal." In the latter case public injury

---

[1] Sess. vii, c. 13.   [2] Matt. vii 6.

would be done to the secret sinner, scandal would be given to others, and other inconveniences would follow, if the sacraments were refused; and these reasons justify the minister in co-operating materially with the sin of unworthily receiving the sacraments. Of course, if the minister only knows of the bad dispositions of the subject from sacramental confession, he can make no use of his knowledge out of confession.

2. It is specially laid down in the new Code of Canon Law and in the synods[1] that the priest should strive to induce all who are going to marry to approach beforehand the sacraments of Penance and the holy Eucharist. If he does not succeed in this, he may nevertheless assist at the marriage even though he knows that one or both parties are not properly disposed to receive the sacrament, for he is not the minister of Matrimony, but only the witness authorized by the Church to assist at it and to bless the parties; to refuse to assist would commonly do more harm than good. Even if one of the contracting parties knows that the other is not in a fit state to receive a sacrament of the living like Matrimony, still he will as a rule be excused from sin in ministering the sacrament to him, because he is not a consecrated minister of the sacrament, and the advantages connected with marriage are a sufficient justification for co-operating materially with the sin committed by the other party by receiving the sacrament in a state of sin.

3. If one who is unworthy were to demand the administration of a sacrament out of contempt for the Faith or to show his hatred for religion, the minister would be bound to refuse it even at the risk of his life. He must protect the sacraments which have been committed to his care from so great an indignity—which indeed would redound on God himself—even at the risk of life. Whether a minister at the risk of his life would be bound to refuse a sacrament to one who was unworthy and who demanded its administration with threats of death in case of refusal, not indeed out of contempt or hatred of the Faith, but for some other reason, is a disputed point among theologians. It is at any rate a probable opinion that the minister would not be bound to expose his life to danger, but that he might administer the sacrament to save himself, as we saw above that he might administer it to a secret sinner to avoid scandal.

4. Innocent XI condemned the proposition that instant and grave fear is a just cause for simulating the administration of the sacraments.[2] From this it follows that not only formal

---

[1] 1 West., d. 22; can. 1033.   [2] Prop. 29.

simulation with the intention of deceiving others is wrong, as being a lie in action, but even material simulation of administering a sacrament, whereby the matter or the form of a sacrament is used without the making of the sacrament, is not justified by grave fear. The minister may not give an unconsecrated host to a sinner as Communion, nor fictitiously absolve a penitent even to avoid death. The reason is because by so doing he would abuse a holy rite, instituted by Christ, and thus be guilty of gross irreverence toward God. It is a less sin for a priest to celebrate unworthily than to pretend to say Mass and not consecrate. However, a priest who instead of absolving a penitent who is not worthy of absolution dismisses him with a blessing so as not to betray him to people who are looking on, does not simulate the administration of the sacrament in the technical sense, and he does nothing reprehensible. He does not make an irreverent use of the sacramental sign or of part of it without completing the sacrament, in which the essence of the simulation of the administration of a sacrament consists in so far as it is wrong and has been condemned by the Church.

According to Canon 731, it is forbidden to administer the sacraments of the Church to heretics and schismatics, even though they be in good faith and ask for them, unless they have first been reconciled with the Church after abjuring their errors.

CHAPTER IV

THE RECIPIENT OF THE SACRAMENTS

1. THE sacraments were instituted to sanctify the souls of men and thus to prepare them for heaven. Only living men, then, can validly receive the sacraments; dead men or other beings cannot receive them validly. Death takes place when the soul is separated from the body, but we do not know the precise moment when that separation takes place. Except putrefaction, there are no absolutely certain signs of death, and it is quite probable that the soul remains united to the body for some time after all apparent signs of life have disappeared. Under these circumstances recent medical men and divines hold that it is lawful to administer the last sacraments to one who has to all appearances been dead for an hour or two. This is especially the case when death is the result of some sudden accident. Men only, not women, are capable of receiving the sacrament of Orders, and only those who have committed actual sins after Baptism can validly receive the sacrament of Penance. As the sacraments were instituted for the Church of Christ, of which men become members by Baptism, this sacrament is a necessary condition for the valid reception of the others.

2. No special disposition or intention is required on the part of infants, who have not come to the use of reason, and of imbeciles for the validity of the sacraments which they are capable of receiving. As they have not the use of reason they are incapable of disposing themselves for the reception of the sacraments, and yet the Church has been accustomed to give them the sacraments. The practice of the Church in such matters has the very greatest authority, as the Angelic Doctor says: " The custom of the Church has the greatest authority, and it should always be followed in all things, because even the teaching of Catholic Doctors receives its authority from the Church. So that we must rather stand by the authority of the Church than by the authority of Augustine or Jerome, or of any Doctor soever."[1] With reference to infant Baptism the Council of Trent passed the following decree: " If anyone saith that little children, for that they have not actual faith,

---

[1] *Summa*, 2-2, q. 10, a. 12.

are not, after having received Baptism, to be reckoned amongst the faithful; and that for this cause they are to be rebaptized when they have attained to years of discretion; or that it is better that the Baptism of such be omitted than that while not believing by their own act they should be baptized in the faith alone of the Church; let him be anathema."[1]

3. On the other hand, God does not sanctify adults who have the use of reason without some co-operation on their side; justification, says the Council of Trent,[2] is the sanctification and renewal of the interior man by the *voluntary* reception of grace and the gifts of the Holy Spirit. Some wish, desire, or intention to receive a sacrament is, then, necessary on the part of adults for its validity. A positive refusal to receive a sacrament, or a neutral state of mind neither willing nor refusing it, would make the reception of a sacrament null and void. The kind of intention which is necessary and sufficient for the validity of a sacrament varies according to its nature. In Penance and Matrimony a virtual intention is required in the subject, as it is required in the minister. For in Penance the acts of the penitent enter into the substance of the sacrament, and so they must be directed by him to its confection. Matrimony is constituted by the mutual consent of the parties, and for this at least a virtual intention is necessary. An habitual intention is required in order to be baptized validly; in other words, the person baptized must have at some time intended to receive the sacrament and not revoked his intention afterward. It is a disputed point among divines whether an habitual and express intention is necessary or whether an implicit intention contained in a desire to do all that God has ordained, or in an act of perfect charity or contrition, is sufficient. The latter opinion is probable, and it may be used in case of necessity when one is in danger of death, and then only. For the sacraments, which confer benefits without imposing any great burden, a general or implicit intention, such as is contained in a desire to die like a Catholic with all the rites of the Church, is sufficient for their validity. For Orders at least an habitual intention is required.

Those, therefore, who are asleep, or are unconscious, can receive the sacraments validly, for they may have all the dispositions which are necessary. The only difficulty is about Penance, but, as we shall see, it is at least a probable opinion that absolution is valid when given to one who is unconscious, but otherwise disposed for the sacrament. However, it is

[1] Sess. vii, c. 13, de Bapt.   [2] Sess. vi, c. 7.

not lawful to administer the sacraments to those who are asleep, unconscious, or out of their mind, except when in danger of death. For the subject should be in a fit state to dispose himself for the reception of the sacraments so that he may receive them with due reverence and fruit.

4. Except in Penance, neither faith nor good dispositions are required for the validity of the sacraments, as is clear from the practice of the Church, which is not accustomed to repeat sacraments received in heresy or in bad dispositions. However, the state of grace is necessary for the lawful reception of the sacraments of the living, as we have seen; and for those of the dead, faith, hope, and sorrow for sin are necessary, as the Council of Trent teaches that they are for the justification of the sinner.[1] Furthermore, for the lawful reception of the sacraments the subject must be free from all censures which deprive him of the right to receive them.

It follows from this that heretics and schismatics even when baptized may not lawfully receive the sacraments at the hands of Catholic ministers, as a general rule.[2] The sacraments are intended for those who are visibly members of the Catholic Church, and they alone have the right to receive them. If anyone else wishes to receive them, let him enter the visible Church of God. However, it is a disputed point whether the sacraments may be lawfully administered to a schismatic or heretic who is in good faith, and who is in danger of death. Although St Alphonsus and others deny that it is lawful to absolve such a person, yet the opposite opinion has its supporters, and it is in keeping with several decrees of the Roman congregations—as, for example, that of the Holy Office, July 20, 1898.[3]

The faithful are not prohibited from asking for the sacraments from ministers who they know lead bad lives, if they have good reason for so doing. Sin, indeed, is committed by the minister if he administers a sacrament while in sin, but if he does so his malice must be imputed to himself, not to those who for good reason exercise their right to receive the sacraments. Moreover, the malice of the minister cannot affect the sacraments.

Although in extreme necessity a Catholic may receive the sacraments from schismatical ministers, yet scandal to be avoided rarely permits of its being done, as Benedict XIV teaches.[4]

---

[1] Sess. vi, c. 6. [2] Can. 731.
[3] *Analecta Ecclesiastica*, 1898, p. 387.
[4] De Syn. vi, c. 5, n. 2.

The faithful may confess to any Catholic priest of any rite who has faculties for confession (Can. 905); and the faithful may receive Holy Communion consecrated according to any rite. But they are to be counselled to receive their Easter Communion according to their own rite. Holy Viaticum should also be received according to the rite of each one, except in case of necessity when it may be received according to any rite (Can. 866).

BOOK III
BAPTISM

CHAPTER I
THE NATURE OF BAPTISM

1. THE first of the sacraments, the door by which men enter into the Church of God, by which they are made her children and the sons of God, is Baptism. The Catechism of the Council of Trent defines Baptism as the sacrament of regeneration by water in the word. This is but expressing in other words what our Lord said to Nicodemus, " Unless a man be born again of water and the Holy Ghost he cannot enter into the kingdom of God."[1] The new birth which takes place in Baptism is the new life of grace which is given to the soul by the sacrament, and by this vivifying grace the soul which was dead to God lives to him with a supernatural life.

Baptism, then, is a total washing of the soul from the stains of sin, both original and actual, if any have been committed, and a complete cancelling of all the debt of punishment which may be due to sin. This is brought about by the infusion of sanctifying grace into the soul, together with the habits of the theological virtues of faith, hope, and charity. Moreover, by Baptism a character is imprinted on the soul by which it is known to God and his angels as that of a baptized Christian; and the person baptized becomes a member of the Church, a child of God, and heir to the kingdom of heaven.

2. By the positive will of Jesus Christ Baptism is necessary for salvation, as may be gathered from the words quoted above. This truth was defined by the Council of Trent,[2] " If anyone saith that Baptism is optional, that is, not necessary unto salvation—let him be anathema." Without Baptism, then, it is impossible to be saved, not merely because Christ commanded all to receive this sacrament, but because it infuses sanctifying grace into the soul, that nuptial garment without which no one can be admitted to the beatific vision. If, however, for one cause or another it is not possible to receive the Baptism of water, its place may be supplied by an act of perfect

[1] John iii 5.   [2] Sess. vii, c. 5, de Bapt.

contrition or of the pure love of God, and by martyrdom. On this account Baptism is said by theologians to be threefold: the Baptism of water, the Baptism of desire, and the Baptism of blood.

Perfect conversion to God by contrition for sin or by charity certainly infuses sanctifying grace into the soul and forgives sin, as Holy Scripture frequently declares, and as the Council of Trent teaches.[1] In this, therefore, its effect is similar to the primary effect of Baptism, and it is rightly called the Baptism of desire. Still, after the promulgation of the New Law the Baptism of desire only produces its effect because explicitly or implicitly it contains a desire and a purpose to receive the Baptism of water, should occasion offer. Although the Baptism of desire reconciles the sinner to God, yet it does not imprint any character on the soul, nor does it necessarily remit all the temporal punishment due to sin. The extent to which it does this will depend on the intensity of the act.

Martyrdom, also, or death patiently endured for the sake of Christ or for some Christian virtue, has the same effect as the Baptism of desire. "Greater love than this," said our blessed Lord, "no man hath, that a man lay down his life for his friends."[2] Still martyrdom does not produce its effect simply as an act of love, but in a manner *ex opere operato*, by a special privilege, as being an imitation of the passion and death of Christ. Thus the Church honours as saints in heaven the Holy Innocents and other children who have been put to death for the sake of Christ. In the case of adults who have committed sin there must at least be attrition for sin in order that martyrdom may produce its effect as a kind of Baptism.

[1] Sess. xiv, c. 4. [2] John xv 13.

CHAPTER II

THE MATTER AND FORM OF BAPTISM

1. THE remote and valid matter of Baptism is natural water in a suitable state for washing one's self. It is quite immaterial whether the water be spring water, rain water, sea water, or water from a river or pond; but frozen water is doubtful matter until it is melted, because it is not suitable for washing one's self; while mud is invalid matter (Can. 737).

For solemn Baptism the Church prescribes the use of water specially consecrated for the purpose, and the same may be used for private Baptism, as also may holy water and common water. For the private Baptism of adults who have been converted from heresy and require to be baptized conditionally, the First Synod of Westminster prescribes the use of holy water.

The proximate matter of the sacrament is its use or application in the act of baptizing. This may validly be done either by infusion, or immersion, or sprinkling, provided that the water touches the head of the person to be baptized and flows so as to express the action of washing. In the Western Church, however, a triple pouring of water on the head of the person to be baptized, or a triple immersion, if such be the custom, is prescribed by the rubrics of the Ritual. Care should be taken that the water touch the skin, as the Baptism would be of doubtful validity if it merely touched the hair. Merely to lay the wet hand or finger on the skin would not be valid Baptism, and even if the wet finger were moved over the skin the validity would still be doubtful (Can. 758).

2. The form of Baptism is: " I baptize thee in the name of the Father, and of the Son, and of the Holy Ghost." Any change in this form which altered the sense would also invalidate the Baptism, as if one should say, " I baptize thee in the name of Christ," or " of the Blessed Trinity." The form should be pronounced by the minister while he pours the water, and it is clear that if one pronounced the words while another poured the water, or if one baptized one's self, the Baptism would be invalid.

CHAPTER III

THE MINISTER OF BAPTISM

1. The ordinary minister of solemn Baptism is a priest, but as it is a parochial sacrament, its lawful administration belongs exclusively to the parish priest or to the priest who has the cure of souls in the district in which the parents of the child have their domicile or quasi-domicile. Such priest may, of course, delegate authority to any other priest to baptize in his name; if there is reasonable cause, as in case of illness or constant occupation in hearing confessions, he may commission a deacon to give solemn Baptism. The children of strangers may be baptized by the parish priest of the place, unless they can easily and without delay be baptized by their own parish priest (Can. 738, sec. 2).

In case of necessity, when there is danger of someone dying without Baptism, anyone who has the use of reason may baptize without the ceremonies. In such cases of necessity the Ritual prescribes that a priest should be preferred to a deacon, a deacon to a subdeacon, a cleric to a lay person, a man to a woman, unless the latter be preferred for the sake of decency or because she is better acquainted with the method of valid Baptism. Those who have the cure of souls should take care that the faithful, especially midwives, are instructed in the right method of administering Baptism. The Ritual also prescribes that a father or mother should not baptize their own child except when it is in danger of death and no one else can do so (Can. 742).

2. The ceremonies prescribed for solemn Baptism are of grave obligation, so that it would be a mortal sin to omit without necessity a notable part of them, as, for example, the anointings or the use of consecrated water. The child is anointed with the oil of catechumens before the actual baptizing, and afterward with the chrism. The holy oils should be kept carefully separated, and they should be renewed every year when the oils are consecrated by the Bishop on Maundy Thursday. The baptismal font, too, should be blessed on Holy Saturday with the oils consecrated on the previous Thursday. If they have not arrived in time the font should

be blessed without them, and they should be added afterward, unless, in the meantime, someone has to be baptized, and then the old oils may be used in blessing the font. If the oils threaten to be exhausted, fresh, unblessed olive oil may be added, always in smaller quantity. The same rule may be followed with regard to the consecrated water in the font. The Ritual admonishes the parish priest to take care that as far as possible names of saints should be given in Baptism, so that, by their example, the baptized person may be moved to live holily, and that he may hope to enjoy their patronage. In solemn Baptism the Latin language should be used, but certain portions may also be rendered in the vernacular, according to the Ritual approved for use in the country.

3. According to the Code of Canon Law, the proper place for solemn Baptism is the baptistery in a church or public oratory. Every parish church should have a baptismal font. If, on account of distance or for other reasons, a person to be baptized cannot be brought to the parish church, the parish priest may and ought to administer solemn Baptism in the nearest church or public oratory. Solemn Baptism should not be administered in private houses unless those to be baptized are the children or grandchildren of those who hold the chief authority in the country, or have the right to succeed to the throne, and they make the request, or if the local Ordinary for good reason in some extraordinary case thinks that it should be allowed. In these cases Baptism should be given with consecrated water, and in the chapel or in some suitable room of the house (Can. 773-776).

Adults should be baptized according to the longer form in the Ritual unless the local Ordinary for a grave reason allow the form for the Baptism of infants to be used (Can. 755, sec. 2).

Those who have attained the use of reason are their own masters in the things of God, and are considered adults with reference to Baptism (Can. 745, sec. 2, ii).

Adults who have been converted from heresy and require conditional Baptism are to be baptized privately with holy water and without the ceremonies, according to the First Synod of Westminster (Can. 759, sec. 2).

In questions concerning Baptism, infants are those who have not attained the use of reason, and those who never have had the use of reason are reckoned as infants (Can. 745, sec. 2).

Canon 760 prescribes that when Baptism is reiterated conditionally, the ceremonies are to be employed if they were not used in the first Baptism; if they were used in the first Baptism they may be used or omitted in the second at the option of the minister. This does not apply to conditional Baptism administered to adult converts.

CHAPTER IV

THE SPONSORS

1. SPONSORS, according to ecclesiastical law, are used in solemn Baptism to answer for the child baptized, to hold him during Baptism, or to receive him immediately after Baptism from the hands of the minister, and to act as his instructors in the Faith which he received and professed in Baptism. With regard to those who have Catholic parents, the sponsors may ordinarily presume that the Catholic education of the child will be sufficiently provided for by them; but otherwise the sponsors will be bound, as far as possible, to provide for it. Sponsors should be employed in private Baptism if at least one can easily be had; if this was not done, they should be employed afterwards when the ceremonies are supplied in the Church (Can. 762, sec. 2).

2. The Council of Trent ordained, " that in accordance with the appointments of the sacred canons, one person only, whether male or female, or at most one male and one female, shall receive in Baptism the individual baptized; between whom and the baptized, and the father and mother thereof, as also between the person baptizing and the baptized, and the father and mother of the baptized, and these only, shall spiritual relationship be contracted. The parish priest, before he proceeds to confer Baptism, shall carefully inquire of those whom it may concern what person or persons they have chosen to receive from the sacred font the individual baptized; and he shall allow him or them only to receive the baptized; he shall register their names in the book, and teach them what relationship they have contracted, that they may have no excuse on the score of ignorance. And if any others besides those designated should touch the baptized, they shall not in any way contract a spiritual relationship, any constitutions that tend to the contrary notwithstanding."[1]

Spiritual relationship between the sponsors and the parents of the baptized person and between the minister of Baptism and the parents was abolished by Canon 768.

[1] Sess. xxiv, c. 2, de Ref.

In order to be sponsor validly a person must be:

(1) Baptized, have the use of reason, and have the intention of being sponsor.

(2) He must not belong to any heretical or schismatical body, nor be excommunicated by a condemnatory or declaratory sentence, nor infamous with the infamy of law, nor excluded from acts of law, nor a deposed or degraded cleric.

(3) He must not be the father, mother, or spouse of the person baptized.

(4) He must be designated by the person to be baptized, or by his parents or guardians, or failing these by the minister of Baptism.

(5) He must physically hold or touch the baptized person in the act of Baptism, by himself or by his proctor, or immediately raise or receive him from the sacred font or from the hands of the person baptizing (Can. 765).

3. To be admitted as sponsor lawfully a person—

(1) Must have reached the fourteenth year of his age, unless the minister judge otherwise for a good reason.

(2) He must not be excommunicated for a notorious crime, or excluded from acts of law, or infamous with the infamy of law, but without sentence having been passed, or under interdict, or otherwise publicly criminal, or infamous by infamy of fact.

(3) He must know the rudiments of the Faith.

(4) He must not be a novice or professed in any religious institute, unless there is necessity and the express leave be had of at least the local superior.

(5) He must not be in sacred orders unless he have the express leave of his own Ordinary (Can. 766).

Others are sometimes prohibited by provincial law, as the following in England: those who have not been confirmed or who have not made their Easter duties, and ecclesiastics.

One may be sponsor by proxy, and then the principal, not the proxy, contracts spiritual relationship with the person baptized.

Sponsors are not necessary when Baptism is reiterated conditionally, unless the same person can be had in the second Baptism as acted as sponsor in the first (Can. 763).

CHAPTER V

WHO MAY BE BAPTIZED?

1. ANY living human being who has not yet been baptized is capable of receiving this sacrament. If he has the use of reason, an habitual intention at least to receive Baptism is necessary for its validity, though, as we saw above, it is probably sufficient if it be implicitly contained in a wish to do all that God requires, or any similar act of the will. In children who have not attained the use of reason and in imbeciles no intention is required for the reception of Baptism; the intention of the Church supplies for it.

For the lawful reception of this sacrament by adults who have the use of reason all those dispositions are necessary which, as the Council of Trent teaches,[1] are required for the justification of the sinner. They must, then, have faith, and believe all those truths which God has revealed and which the Church proposes to our belief. In particular they must know and believe explicitly the being of God, that he rewards and punishes men according to their deserts, the Blessed Trinity, the Incarnation, the Apostles' Creed, the Decalogue, and the Lord's Prayer. In other words, they should be properly instructed in the catechism. They should also approach the sacrament with hope, and at least with that kind of sorrow for sin which is called attrition.

2. Catholic parents are bound to see that their children are baptized, and that as soon as can conveniently be done. According to approved theologians, it would be a serious sin if the Baptism of a child were put off for a month without good reason. As Catholic parents are subjects of the Church, and they are bound to obey her laws, no injustice would be done if a child of such parents were baptized without or against their wish. Non-baptized parents are not subject to the Church, and, as St Thomas teaches, it would be against natural justice if an infant of theirs who is in no danger of death were to be baptized without their consent. When a non-baptized child is in danger of death the necessity of providing for its eternal salvation overrides all other private considerations (Can. 750, sec. 1).

---

[1] Sess. vi, c. 6.

When a child comes to the use of reason he becomes his own master in the things of God, and absolutely he may ask for and receive Baptism without the consent of his parents. Still in practice great caution is needed in such a matter. Of course, if the parents agree to allow the child to be brought up a Catholic, and it has Catholic sponsors, the difficulty will cease. But if it is baptized against their will, and remains subject to their control in other respects, the faith of the child will be in constant danger, especially as it can hardly be very firmly established before mature age. Ordinarily, then, children should not be baptized without their parents' consent until they reach an age when their convictions are firmly rooted and there is every prospect of their perseverance.

3. It would be a grave sin knowingly to baptize again one who has already been validly baptized. So that when a child has been baptized by a nurse or midwife by reason of apparent danger of death, inquiry should indeed be made as to the manner of the Baptism, but if the matter and form were rightly applied the Baptism must not be repeated; only the ceremonies must be supplied in the Church. In case of doubt concerning the validity of the former Baptism, it should be repeated conditionally.

When heretics are converted to the Faith, inquiry should be made in every case concerning their Baptism. If it is found either that they were never baptized, or that the Baptism was invalid, they must be baptized again absolutely. If, after inquiry, a prudent doubt remains as to whether they were ever baptized, or as to whether their Baptism was valid, they should be baptized again conditionally, and in secret so as to avoid scandal.

If it is found that their Baptism was valid, they should only abjure their errors, and make a profession of the Catholic faith.

4. An aborted fœtus, if it is still living, should be baptized, rupturing the membranes if necessary, and pouring water over it while at the same time pronouncing the form of Baptism (Can. 746).

The Ritual admonishes ministers of the sacrament to be cautious about baptizing monsters. If a monster has not a human shape, but is a mere mass of fleshy growth, it should not be baptized at all. If there are two heads and two bodies, there are two persons, and both should be baptized, separately if there is time, otherwise under a common form. If it is doubtful whether there are two persons or only one, Baptism should be given absolutely to one, and again conditionally to the other, under the form, " If thou art not baptized, I baptize thee," and so forth.

The Ritual also prescribes that if a woman dies in pregnancy the fœtus should be extracted, and if still living should be baptized. This, of course, supposes that there is a skilled person present who judges that the fœtus is still alive, and who is capable of performing the necessary operation.

The question also occurs whether a mother, who is still living but who cannot bring forth her child alive, is bound to undergo a serious operation like Caesarian section in order to insure the eternal welfare of her child by Baptism. Of course she may not undergo the operation if it would be the immediate cause of her own death. The mother must not be killed even for the salvation of the child. Even if her health and condition are such that in all probability she could stand the operation, yet it is probable that she is under no obligation to submit to it. The child can with sufficient certainty be baptized in the womb, and even if the operation were performed, greater certainty that the child would still be alive and capable of Baptism can seldom be obtained. In such circumstances no strict obligation to undergo a serious operation can be imposed on the mother.

BOOK IV
CONFIRMATION

CHAPTER I
THE MATTER OF CONFIRMATION

1. CONFIRMATION is a sacrament by which a baptized person receives grace boldly to profess and defend the Faith which he received in Baptism. It is, then, complementary to Baptism; as Baptism makes a man a follower of Christ, Confirmation makes him a soldier of Christ. It is a sacrament of the living, and gives an increase of sanctifying grace to the soul together with the right to receive those actual graces which will be needed to resist temptation and to lead a good Christian life. It is also one of the three sacraments that imprint a character on the soul.

2. Divines are not agreed as to what constitutes the matter of Confirmation. Some hold that the general imposition of hands by the bishop who confirms at the beginning of the rite is the essential matter; while the subsequent anointing of each person to be confirmed belongs to the matter accidentally. Others maintain that this general imposition of hands and the anointing form the essential matter of the sacrament. The common opinion is that the anointing with chrism, together with the simultaneous imposition of the hand of the Bishop on the forehead of the confirmed person while he makes on it the sign of the cross with the chrism, is the adequate and essential matter of the sacrament.

Chrism, which is thus the remote matter of Confirmation, is made of olive oil and balsam. It is a disputed point whether the mixture of balsam is only of precept or whether it is necessary for the validity of the sacrament. However, balsam of any country will suffice. The chrism thus made must be blessed by a bishop, and this, according to the common opinion, is necessary for the validity of the sacrament.

Three kinds of holy oils are blessed by the bishop on Maundy Thursday—the oil of the sick, with which Extreme Unction is given; the oil of catechumens, with which those about to be baptized are anointed in administering Baptism; and chrism.

It is probable that any one of these holy oils will serve for the others, so that Confirmation given with oil of the sick would be probably valid. Still it is not lawful to follow this opinion except in case of necessity.

A fresh supply of holy oils should be procured every year after they have been blessed by the bishop on Maundy Thursday, and the old ones burned. However, if the new oils cannot be obtained at the proper time, especially in the missions where Vicars Apostolic without episcopal consecration have faculties to give Confirmation, the old oils may be used as long as the difficulty of obtaining new ones lasts.

3. The form of Confirmation is, " I sign thee with the sign of the cross, and I confirm thee with the chrism of salvation, in the name of the Father, and of the Son, and of the Holy Ghost." There is some doubt as to whether the invocation of the Blessed Trinity is an essential part of the form, chiefly because it does not appear along with the other part in the form used in the Eastern Church. The question belongs to dogmatic theology, but briefly we may say that if it is an essential part of the form, the invocation is elsewhere in the Oriental rite.

CHAPTER II

THE MINISTER OF CONFIRMATION

THE ordinary minister of Confirmation is a bishop, but the Pope may, and in the missions frequently does, delegate faculties to a priest to administer the sacrament with chrism blessed by a bishop. In other words, a bishop is the ordinary official in the hierarchy who has the power to admit Christians into the army of our Lord by confirming them, but the General of the army in special cases empowers a simple priest to do this. It is a disputed point whether the Pope could empower a simple priest to bless the chrism.

By law Cardinals, Abbots and Prelates *of no diocese*, Prefects and Vicars Apostolic have the faculty of giving Confirmation within their territory during their tenure of office (Can. 782, sec. 3).

A bishop may not give Confirmation outside his diocese without the leave of the bishop of the place; but within his diocese he may confirm all who come to him, whether they are his subjects or not, unless their own bishop has expressly forbidden it (Can. 783). A bishop is bound to give his subjects who have not been confirmed the opportunity of receiving the sacrament.

He must also be prepared to administer Confirmation when a reasonable request is made for it by any of the faithful subject to his charge.

In case the bishop himself is prevented from administering Confirmation he should provide that his subjects have the opportunity of receiving it at least every five years (Can. 785).

CHAPTER III

THE SUBJECT OF CONFIRMATION

1. ANYONE is capable of being confirmed who has not yet received this sacrament and who has been baptized. For the validity of the sacrament the use of reason is not necessary, but adults who have the use of reason must have at least an habitual intention of receiving the sacrament. No one may lawfully receive this sacrament who is not in the state of grace. Moreover, according to modern discipline, Confirmation is only given to those who have been well instructed in Christian doctrine and know well what is required of a good Catholic. Before Confirmation is administered, the opportunity should be taken to give special instructions in Catholic faith and practice to those who are about to receive the sacrament (Can. 1330).

2. The First Synod of Westminster[1] prescribes that priests who have the cure of souls should do all in their power to have children confirmed, especially if they be of the humbler sort, so that they may be able to resist the temptations to which their faith will afterward be exposed. Canon 787 says that no one may neglect to receive Confirmation on occasion being offered, and that parish priests are to take care that the faithful receive it opportunely.

3. For Confirmation there should be one sponsor who presents one or two to be confirmed. He himself should be confirmed, should have the use of reason, and should have the intention of fulfilling his office. He should not be a heretic or schismatic, or criminal, nor the father, mother or spouse of the person to be confirmed. He should be lawfully designated, and should physically touch the person confirmed by personal contact or by proxy.

That he may be lawfully admitted he should not be the same who acted as sponsor in Baptism, and he should be of the same sex as the person confirmed (Can. 794-796).

Spiritual relationship arises between him and the person confirmed (Can. 797). But it is not a diriment impediment of marriage (Can. 1079).

[1] d. 17.

BOOK V

THE HOLY EUCHARIST

Part I

THE SACRAMENT OF THE EUCHARIST

CHAPTER I

THE NATURE AND EFFECTS OF THE EUCHARIST

1. THE Council of Trent teaches " that in the august sacrament of the holy Eucharist after the consecration of the bread and wine our Lord Jesus Christ, true God and man, is truly, really, and substantially contained under the species of those sensible things. For neither are these things mutually repugnant—that our Saviour himself always sitteth at the right hand of the Father in heaven, according to the natural mode of existing, and that nevertheless he be in many other places sacramentally present to us, in his own substance, by a manner of existence which, though we can scarcely express it in words, yet can we by the understanding, illuminated by faith, conceive, and we ought most firmly to believe, to be possible unto God; for thus all our forefathers, as many as were in the true Church of Christ, who have treated of this most holy sacrament, have most openly professed that our Redeemer instituted this so admirable a sacrament at the Last Supper, when, after the blessing of the bread and wine, he testified in express and clear words that he gave them his own very body and his own blood. And this faith has ever been in the Church of God, that immediately after the consecration the veritable body of our Lord and his veritable blood together with his soul and divinity are under the species of bread and wine."[1] It does not belong to the province of moral theology to prove or to defend this dogma of our Faith. We accept the teaching of the Church that the holy Eucharist is a sacrament in which under the species of bread and wine we receive Jesus Christ, the spiritual food of our souls. It is not merely a sacrament while it is received by the communicant, or while it is consecrated

[1] Sess. xiii, c. 1, 3.

by the priest in Mass. It is a permanent sacrament, under which our Lord remains present as long as the sacred species remain unchanged. It gives sacramental grace to the soul while it is being swallowed as food, and the divine presence remains in the communicant until the species of bread and wine are corrupted.

Although in the consecration there is a twofold matter and form, yet these constitute only one sacrament, for the species of bread and wine together signify a complete spiritual repast, just as food and drink go to make one meal for the body.

2. The effects which the holy Eucharist produces in the soul are set forth by the Council of Trent: " Our Saviour wished that this sacrament should be received as the spiritual food of souls, whereby may be fed and strengthened those who live with his life who said, ' He that eateth me, the same also shall live by me '; and as an antidote, whereby we may be freed from daily faults, and be preserved from mortal sins. He would, furthermore, have it be a pledge of our glory to come, and everlasting happiness, and thus be a symbol of that one body whereof he is the head, and to which he would fain have us as members be united by the closest bond of faith, hope, and charity, that we might all speak the same things, and there might be no schisms amongst us."[1] Besides being an antidote by which we are preserved from mortal sin, it is a very probable opinion that if the Eucharist is received by one in a state of mortal sin, of which he is not conscious and to which he is not attached, that sin will be forgiven. For the sacraments give grace to all who put no obstacle in their way, and such a communicant cannot be said to put an obstacle to the grace of the sacrament. But the entrance of grace expels all mortal sin from the soul. This is the teaching of St Thomas[2] and many other theologians.

[1] Sess. xiii, c. 2.   [2] *Summa*, 3, q. 79, a. 3.

CHAPTER II

THE MATTER AND FORM OF THE EUCHARIST

1. THE remote matter of the Eucharist is twofold—wheaten bread and wine of the grape. Barley bread, or bread made from oats or rye, or any other kind of grain or vegetables or fruits, is invalid matter. The wheaten bread must be baked with water, not boiled, or mere dough. If baked with oil or milk or butter, it will be doubtful matter. The wine must be genuine juice of the grape, not made artificially; wine made from any other kind of fruit will be invalid matter. If the wine has become vinegar, it is changed substantially, and will not serve for Mass; if it has only begun to get sour, it will be consecrated validly, but the priest who uses it sins grievously. There is some controversy as to whether frozen wine could be consecrated. The rubrics prescribe that if the precious blood is frozen after the consecration it should be liquefied again by putting warm cloths about the chalice and then consumed. It is clear, then, that freezing does not change the species substantially so as to render our Lord no longer present under them; it follows from this that freezing does not prevent the wine being consecrated.

Unfermented bread is used for the Eucharist in the Western Church, and fermented in the Oriental rites. Members of the two Churches are bound under grave precept to follow their respective rites, even if a Western priest were for a time in the East (Can. 816).

Because water came forth from the opened side of our Redeemer with his blood, the Church has commanded that in saying Mass a little water, not more than a fifth or at most a third part of the wine, should be mixed with the wine in the chalice. If the wine of a country is of a poor quality and difficult to keep, a little alcohol may be added to it to preserve it, but not so as to make more than 12 or 18 per cent. of the whole. No other matter may be added either to the flour or to the wine which are used for the Blessed Eucharist, and the greatest care should be taken both by bishops and priests to insure the use of only genuine matter in the confection of this sacrament.

2. The form of consecration for the bread is, "For this is my body," and for the chalice, "For this is the chalice of my blood of the New Testament, the mystery of faith, which shall be shed for you and for many unto the remission of sins." Any change in these forms which would make the sense different would also make them invalid.

There is a controversy among theologians as to whether the whole of the above form for the consecration of the chalice is essential, or whether it would be sufficient for the validity of the consecration to say only, "This is the chalice of my blood." It is very probable that these words alone constitute the essential form for the consecration of the chalice, though, of course, the fuller form must always be used. For these words alone signify the real presence of our Lord; the rest are merely a further declaration or explanation of them. Besides, "This is my body" constitutes the valid form for the consecration of the bread, and so, by analogy, "This is the chalice of my blood" should constitute the valid form for the consecration of the wine.

3. For the valid consecration of the Eucharist the priest must not only use the proper matter according to the institution of Christ, but that matter must be physically present, not far distant from him, when he pronounces the form of consecration. This essential condition is required by the sense of the form, "This is my body," which indicates that the matter to be consecrated is near the priest, so that it can be indicated by the demonstrative pronoun. Hence a priest in one room could not consecrate bread and wine in another, or behind his back, or, as it would seem, locked up in the tabernacle. Moreover, the matter must be determined by the intention of the priest; he would not consecrate a host which had been left on the altar for him to consecrate, but about which he knew nothing, and which he had no intention to consecrate. A difficulty sometimes arises when a priest has been asked to consecrate the ciborium which is placed on the altar by the sacristan, but which the priest afterward forgets to take and place on the corporal for consecration. What is intended for consecration should be placed on the corporal and on the altar-stone of sacrifice. Inasmuch as this was not done, and it would be wrong to intend to consecrate a ciborium which had not been placed on the corporal, it would seem at first sight that such a ciborium is not consecrated. It is, however, better to make a distinction. If the priest had intended to consecrate the ciborium and during Mass had noticed its presence, though he did not advert to its being off

the corporal, it would certainly be consecrated. If, on the contrary, after being notified in the sacristy about consecrating the ciborium, he forgot all about it, and never adverted to its presence on the altar, the consecration will be doubtful; and hosts thus doubtfully consecrated should on no account be given as Communion to the faithful, but should be consecrated conditionally in another Mass, or if they are few in number they might be consumed by the priest before taking the ablutions.

Furthermore, for the lawful consecration of the matter, the hosts must be whole, clean, and of the usual size and shape; the chalice and ciborium must be uncovered, and the consecration must be in Mass as it is prescribed to be said and under both kinds. If the ciborium or chalice are by mistake left covered, the consecration will be valid, for all the conditions required for validity are fulfilled. Hosts to be consecrated should be on the corporal at the offertory when the victim is set aside for the sacrifice, but if this has not been done, they may be received up to the canon, or for grave reason even up to the consecration, but the oblation should be mentally supplied.

CHAPTER III

THE MINISTER OF THE EUCHARIST

1. ONLY a priest can say Mass and consecrate the Eucharist, and a priest is also the ordinary minister who distributes Holy Communion to others. If, however, the priest is occupied and is unable to give Holy Communion himself, he may delegate faculties to a deacon who is the extraordinary minister of the Eucharist. In case of necessity, especially when there is danger of dying without receiving the Viaticum, and there is no priest or deacon to give it, a simple cleric, or even a lay person, may administer Holy Communion to himself or to another. It was not very unusual in the primitive Church for laymen to do this, but nowadays the occasion would seldom arise.

2. Any priest within Mass, and if he celebrates privately, also immediately before and immediately after Mass, can administer Holy Communion. This may be done wherever he says Mass, even in a private oratory, unless for some good reason the local Ordinary forbids it in particular cases (Can. 846, 869).

It is the right and duty of the parish priest within his parish to carry Holy Communion publicly to the sick, even though they be not his parishioners. Other priests can only do this in case of necessity, or with at least the presumed leave of the parish priest or of the Ordinary (Can. 848).

To carry Viaticum to the sick, whether publicly or privately, also belongs exclusively to the parish priest. Any priest can carry Holy Communion to the sick privately (Can. 849).

3. All who have the cure of souls are bound to administer the Eucharist to their flock, not only when these are under an obligation to receive it, but whenever they reasonably ask for it. This obligation is grave, but it does not bind with proximate danger of death from catching disease or from some other cause, nor is a single refusal of the sacrament necessarily a grave sin, for the loss of it may easily be made up on another occasion. Priests who have not the cure of souls may sometimes be bound to administer Holy Communion, not out of justice, but out of charity.

4. For the lawful administration of Holy Communion the minister must be free from all censures which deprive him of

the right to administer it; he must be in the state of grace, and he must follow the rubrics laid down by the Church in the Missal and Ritual.

According to Canon 867, Holy Communion may be administered on any day, but on Good Friday only as Viaticum to the sick.

On Holy Saturday Holy Communion may not be given to the faithful except in High Mass, or immediately after it and in continuation of it.

Holy Communion can only be administered at the times when Mass may be said, unless there be some reasonable cause for doing otherwise.

But Viaticum may be given at any time of the day or night.

The Blessed Sacrament should not be taken from the church except when it is carried to the sick, and then with all the marks of honour prescribed by the rubrics of the Ritual. However, in English-speaking countries the Holy Eucharist cannot be taken to the sick publicly, so it is carried in a small pyx enclosed in a bag specially made for the purpose, and suspended by a cord or chain from the priest's neck. The priest should have on a stole underneath his coat.

5. If a consecrated host falls on the ground or on the Communion cloth, the place should be marked and afterward washed, and the water poured into the piscina. If the Precious Blood is spilled, the priest should suck it up as far as possible, and afterward the place should be well washed, scraped, and the water and scrapings poured into the piscina. If a consecrated host fall on the beard or clothes of a communicant, the place on which if fell need not be washed. If it falls on the breast or dress of a woman, she should take it reverently in her fingers and give it to the priest, who will then administer it to her as Communion.

If, while he is still vested, a priest discovers what seem to be particles consecrated in his Mass, the rubrics direct that he should consume them, even though no longer fasting; if he has put off the sacred vestments, or if the particles do not belong to his Mass, they should be reserved for another priest to consume after his own Communion, or placed in the tabernacle.

If the Blessed Sacrament is vomited by a sick man, the sacred species should be carefully separated and placed in a vessel in the tabernacle until they corrupt, when they should be thrown into the piscina. Corruption will more quickly take place, and any disagreeable odour will be avoided, if a little water be put into the vessel.

CHAPTER IV

THE RESERVATION OF THE EUCHARIST

1. THE Ritual prescribes that the parish priest, or one who has the cure of souls, should take care that some consecrated particles, in sufficient number for the use of the sick and for the Communion of the rest of the faithful, should be always reserved in a clean pyx of solid and decent material, well closed with its own lid, covered with a white veil, and as far as possible in an ornamented tabernacle kept locked with a key. This key should be in the keeping of the priest, not in that of the sacristan or other person. As a rule the pyx or ciborium is of silver, and gilded inside. There seems to be no strict law prescribing that it should be consecrated or even blessed, though there is a form for blessing it in the Ritual.

The Blessed Sacrament, then, must be thus reserved for the use of the faithful in all cathedrals, parish churches, and chapels of ease attached to parochial churches. Religious orders of men and women who take solemn vows have the privilege of reserving the holy Eucharist in their churches. It can only be reserved in other churches or oratories by special indult from the bishop, or from the Holy See in the case of strictly private oratories (Can. 1265).

2. The Ritual further prescribes that the tabernacle should be decently covered with a veil, that nothing else besides the Blessed Sacrament should be put in it, and that it should be placed on the high altar, or on another if this would conduce to greater reverence toward the holy Eucharist, so that it would be no obstacle to sacred functions or ecclesiastical offices. Several lamps, or at least one, should always be kept burning before it night and day. The lamps should be fed with olive oil, but if the church is very poor the bishop may allow vegetable or mineral oil to be used. Gas or electric lamps should not be tolerated. One lamp must be kept burning under pain of grievous sin.

The veil of the tabernacle should be white or in keeping with the colour of the day, but never black (Can. 1269-1271).

3. The particles taken for consecration should be fresh, not more than fifteen days or at most a month old, and they should be renewed every eight, or at most fifteen, days, though in this matter regard should be had to the dampness or dryness of the place and season (*cf.* Can. 1272).

CHAPTER V

THE SUBJECT OF THE EUCHARIST

Article I

The Necessity of the Eucharist

1. The holy Eucharist can be received only materially by one who is not baptized and who consequently is incapable of receiving the other sacraments; it is received spiritually by one who ardently desires to receive it with the proper dispositions; it is received sacramentally when it is really received by one who has been baptized. The sacramental reception of the Eucharist is not a necessary means of salvation, for it is a sacrament of the living and supposes the grace of God in the soul, and a soul in the state of grace has everything which is necessary for salvation. Divines dispute whether the Eucharist is a necessary means for preserving the life of grace in the soul. It is, indeed, the ordinary food of the Christian soul, as bread is the ordinary food of the body, but as there is other spiritual food which may be taken, and notably prayer, and this may supply for the want of the ordinary food, the better opinion holds that the Eucharist is not strictly necessary even for the preservation of the life of grace in the soul. However, it is certainly necessary by divine and ecclesiastical precept. The divine precept is manifest from the words of our Lord: " Unless you eat the flesh of the Son of man and drink his blood you shall not have life in you."[1] Not that these words imply that Communion under both kinds is of divine law, for he who receives the sacrament under one species receives the body and blood of Christ with his soul and divinity. Moreover, as the Council of Trent explains,[2] he who made use of those words also said, " He that eateth this bread shall live for ever."[3] The Church, therefore, for just and weighty reasons has forbidden Communion under both kinds, using the power given to her by Christ with reference to the dispensation of the sacraments, though she has no authority to change their substance.[4]

[1] John vi 54.
[2] Sess. xxi, c. 1.
[3] John vi 59.
[4] Trent, sess. xxi, c. 2.

This divine precept must be fulfilled at least at the time of death, when it is of the greatest importance, and also sometimes during life. How often it must be received to satisfy the divine precept is uncertain, but the Church has determined the divine law by ordering all the faithful who have come to years of discretion to receive Holy Communion at least once a year, at Easter.[1] Those, however, who desire to lead a good Catholic life, are by no means content with yearly Communion; they receive it once a month or still more frequently.

2. According to the general rule, children become subject to and bound to obey the positive laws of the Church when they reach the age of seven. However, before the new Code of Canon Law came into force it was usual to defer a child's first Communion until he had reached the age of nine or twelve. The Code (Can. 859) interprets the phrase "years of discretion," used by the Lateran Council, to mean the same as to attain the use of reason, and so, now, children are bound to make their Easter Communion when they are seven years of age, unless, indeed, for some good reason it is judged advisable to abstain for a time. This obligation, as far as it affects those under the age of puberty, falls chiefly on those who have care of them—that is, on parents, guardians, confessors, teachers, and parish priests (Can. 860).

Canon 863 prescribes that the faithful are to be exhorted to receive Holy Communion frequently, and even daily, according to the rules laid down in the decrees of the Holy See, and that those who attend Mass should dispose themselves to receive Holy Communion not only spiritually, but sacramentally.

Daily Communion may not be refused to anyone who is in the state of grace and who has a right intention. There should be suitable preparation and thanksgiving, and that daily Communion may be practised with more prudence and with greater fruit, the advice of the confessor should be asked.

It is a disputed point whether one who is now in danger of death and who has within the last few days received Holy Communion is bound by divine precept to receive Viaticum. Although any good Catholic would certainly receive it again, yet the obligation to do so is not clear, because the previous Communion in all probability satisfies the divine law. If one becomes dangerously ill on the day on which he has received Holy Communion out of devotion, it was similarly a disputed point whether he might, or was bound to, receive it again as Viaticum. Ordinarily, indeed, no one should receive Holy

---

[1] 4 Lat., c. 21; can. 859.

Communion twice on the same day, but in this case he may do so, though he is not bound to do so, for the Code only says that it is very much to be desired (Can. 864, sec. 2).

3. Holy Communion should not be given to those who have lost the use of reason, but if they have lucid intervals it may then be given if there be no danger of irreverence. To those who are in danger of death, and have lost the use of their senses, it may be given if they can swallow, and there is no danger of irreverence; and it should be given as Viaticum to criminals condemned to death if they are in the proper dispositions. Reverence forbids it to be given to those who are suffering from constant coughing, and to those who cannot retain any food on the stomach, unless they have been free from vomiting for six hours or so.

Article II

The Dispositions Requisite for the Reception of the Eucharist

Section I

The Dispositions of the Soul

1. Besides having sufficient knowledge of what the Eucharist is, he who receives it should be in the state of grace and free from mortal sin. The presence in the soul of venial sin unrepented of is indeed a defect and an obstacle to the fullest outpouring of God's grace, but it is not a new sin to receive Holy Communion with only venial sins on the soul. But it is a grievous sacrilege to receive the Eucharist while conscious of being in mortal sin, " For he that eateth and drinketh unworthily, eateth and drinketh judgement to himself, not discerning the body of the Lord." It is not sufficient for one who is conscious of mortal sin to recover the state of grace by making an act of perfect contrition before Communion; he is bound to go to confession. This is taught us by the Council of Trent:[1] " Wherefore he who would communicate ought to recall to mind the precept of the Apostle, *Let a man prove himself*. Now ecclesiastical usage declares that necessary proof to be, that no one conscious to himself of mortal sin, how contrite soever he may seem to himself, ought to approach to the sacred Eucharist without previous sacramental confession. This, the Holy Synod hath decreed, is to be invariably observed

[1] Sess. xiii, c. 7.

by all Christians, even by those priests on whom it may be incumbent by their office to celebrate, provided the opportunity of a confessor do not fail them; but if in an urgent necessity a priest should celebrate without previous confession, let him confess as soon as possible." No one, then, who is conscious of mortal sin may go to Holy Communion without sacramental confession, unless he is under some necessity of receiving the Eucharist and there is no opportunity of going to confession. There will be such necessity as is here contemplated if a priest has to say Mass for his people on a day of obligation, or to consecrate the Viaticum for a dying person, or if Communion must be received to avoid scandal or to satisfy the Easter precept. There is no opportunity of going to confession if there is no priest present who can give absolution, and it would be a serious inconvenience to go to one at a distance. Even when in these circumstances a priest who is in sin has said Mass with contrition indeed, but without confession, he is commanded by the Council of Trent to go to confession as soon as possible afterward. This is a strict ecclesiastical law, but according to the mind of the Council it only binds priests, not laymen (Can. 807, 856).

2. When one has been to confession with a view to going to Holy Communion, but forgot to mention some grievous sin which he afterward remembers, he is not obliged to repeat his confession before Communion; it will be sufficient if he mentions it in his next confession. The reason is because the forgotten sin was indirectly forgiven by the absolution which he received, and he has proved himself sufficiently according to the words of the Apostle.

Even if there be not sufficient time to make a full confession before Communion, still confession is obligatory, as it is also when the penitent has reserved cases, for now in case of necessity any confessor may absolve directly from reserved cases.

Section II

The Dispositions of the Body

1. Although God looks to the soul and its dispositions rather than to externals, yet, as the Ritual says, those who communicate should approach the altar with humble deportment, and their dress and everything about them should show forth the reverence which they feel for the Blessed Sacrament. Reverence taught the first Christians that the holy Eucharist should be the first food taken in the day, so that fasting Com-

munion very soon came to be a universal practice in the Church. St Augustine says that it was the custom throughout the whole world in his time, and he traces it back to the times of the Apostles.[1] The Council of Constance says: " This present council declares, decrees, and defines, that although Christ instituted and gave this venerable sacrament to his disciples under both species of bread and wine after supper, yet notwithstanding, the laudable authority of the sacred canons and the approved custom of the Church has and keeps this observance that this sacrament ought not to be consecrated after supper nor received by the faithful unless they be fasting, except in case of sickness or of some other necessity allowed and admitted by law and by the Church."[2]

The rubrics of the Missal[3] contain the following: " If anyone has not kept fast after midnight, though he has taken only water or other drink or food, even as medicine, and in however small a quantity, he cannot communicate or celebrate. If remnants of food remaining in the mouth are swallowed, they do not hinder Communion, since they are not taken as food, but with the saliva. The same holds good if in washing the mouth a drop of water is swallowed inadvertently " (cf. Can. 858).

The law of the Church, then, with reference to fasting Communion is that the Eucharist may not be received by one who has not kept strict fast from all food and drink, even in the smallest quantity, since midnight. If Holy Communion is received shortly after midnight, there is no obligation to fast for some time before midnight, although reverence would dictate the advisability of such a course. The law of fasting has been made out of reverence for the Blessed Sacrament, so that violations of it are against the virtue of religion and sacrilegious.

To constitute a violation of the fast, what is taken must be of the nature of food or drink. Pebbles, wood, paper, hairs are not food, and if swallowed do not hinder Communion. The same is probably to be said of bits of the nails of the fingers, which some people have a habit of biting. The food or drink must also be taken as food or drink, not *per modum respirationis*, as is said, and must be from without, not from within the mouth. Taking snuff, or smoking, or inhaling a flake of snow with the breath, do not, then, hinder Communion, nor the swallowing of blood from the gums or from inside the lips.

[1] Decretum Gratiani, c. 54, D. 2, de consec.
[2] Sess. xiii.   [3] De def. ix.

THE SUBJECT OF THE EUCHARIST

Midnight may be reckoned according to the time publicly observed in the place, or by the true time according to the sun, or by the mean time.

2. The law which prescribes fasting Communion is a positive ecclesiastical law and admits of exception and excuse. Thus, when in danger of death, from whatever cause, one may receive Holy Communion not fasting. This may also be done if it is not possible to abstain from Communion without grave scandal or serious loss of reputation; or when the Blessed Sacrament is in danger of being profaned; or in order to complete the sacrifice of the Mass left unfinished by another priest from sudden illness; or probably in order to consecrate the Viaticum for a dying person who otherwise would be deprived of it. The common opinion is that Mass may not be said by a priest not fasting merely in order that his people may hear Mass on a Sunday; but this reason, taken together with some other, might justify the action.

There used to be a controversy among divines as to whether one who is sick but not in danger of death, and yet cannot observe the fast before Communion, may be allowed sometimes to communicate not fasting. This controversy has been set at rest by the decree of Pius X, December 7, 1906, and by Canon 858, sec. 2. The law now allows those who have been sick in bed for a month, without a well-grounded hope of their speedy recovery, although they may have taken something by way of drink or medicine, to receive with the advice of their confessor Holy Communion once or twice in the week.

After receiving Viaticum a sick person who continues to live for some time afterward may receive Holy Communion again, practically as often as his devotion urges him thereto and the priest's occupations will allow of its being brought to him. As long as he remains in danger of death, Holy Communion should be given as Viaticum, with the form, *Accipe frater*. No merely material uncleanness without moral fault, or mere bodily unsightliness, is a bar to Holy Communion. Married people are advised to abstain from marital intercourse before going to Holy Communion, but there is no strict obligation to do so.

Viaticum should be given to children in danger of death if they can distinguish it from ordinary food and pay it reverent adoration (Can. 854, sec. 2).

Part II

THE EUCHARIST AS A SACRIFICE

CHAPTER I

THE NATURE OF THE SACRIFICE OF THE MASS

1. THE Council of Trent teaches that the Eucharist is not only a sacrament but is also a sacrifice, instituted by our Lord at the Last Supper to represent and perpetuate the memory of the sacrifice which he was about to offer on the Cross, and to apply its fruits to the souls of men. " He therefore, our God and Lord, though he was about to offer himself once on the altar of the Cross unto God the Father by means of his death, there to operate an eternal redemption; nevertheless, because that his priesthood was not to be extinguished by his death, in the last supper, on the night in which he was betrayed —that he might leave to his own beloved Spouse the Church a visible sacrifice, such as the nature of man requires, whereby that bloody sacrifice, once to be accomplished on the Cross, might be represented, and the memory thereof remain even unto the end of the world, and its salutary virtue be applied to the remission of those sins which we daily commit—declaring himself constituted a priest for ever according to the order of Melchisedec, he offered up to God the Father his own body and blood under the species of bread and wine; and under the symbols of those same things he delivered (his own body and blood) to be received by his Apostles, whom he then constituted priests of the New Testament; and by those words, *Do this in commemoration of me*, he commanded them and their successors in the priesthood to offer (them); even as the Catholic Church has always understood and taught."[1]

A sacrifice is defined to be an offering of some visible object made to God by the performance of a sacred action on the part of a priest or publicly deputed minister, by which we confess the supreme lordship of God. A sacrifice, therefore, differs from an ordinary offering in that it is an act of public worship paid to God alone by a duly authorized minister, who,

---
[1] Trent, sess. xxii, c. 1.

by slaying the victim or in some way changing it, proclaims the supreme dominion of God over all things.

The sacrifice of the Eucharist is called the Mass, and it may be offered for all the ends for which the various sacrifices of the Old Law were instituted by God. It is the supreme act of worship which we pay to God, and under this respect it is called latreutic; it is eucharistic, inasmuch as through it we render thanks to God for his graces and benefits; it is impetratory, inasmuch as it placates the anger of God, which has been roused against sin and the sinner; and it satisfies the justice of God and thus remits the punishment due to sin.

The introductory portion, up to the offertory, is called the Mass of Catechumens, the principal parts of the Mass being the offertory, the consecration, and the communion. There is much difference of opinion among divines as to what constitutes the essence of the sacrifice of the Mass. Some place its essence in the communion, others in the consecration, others in the consecration together with the communion. More probably the consecration of both species, by which the death of Christ is mystically represented by the separate consecration of the bread and wine, contains the whole essence of the sacrifice. The question belongs rather to dogmatic than to moral theology.

2. The Mass is a representation and a reproduction in an unbloody manner of the sacrifice of our Lord on the Cross. The principal minister, Jesus Christ, is the same; the victim is the same; the only difference is the manner of offering, as the Council of Trent teaches. A rightly ordained priest is the secondary minister, who in the name of Christ and of the Church offers the sacrifice to God. In so far as it is the action of Christ, the Mass produces its effect like the sacraments *ex opere operato*, and does not depend for its efficacy on the holiness or other dispositions of the priest. But it is also the action of the priest, and of the faithful in whose name he acts; and under this respect it produces its effect *ex opere operantis*.

All the faithful, by virtue of the Communion of saints, but especially those who assist at Mass, partake of its fruits and benefits. Those fruits are, as we have seen, latreutic, eucharistic, impetratory, propitiatory, and satisfactory; so that in the Mass we have a most excellent means of fulfilling all the ends of religion. By it and through it we offer to God the highest act of worship which it is in our power to offer; we give him thanks for his continual benefits to us, we ask in the most efficacious manner for what we and others stand in need of, we propitiate his just anger, and make satisfaction for our sins.

The priest who celebrates performs an action in the highest degree pleasing to Almighty God and meritorious for himself. Moreover, just as prayer may be offered for a special intention, and as the sacrifices of the Old Law were offered for the needs of those who presented the victim, so the Mass also may be celebrated by the priest for some definite intention. The special or ministerial fruit of the Mass is thus applied by the priest according to the intention with which he offers it.

3. Apart from special prohibitions, the Mass may be offered for all those for whom the sacrifice of the Cross was offered, and whom it can benefit. It may be offered for all the faithful living and dead. The Council of Trent defined that the souls in purgatory are helped by the sacrifices of the faithful, and it is at least theologically certain that the fruits of the Mass are to some extent, which is known to God, applied to them *ex opere operato*, when Mass is said for that intention. It may also be offered for the conversion of infidels, and in thanksgiving for all the graces and glory which God has bestowed on the blessed in heaven. The damned in hell can receive no benefit from our prayers or sacrifices. According to the new Code, Mass may be offered for anybody, living or dead, but only privately, and with precautions to avoid scandal for excommunicates, and, moreover, only for their conversion, if they are to be avoided as excommunicates (Can. 809; 2262, sec. 2, ii).

4. Infinite is the worth and dignity of the sacrifice of the Mass, for it is the same as the sacrifice on Calvary, which was capable of redeeming innumerable worlds. This is acknowledged by all theologians, but they are not agreed as to whether the actual fruit derived from a Mass is also infinite. Those fruits are, indeed, greater or less in proportion to the dispositions of the person to whom they are applied. But while St Alphonsus and others are of opinion that a Mass offered for any number of intentions will benefit each one as much as if it were offered for him alone, others hold that the fruit of a Mass is determinate in quantity, and that if it is offered for many each one receives less than he would do if it were offered for him alone. The latter seems the preferable opinion, as it explains better the practice of the Church according to which Mass is offered for individuals, living and dead. If the first opinion were correct, charity would require that every Mass should be offered for all who are in need, for no individual would be the loser; everyone would derive all the benefit from

the Mass of which he was capable. This opinion, too, is more in keeping with the nature of the sacraments, of which the fruits seem to be limited in quantity. Otherwise there would be no use in administering several sacraments to a dying person when out of his senses, as is the practice of the Church. Whichever opinion be true, it is against justice to offer only one Mass in satisfaction of the obligation of saying several, when several stipends have been received. Alexander VII condemned the following proposition: " It is not against justice to receive stipends for many Masses and to say only one. Neither is it against fidelity, even if I promise on oath to him who gives a stipend that I will not offer the Mass for anyone else."

Nothing, however, prevents the priest from having a second intention, as it is called, even when he says Mass for a stipend. By this second intention the priest intends that if for any reason the Mass cannot benefit him for whom the first intention offers it, then the fruit may go to the second. Or, if in fact it be true that the fruit of a Mass is infinite, and capable of equally benefiting any number of persons, then the priest by his second intention desires that others should benefit by his Mass.

CHAPTER II

THE APPLICATION OF MASS

1. THE application of a Mass is the intention with which the priest who says it wishes that it should accrue to the benefit of a certain person or persons. Such a special act is only required for the application of the ministerial or special fruit, as it is called; for the priest himself derives fruit from his Mass, as likewise do those who assist at it, and the faithful in general, without any special application.

As it belongs to one who prays to choose the intention for which he offers up his prayer, so the application of his Mass belongs to the priest. A superior may indeed prescribe the intention for which a Mass is to be offered, but he who celebrates the Mass must make the actual application. This should be done before the consecration is finished, for, according to the *common opinion*, the essence of the Mass consists in the consecration, and an action cannot receive its direction from an intention which is only formed after the action is accomplished. Probably, however, it will be sufficient if the intention is formed between the two consecrations.

2. It is not necessary that the intention by which Mass is applied should be actual or even virtual; it is sufficient if it be habitual, or made once for all and not afterward revoked.

When Mass is said for a stipend it is not necessary for the priest to know precisely what the intention is for which he is desired to say Mass; it is sufficient if he say Mass for the intention of the giver of the stipend. Clement VIII forbade priests to offer Mass for the first who should give a stipend for that purpose, and if no one actually intended to ask for a Mass when a priest celebrated with such an intention the Mass would not be applied.

A priest does not sin if he celebrates without any special intention, but it is always better to have one, as then the Mass will be more fruitful. When a priest celebrates for a stipend he may not divide the fruits of the Mass, applying the satisfactory or other fruit to the intention of the giver, and another fruit to some other intention. The whole fruit of the sacrifice must go to the giver of the stipend. When, however, a Mass is ordered by a superior in thanksgiving for some blessing, it will not be wrong to apply the other fruits for other intentions which in no way interfere with that prescribed by authority.

CHAPTER III

THE OBLIGATION OF APPLYING MASS

1. Priests may be bound to say Mass for a definite intention on various grounds. Those who hold a benefice are frequently obliged to say Mass, either every day or on certain fixed days, for the intentions prescribed by the founder of the benefice. The conventual Mass, which should be said every day in cathedral, collegiate, and conventual churches, ought to be applied for the benefit of the souls of benefactors.

The Council of Trent[1] declares that by divine precept it is enjoined on all who have the cure of souls to offer sacrifice for their flock. Bishops, therefore, and regular prelates, who have the full cure of souls, are bound by divine law to say Mass for those committed to their charge. Parish priests are of ecclesiastical institution, and they have not the full cure of souls committed to them. How far their duties extend depends on ecclesiastical law. That law obliges them as well as bishops to say Mass for their flock every Sunday and holy day of obligation, even on those feast-days of obligation which have been suppressed. This obligation is at the same time real and personal. It is real in the sense that if for any reason a bishop or parish priest cannot fulfil it on any particular day, he is under the obligation of providing that it should be fulfilled by some other priest. It is personal in the sense that they must as far as possible fulfil it in person; but if a parish priest be lawfully absent from his parish, he may either apply Mass for his people in the place where he is, or have one applied in his parish by the priest who takes his place (Can. 466, sec. 5).

Quasi-parish priests are bound to offer Mass for their people on the more solemn feasts mentioned in Canon 306.

2. The ecclesiastical superiors of priests may issue a command that Mass be applied for some special intention. When this is done the command must, of course, be obeyed by all whom it concerns. The matter of such a precept is certainly grave, and so there will be a serious obligation of complying with it, if the superior intended to issue a strict precept. This, however, is not always or necessarily the case; and in particular

[1] Sess. xxiii, c. 1, de Ref.

THE OBLIGATION OF APPLYING MASS

instances, if there is question of determining the gravity of an obligation arising from such a precept, the intention of the superior who gave it will have to be examined according to the ordinary rules of interpretation.

3. A priest may bind himself by promise to say Mass for a particular intention, and then he will be bound to say it either in justice, or at least out of fidelity, just as he is bound to fulfil his other promises.

4. Finally, priests are bound in justice to say Mass for the intention of those from whom they have received a stipend for the purpose. The stipend is not the price of the Mass, for this cannot be bought and sold without committing the grave sin of simony. The stipend is given to provide for the support of the priest, who in return undertakes to say Mass for the giver of the stipend. In the early Church the faithful used to bring bread and wine to the priests, who selected from what was offered enough for the sacrifice, and reserved the rest for their support. This was found to be inconvenient, and in course of time the faithful who wished Mass to be offered for their intention contributed a sum of money for the support of the priest. This method, after all, is in substance what St Paul alludes to: " Know you not that they who work in the holy place eat the things that are of the holy place; and theyt hat serve the altar partake with the altar?"[1] Simony may, indeed, be committed in transactions concerned with the Mass and stipends, but such sordid practices should not be presumed to be of ordinary occurrence (Can. 824).

Although a priest who accepts a stipend for a Mass does not sell the Mass, yet he enters into a strict contract with the giver of the stipend, and binds himself in justice to apply the Mass for his intention. He will, therefore, commit a grave sin against justice if he fail to fulfil his obligation, and he must restore the stipend which he received, but which he has no title to keep. Not only is the priest who has accepted a stipend bound in justice to say a Mass, but justice also requires that he should observe all the conditions of the contract into which he entered concerning the quality of the Mass, the place, and the time of celebration.

The law of the Church on the matter may be stated as follows:

According to the received and approved custom and practice of the Church, it is lawful for any priest who says and applies Mass to receive an alms or stipend for it.

[1] 1 Cor. ix. 13.

But whenever a priest says Mass more than once in the day, if he has applied one Mass by a title of justice, except on Christmas Day, he cannot receive a stipend for another Mass on the same day, but he may receive some compensation due for some extrinsic reason.

It is never allowed to apply Mass for the intention of someone who will offer a stipend and ask for the application of a Mass but has not yet done so, and retain a stipend given afterwards for a Mass said beforehand.

Nor is it allowed to receive a stipend for a Mass which is due in justice and applied by another title. Nor to receive a double stipend for the application of the same Mass. Nor to receive one stipend for the mere celebration of Mass, and another for the application of the same Mass, unless it is certain that one stipend was offered for the mere celebration of the Mass without its application.

Those are called *manual* stipends which are offered for Masses by the faithful, as it were, out of *hand*, whether in order to satisfy their own devotion or to fulfil an obligation imposed on them by the will of a testator even in perpetuity.

The stipends of funded Masses are said to be *like manual* Masses which cannot be applied in the proper place, or by those who ought to apply them according to the laws of the foundation to which they belong, and so by law or by an indult of the Holy See they have to be given to other priests to be satisfied.

Other stipends which are received from the revenue of foundations are called *funded* or *foundation* Masses.

Let all appearance even of trading or trafficking with stipends for Mass be altogether avoided.

As many Masses must be said and applied as stipends were given and accepted, however small they were.

The obligation does not cease even though the stipends already received for Mass have been lost without any fault on the part of him who was burdened with their celebration.

If anyone offers a sum of money for Mass stipends without indicating the number of Masses which he wishes to be said, let the number be computed according to the tax of the place where he lived, unless it must be lawfully presumed that his intention was different.

It belongs to the local Ordinary to determine the manual stipend for Masses in his diocese by a decree made in diocesan synod as far as possible; nor is it lawful for a priest to exact a larger sum.

Where there is no formal decree of the Ordinary on the point, let the custom of the diocese be observed.

Religious, even though they be exempt, ought to abide by the local Ordinary's decree or the custom of the diocese in the matter of the manual stipend of Masses.

A priest may receive a larger stipend for the application of Mass if it is offered voluntarily, and also a less, unless the local Ordinary has forbidden it.

It is presumed that the offerer of a stipend asked only for the application of Mass, but if he expressly stipulated that any circumstances should be observed in the celebration of Mass, the priest who accepts the stipend should comply with the desire expressed.

If the time for the celebration of Masses was expressly determined by the offerer of the stipend, the Masses must by all means be celebrated at that time.

If the offerer expressly determined no time for the celebration of manual Masses—

(1) Masses offered for an urgent intention must be offered at the time required by the circumstances and as soon as possible.

(2) In other cases the Masses must be offered within a reasonable time in proportion to the greater or less number of Masses. The decree of the Sacred Congregation of the Council, May 11, 1904, assigned one month from the time of receiving the stipend as the limit within which one Mass is to be said, six months as the limit for one hundred Masses, and a longer or shorter period for a greater or less number.

If the offerer expressly left the time of celebration to the judgement of the priest, the priest may say the Mass at what time he pleases, but no one is allowed to receive more stipends than he can satisfy in one year.

In churches in which, on account of the special devotion of the faithful, stipends for Mass are so abundant that all cannot be said there within the proper time, let the faithful be informed by a notice placed in an open and conspicuous place that the stipends offered will be satisfied either there, when it can be done conveniently, or elsewhere.

Let one who has Masses to be said by others distribute them as soon as may be, but the lawful time for their celebrating begins from the day on which the priest who has to say them received the same, unless the contrary is certain.

Those who have a number of Masses of which they can freely dispose may give them to priests on whom they can rely, provided that they know that they are unexceptionable, or are recommended by the testimony of their own Ordinary.

Those who have given Masses, which they have received from the faithful or which are entrusted to them, to others to be said by them, remain bound by their obligation until they receive notice that the stipends have been received and the obligation accepted.

One who sends manual stipends to others ought to send the whole sum which he has received, unless either the offerer expressly allows him to retain a portion, or it is certain that the excess above the diocesan tax was given out of personal considerations.

In Masses which are *like* manual Masses, unless the intention of the founder forbids it, any excess may lawfully be retained, and it is sufficient to send only the manual stipend of the diocese in which the Mass is celebrated, if the large stipend takes the place of a part of the dowry of the benefice or pious foundation.

Each and all administrators of pious foundations or persons who are bound in any way to fulfil obligations of having Mass said, whether ecclesiastics or laymen, towards the end of each year must give the Masses which have not yet been said to their Ordinaries according to the method to be defined by them.

This period is to be interpreted in such a way that in the Masses *like* manual Masses the obligation of handing them over runs from the end of the year within which they ought to have been said; but in manual Masses after a year from the day of undertaking them, unless the offerer determined otherwise.

The right and the duty of seeing that Mass obligations be fulfilled belongs to the local Ordinary in secular churches; in the churches of religious it belongs to their superiors.

Let rectors of churches and of other pious foundations, whether secular or religious, in which Mass stipends are wont to be received, have a special book in which they note the number of stipends for Mass received, the intention, the amount of the stipend, and the celebration of the Masses.

The Ordinaries are under the obligation at least every year of examining these books in person or by deputy.

Moreover, local Ordinaries and religious superiors who give Masses to their subjects or to others to be said should at once put down in order in a book the Masses which they have received with their stipends, and should take care, as far as they can, that the Masses be said as soon as possible.

Indeed, all priests, whether secular or religious, ought to note accurately what Mass intentions they have received and which they have satisfied (Can. 824-844).

CHAPTER IV

THE TIME FOR SAYING MASS

1. By the common law of the Church Mass may only be said once in the day except on Christmas Day and on the day of the Commemoration of the Holy Souls (November 2), when a priest may say three Masses. Mass may be said on every day in the year, but on the three last days in Holy Week Low Mass is forbidden. On those days in cathedral, collegiate, and parish churches, High Mass should be sung as far as possible. In parish churches where High Mass cannot be sung, but three or four clerics can be got to serve, the ceremonies should be carried out according to the memorial of rites drawn up by command of Benedict XIII. In parish churches where not even this can be done, the bishop may give leave for a Low Mass on Holy Thursday, and he may also, for the convenience of the sick, allow a Low Mass to be said in other churches before the High Mass.

2. Mass may be said twice by a priest on the same day if the necessity of the people requires it. The bishop is the judge as to when it is necessary, as it will be if the people cannot all get to one Mass on account of the distance at which they live from the church, or because the church is too small to contain them all at once. Moreover, in missionary countries it is quite common for priests to have a special faculty of celebrating twice in the day on Sundays and holy days of obligation. The only cause recognized for the lawful use of this faculty is the necessity of the people, of which again the bishop is the judge, and it is expressly forbidden to take a stipend for the second Mass. The use of the faculty is not lawful when another priest can be got to say the Mass required by the necessity of the people.

3. According to the present discipline of the Church, Mass may not be begun before one hour before daybreak nor after one hour after midday (Can. 821, sec. 1). The necessity of the people or of the priest is a sufficient reason for celebrating somewhat earlier and later than the ordinary times, and regulars have privileges by which they may for just cause begin Mass much earlier and much later than the legal time.

THE HOLY EUCHARIST

His Holiness Pius X, by a decree of the Holy Office dated August 1, 1907, graciously permitted a priest in future to say three Masses or only one according to the rubrics on the night of the Nativity in all convents of nuns who have enclosure, and in other religious institutions, pious houses, and clerical seminaries, in which the Blessed Sacrament is habitually reserved. Holy Communion may be administered to all who ask for it at these Masses, and anyone who hears one or more of them satisfies the precept of hearing Mass on that day.[1]

[1] *Acta Sanctae Sedis*, xl, p. 478; Can. 821, sec. 3.

CHAPTER V

WHERE MASS MAY BE SAID

1. By ecclesiastical law Mass may regularly be said only in churches and oratories dedicated solely to the service of God, and therein on duly consecrated altars.[1] If, however, there be no church in the place, or if it be in ruins, or if it be too small to hold the number of worshippers, Mass may be said in a tent or in the open air on a portable altar with the leave of the bishop, if time permits of this being asked.

A bishop can erect public oratories in which Mass may be said in religious institutions, in monasteries and convents, in seminaries, hospitals, prisons, and in the bishop's own residence. bishops also enjoy a personal privilege of saying Mass on a portable altar even in private houses where they happen to be staying.

The Council of Trent[2] forbade bishops to allow priests to say Mass in private houses, and in consequence of this law and of repeated answers of the Roman Congregations, it is now settled that bishops have no power to grant leave for purely domestic oratories in private houses (Can. 822).

The power to do this is now reserved to the Holy See.

If there is an oratory duly erected on board ship, Mass may be said there when circumstances permit. The Holy See also grants leave for Mass to be said on board ship on a portable altar even when there is no permanently erected oratory on board. A priest who has obtained and desires to use this privilege is bound to observe the conditions under which it is granted. Those conditions are that the ship is safe and at a distance from shore, that the sea is tranquil, and that another priest or a deacon is at hand to hold the chalice in case of danger when the ship rolls. Mass should not be said in the passengers' berths unless everything has been arranged so as to show due reverence to the Blessed Sacrament.

2. If a church or public oratory has been polluted by the perpetration therein of certain crimes, it is forbidden to say Mass there until it has been reconciled. The crimes which

---

[1] Trent, sess. xxii, Decree on things to be observed in Mass.
[2] *Loc. cit.*

pollute a church, provided that they are certain, notorious and committed in the church itself, are: homicide, the grave and injurious shedding of blood, the putting of the church to impious or sordid uses, the burial therein of an unbaptized person or of an excommunicated person after a declaratory or condemnatory sentence (Can. 1172).

It is not allowed to celebrate the divine offices, to administer the sacraments, or to bury the dead in a polluted church before it has been reconciled.

If the church is only blessed it can be reconciled by its rector or by any priest with the presumed leave at least of the rector.

If the church is consecrated, its reconciliation belongs to the Ordinary of the place or to the higher superior if it is a church of exempt religious, or to a priest delegated by either of them. But in a case of grave and urgent necessity, the rector of a consecrated church can reconcile it and inform his Ordinary afterwards. The reconciliation of a blessed church can be done with common holy water. If the church is consecrated, the water should be specially blessed, but the priest who is deputed to reconcile the church can bless the water as well as the Ordinary (Can. 1176, 1177).

Private oratories are not polluted, even if any of the above crimes be committed in them, and so they do not need reconciliation.

Mass may not be said in a church or oratory which has lost its consecration. This happens when the greater part of it is destroyed at one and the same time, or when a new portion is added to it and what is added is greater than the old part. A church does not lose its consecration if the roof falls in or if the plastering of the walls is renewed. When a church loses its consecration it must be reconsecrated, or at least blessed, before Mass be again said in it.

When a church is polluted the altars in it are also polluted, but altars do not lose their consecration merely because the churches in which they are placed are desecrated. A fixed altar loses its consecration if the altar-stone is loosed from its foundation, and both fixed and portable altars lose their consecration if the tomb where the relics are placed is violated, or in consequence of a large fracture.

3. The sacred vessels and vestments lose their consecration when they are broken or torn so as to lose their shape, or when they are put to improper uses or exposed for public sale (Can. 1305). When the sacred vessels or vestments have lost their consecration, they must be mended and be reconsecrated before use.

CHAPTER VI
REQUISITES FOR SAYING MASS

BESIDES what we have seen in the last chapter, the Missal prescribes various other requisites for the due celebration of Mass. The following especially call for mention here: three altar-cloths, two wax candles, the ordinary priestly vestments, a server, a chalice and paten, clean corporal and purificator of linen, and a Missal. The altar linen and the vestments should be blessed by a bishop or by a priest with specially delegated faculties for the purpose.

The chalice and paten should be of silver, and gilded at least on the inside. They should also be consecrated by a bishop. The difficulty of procuring wholly wax candles was reported to the S.R.C., which answered, December 14, 1904, that bishops should as far as possible see that the two candles for Mass should at least have a greater proportion of beeswax than of other material, and that private priests need not anxiously inquire about the quality of the wax.

Of the vestments, at least the alb, chasuble, stole, and maniple are required under grave precept; the amice and the girdle, as also a pall, purificator, and crucifix, are required under a less serious obligation.

The server should be a Catholic and of the male sex, but if one cannot be procured, a woman may make responses from outside the altar rails (Can. 813).

It is a disputed point among theologians whether the proper colour of the sacred vestments is of strict precept; and they deny that there is a strict precept with regard to the use of a veil for the chalice, a burse, and a stand for the Missal.

CHAPTER VII
THE RUBRICS OF THE MISSAL

1. IN the rubrics of the Missal the Church has laid down a series of minute rules for the celebration of Mass. Their number and minuteness show her solicitude concerning the proper performance of this divine sacrifice. Those which have reference to the Mass itself are in general preceptive and bind under pain of sin. Grave sin, then, is committed by violating the rubrics of the Mass in serious matters; venial sin is committed by their violation in smaller matters. If a notable or important portion of the rite is omitted, or if notable additions are made to it by private authority, or any considerable change be made in it, there is a serious violation of the law. The rubrics which ordain that certain portions of the Mass be said in a loud or low or middle tone of voice only bind under venial sin, and so, if their observance would cause annoyance to other priests who are saying Mass, they cease to bind. Similarly, if through infirmity a priest is unable to observe some smaller rubrics, it is not the mind of the Church that he should be obliged to abstain from celebrating the holy mysteries.

It is a probable opinion that those rubrics in the Missal which have reference to what should be done out of Mass are only directive, not strictly preceptive so as to bind under pain of sin.

2. The general rule is that the Mass must agree with the office which the calendar prescribes to be said. However, by the decree S.R.C., December 7, 1895, when Mass is said in a church or public oratory which is not one's own, which uses a different calendar, and celebrates a feast of double or higher rite, the Mass must always agree with the calendar of the church or public oratory, and not with the office of the celebrant.

3. When Mass has been once begun it may not be broken off without grave reason, even before the consecration. After the consecration a still graver cause is required, as, for example, the sudden breaking out of fire in the church, when the sacred species might be at once consumed and the Mass brought to

an end. Moreover, even temporary interruptions of Mass are forbidden except after the Gospel, according to custom. The prohibition is stricter according to the greater solemnity of the part of the Mass where there is question of interruption. However, for good cause, an interruption may be permitted before the offertory; to justify an interruption between the offertory and the consecration a graver cause is required, and a very grave cause after the consecration.

BOOK VI

THE SACRAMENT OF PENANCE

CHAPTER I

THE NATURE OF PENANCE

1. PENANCE is both a virtue and a sacrament of the New Law. For as the Council of Trent teaches: " Penitence was indeed at all times necessary in order to attain to grace and justice for all men who had defiled themselves by any mortal sin, even for those who begged to be washed by the sacrament of Baptism: that so, their perverseness renounced and amended, they might with a hatred of sin and a godly sorrow of mind detest so great an offence of God. Wherefore the prophet says, ' Be converted and do penance for all your iniquities, and iniquity shall not be your ruin.' The Lord also said, ' Except you do penance, you shall all likewise perish '; and Peter, the prince of the Apostles, recommending penitence to sinners who were about to be initiated by Baptism, said, ' Do penance and be baptized every one of you.' "[1] God, therefore, has always required repentance or penance on the part of the sinner as a necessary condition for forgiveness. The virtue of penance may be defined as a habit inclining the sinner to hatred and detestation of his sin. He may be moved to this hatred and detestation by various motives, as, for example, by the thought of the goodness of God, who deserves better treatment than to be offended by the sinner, by the feeling of gratitude toward God for his benefits and mercies, by the sentiment of justice which induces the sinner to make reparation for the wrong which by sin he has inflicted on the majesty of God. Penance may thus be a general virtue with various motives, but theologians agree that it is also a special virtue with a particular motive of its own. More commonly they assign as this motive the hatred of sin as being an offence against God, something at which God is rightly and justly angered and displeased, and for which satisfaction must be made to God before peace and harmony can be again established between him and the sinner.

[1] Sess. xiv, c. 1.

Our Lord Jesus Christ instituted the sacrament of Penance, by which the sins committed after Baptism might be forgiven on the sinner's repentance. As the Council of Trent teaches: "Nevertheless, neither before the coming of Christ was penitence a sacrament, nor is it such since his coming for anyone previously to Baptism. But the Lord then principally instituted the sacrament of Penance when being raised from the dead he breathed upon his disciples, saying, 'Receive ye the Holy Ghost: whose sins you shall forgive they are forgiven, and whose sins you shall retain they are retained.' By which action so signal, and words so clear, the consent of all the Fathers has ever understood that the power of forgiving and retaining sins was communicated to the Apostles and their lawful successors for the reconciling of the faithful who have fallen after Baptism."[1]

Penance may be defined as a sacrament of the New Law instituted by Christ after the manner of a judicial process for the remission of sins committed after Baptism by a priest's absolution given to the contrite sinner who has confessed his sin to him.

This sacrament is instituted after the manner of a judicial process, which may be gathered from the very words of institution: "Whose sins you shall forgive they are forgiven, and whose sins you shall retain they are retained," said our blessed Lord; not, of course, that the Apostles were empowered to forgive or not to forgive sins according to their own pleasure. They were bound to exercise the power entrusted to them according to the intention of him who had given it, so that as faithful dispensers of the mysteries of God they were to forgive the sins of those who were worthy of forgiveness, and to dismiss without forgiveness those who were unworthy. But how could they know who was worthy and who was unworthy, and what sins they could forgive and what they could not? Evidently only by the sinner acknowledging his sins and showing that he repented of them, or on the contrary by his showing the want of the necessary dispositions. And so we gather from the words of institution of this sacrament what the tradition of the Church teaches, that for the forgiveness of sin in the sacrament of Penance the sinner must in sorrow confess his sin, and then it will be forgiven by the absolution of the priest. In this we have the substance of a judicial process, inasmuch as the sinner is the criminal who is witness against himself, and the priest is the judge who, according to the merits of the case, absolves the sinner and remits the sin

[1] Sess. xiv, c. 1.

in the name of God, or by not absolving the unworthy sinner retains his sin and condemns him to go unpardoned.

2. The effects of a fruitful reception of this sacrament are the forgiveness of all mortal sins and of all venial sins which are confessed with due sorrow, the consequent remission of the eternal punishment due to mortal sin, and a partial remission according to the dispositions of the penitent of the temporal punishment which his sins have deserved.

Sins which are confessed to a priest who has the requisite jurisdiction to absolve them are forgiven directly by virtue of the power of the keys. On the other hand, if without fault on the part of the penitent some sin is not confessed and the penitent has the requisite sorrow, the sin will be forgiven indirectly, inasmuch as the absolution will take its effect and infuse sanctifying grace into the soul, and this sanctifying grace expels all grievous sin from the soul. The absolution will also be indirect when the priest has not faculties for some sin or sins confessed, but for some special reason he is justified in giving the penitent absolution.

3. The Council of Trent[1] teaches that " This sacrament of Penance is for those who have fallen after Baptism necessary unto salvation, as Baptism itself is for those who have not as yet been regenerated." This sacrament, then, like Baptism, is a necessary means for salvation for all who have committed grave sin after Baptism. There is, consequently, for all such a divine precept which obliges them to go to confession. They must fulfil this precept at any rate before death, and the Church, using the power given her by her divine Founder, has obliged all who are conscious of being in mortal sin to go to confession at least once a year (Can. 906). If there is no opportunity of going to confession, one who has fallen into grievous sin can through the mercy of God obtain pardon for it by making an act of perfect contrition or of pure love of God. These acts implicitly contain a desire to receive the sacrament of Penance and to fulfil all other obligations imposed by God and by lawful authority. Even after sin has been forgiven by an act of perfect contrition or of pure love of God, there will always remain the obligation of confessing it, if it be mortal, when the time for the annual confession arrives or the opportunity occurs. Those who do not fall into grievous sin are under no obligation of going to confession, though, of course, they are the last to neglect the use of so powerful a means as frequent confession to attain purity of soul and to obtain great graces from God.

[1] Sess. xiv, c. 2.

CHAPTER II

THE MATTER OF PENANCE

1. THE remote matter of the sacrament of Penance is the sins which have been committed after Baptism, for sins committed before Baptism, when this is received in adult age, are forgiven by Baptism. The matter of Penance is necessary, or free but sufficient. Mortal sins which have never been directly absolved are the necessary matter of confession, for as the Council of Trent teaches,[1] every mortal sin committed after Baptism must be submitted to the keys. The same council teaches that venial sins may be confessed, but that there is no necessity to do so, and so they are sufficient but free or optional matter of the sacrament. The same is true also of mortal sins which have been already absolved directly, for the penitent may with fruit renew his sorrow for them, and nothing prevents the sentence of absolution being repeatedly pronounced over them. The previous sentence of absolution is, as it were, confirmed anew, and thereby fresh grace is infused into the soul (Can. 901, 902).

2. A doubt may sometimes arise as to whether a person has ever been baptized, or as to whether his Baptism was valid, and after Baptism has been conditionally administered in such a case so as to make so important a matter secure the question remains whether this person must make a general confession of past sins or not. If a Catholic has been in the habit of going to confession and making good ones as far as he knows, there will be no necessity to repeat those confessions after conditional Baptism. For if he was baptized before, his confessions would be valid, and if he was not baptized, his past sins are not matter for confession.

A non-Catholic, however, who receives conditional Baptism is in a different position. His past sins have not been confessed; if he was baptized before, he is bound to confess them; if he was not baptized before, they are not matter for the sacrament of Penance. What is he bound to do when the fact of Baptism is uncertain, and at most it can be said that there are probabilities on either side?

[1] Sess. xiv, c. 5.

The First Synod of Westminster[1] prescribes that a non-Catholic already probably baptized who is received into the Catholic Church must, after conditional Baptism, make a full confession of the sins of his past life. This decree was confirmed by the Holy Office, December 17, 1868, and several other decrees and instructions in the same sense have been issued. In practice, then, and in countries which are bound by these decrees and instructions, as are England and the United States, the question is settled by positive law. With regard to other countries which are not directly subject to the foregoing decrees and instructions, it is still a matter of controversy among divines whether a full confession is obligatory. In the opinion of several, there is no universal law, divine or human, which makes confession obligatory in such a case.[2]

3. The proximate matter of Penance, according to the more common opinion, is the acts of the penitent: contrition, confession, and satisfaction. According to the Thomist doctrine, the acts of the penitent constitute the material part of the sacrament, so that they are the matter out of which the sacrament is made, and are an essential part of the sacramental sign. If the Council of Trent calls them the quasi-matter,[3] it is not because they are not the true matter in the sense just explained, but because they are not the matter which is used externally in the confection of the sacrament, as is water in Baptism, or chrism in Confirmation.

On the other hand, the Scotists allow, indeed, that contrition, confession, and satisfaction on the part of the penitent are necessary conditions for the administration of Penance, but they hold that the whole sacramental sign is contained in the words of absolution. These words alone are used by the minister of the sacrament, and they signify the grace conferred by the sacrament. Taken materially, they constitute its matter; inasmuch as they signify the giving of grace for the remission of sins, they constitute its form. This opinion has never been condemned by the Church, and it remains probable, but the question belongs rather to dogmatic than to moral theology.

4. It is not sufficient to confess one's sins in general terms, and if they are grievous the law of God requires that they be confessed according to number and species, as the Council of Trent teaches.[4] As we have seen, venial sins are sufficient matter for absolution, but there is no necessity to confess them. But supposing that a penitent has only venial sins, and he

---

[1] D. xvi, n. 8. [2] Ferreres, *Comp. Theol. Mor.*, ii, n. 527.
[3] Sess. xiv, c. 3. [4] Sess. xiv, c. 5.

wishes to confess them, what kind of confession is necessary and sufficient? Will it be enough to say, "I accuse myself of some small sins and ask for absolution"; or "I accuse myself of all the sins of my past life, and I have nothing serious"?

All divines agree that it will be sufficient to mention some one sin in particular in this case, or to mention the virtue or obligation which has been violated, as by saying, "I accuse myself of slight negligence in prayer," or "of small faults against charity." They differ about the lawfulness of using a mere general formula. Such a method of confessing is against the practice of the Church, which, as St Thomas says, we should always follow; it is also liable to abuse, for penitents cannot always decide what is serious and necessary matter for confession or not, and shame might easily lead them to be content with generalities when they should give particulars. However, there is something to be said for the other view, inasmuch as some sort of confession is all that is required for the essence of the sacrament, and when there are only venial sins to be confessed there is no certain law which prescribes confession according to number and species, or even more than in general terms. This opinion is at any rate sometimes of use, as it may at times enable confessors to be satisfied with generalities when they cannot get more.

5. The solution of questions about the obligation of confessing doubtful sins largely depends on what system of moral theology is followed. The following principles are generally approved by probabilists:

(*a*) When the penitent doubts whether he has been guilty of some sinful act or not, he is not bound to confess it, for he cannot be said to be conscious of sin, and a certain obligation cannot arise from an uncertain source.

(*b*) When the doubt is as to whether full consent was given to what would have been a grave sin if that were the case, the question should be settled by recourse to presumptions. If in other cases consent has usually been given, the presumption is against the penitent, and he should confess the sin as it is in his conscience; otherwise there will be no obligation to do so.

(*c*) If the doubt is whether the sin were mortal or venial, there is no obligation to confess it, for the penitent is not conscious of mortal sin; and only such are bound to confess.

(*d*) If the doubt is whether a mortal sin which was certainly committed has ever been confessed, we must distinguish; if there be no good ground for thinking that it has been confessed, the obligation will still remain; if, on the contrary, there be good ground for thinking that the sin has been confessed, there will be no obligation of confessing it again.

(e) It is generally better for penitents, unless they are scrupulous, to confess doubtful sins, as it conduces to peace of conscience, and is a meritorious act of humility.

When a doubtful sin has once been confessed as such there will be no obligation to confess it again, even though subsequently the penitent becomes sure that he committed the sin. The sin was confessed as it was on the penitent's conscience, and it was absolved directly.

According to the common opinion, although there is no strict obligation to confess a mortal sin which is doubtful, or which has probably been confessed, yet one should not go to Holy Communion in such a state of doubt without either going to confession and confessing at least some sin, or making an act of contrition. For a man should prove himself before receiving Holy Communion, and have a well-grounded belief that he is in a state of grace.

If a penitent mentions only doubtful matter for absolution, the confessor should secure certain matter before giving absolution. Although a penitent may confess only optional matter, yet he has a right to absolution founded on the tacit contract which the confessor entered into with him when he admitted him to confession.

CHAPTER III
CONTRITION

CONTRITION is the first of the acts of the penitent which constitute the matter of the sacrament of Penance. It is defined by the Council of Trent to be a heartfelt sorrow and detestation of sin committed, with a purpose of not sinning again. In this section we will treat of contrition apart from the purpose of amendment, and in the following section, of the purpose of amendment.

SECTION I
The Nature of Contrition

1. A heartfelt sorrow is not quite the same thing as a hatred or detestation of sin. Sorrow is a pain which we feel on account of the presence of some evil or the absence of some good; hatred is an aversion for some evil which is past. Hatred of sin, consequent aversion for it, and a turning away from it is the chief element in contrition; for if we have this hatred we shall have sorrow for sin regarded as a present evil, we shall turn away from it as a past evil, and we shall propose to flee from it in the future. If, then, we have this hatred of sin, we shall have sorrow and a purpose of amendment; we shall have true contrition.

That sorrow for sin which arises from the perfect love of God is called contrition in the full and strict sense; sorrow for sin arising from less perfect motives, as from the fear of hell or the moral turpitude of vice, is called attrition. Ordinarily the word contrition is used indifferently of both kinds of sorrow.

2. Contrition or penitence or repentance is, as we have already seen, according to the teaching of the Council of Trent, a necessary condition for the forgiveness of sin by God. God will not forgive sin unless the sinner turn from his sin and approach him by sorrow of heart. Contrition, then, is a necessary means of salvation for all who have fallen into grievous sin. It is also matter of divine precept which must be fulfilled at least when the sinner is in danger of death, for then it becomes of supreme necessity, and also sometimes during life. The

Church has determined this divine precept by commanding all who have come to the use of reason and have fallen into sin to go to confession at least once a year. Moreover, repentance for sin becomes necessary when any action has to be performed which for its due performance requires the agent to be in the state of grace. Furthermore, inasmuch as one who is deprived by sin of the grace of God cannot long resist temptation and will fall again and again before long, the sinner is obliged to rise from his sin in order to avoid repeated falls. Of course it is better, and the sinner is to be urged, by all means, to rise at once when he has had the misfortune to fall into sin. He should never sleep while he is conscious of being out of the friendship of God. Still he is not bound under pain of committing a new sin to repent immediately after committing sin. It will be sufficient if he repent at least when repentance becomes necessary according to the doctrine which has just been laid down.

3. Not every sort of sorrow is sufficient to justify the sinner, even with the help of the sacrament of Penance. Although perfect love of God suffices to reconcile the sinner with God, though it leaves the obligation of confessing the sin it remits, still this love will not serve by itself as a preparation and disposition for the reception of Penance. A material part of the sacrament of Penance is contrition, and contrition is not love. The sinner, then, who wishes to receive the sacrament of Penance must have true and sincere sorrow for his sin; he must detest it and turn away from it in order to be reconciled with God, whom it offends. Mere natural sorrow for sin because of the temporal evils which it causes is not sufficient. I may well be sorry because sin has ruined my good name, or my health, or my fortunes, but such motives are merely natural, and have no relation to God. The sinner in the sacrament of Penance seeks reconciliation with God, and so the motives of his sorrow must have reference to God; they must be supernatural, founded on revelation and on faith. Without faith no act can be of avail for salvation, as "without faith it is impossible to please God."[1] The sinner must regard sin as the greatest of all evils, as in reality it is. He must be prepared to do and to suffer anything rather than commit sin again. Otherwise he cannot be said to fulfil that greatest of all the commandments, which bids us love God with our whole heart, with our whole soul, with all our strength, and with all our mind. Inasmuch as any one mortal sin deprives us of the friendship

[1] Heb. xi 6.

of God, the sorrow of the sinner must also be universal and embrace all the sins by which he has grievously offended Almighty God. For this it is not necessary that there should be a separate and distinct act of sorrow for every sin committed; it will be sufficient if the motive be universal, so as to embrace all sins. Thus, inasmuch as all mortal sins are directly opposed to charity, and any such sin deserves the punishment of hell, if our sorrow is motived by love toward God, or by fear of hell, it will be universal in the sense required.

Provided that there be sorrow for all mortal sins confessed, a want of sorrow for venial sins will not invalidate the sacrament. For venial sins are compatible with the state of grace and the friendship of God. Still there must be some sorrow for sin confessed; otherwise an essential part of the sacrament of Penance will be wanting. And so if the penitent have only venial sins to confess, for none of which he is sorry, the sacrament would be invalid and sacrilegious. He must at least be sorry for one sin confessed, and he should not confess venial sins for which he is not sorry unless he has some good reason, as if he wishes to ask the advice of his confessor about them, or to make the state of his soul more fully known to him.

4. As contrition, according to the common view, forms a part of the sacramental sign in Penance, it should in some manner be expressed outwardly, not indeed that any form of words is necessary, but the sorrow of the penitent should appear from his confession, from his demeanour, or from his words or other signs. It must exist, if not before, at least when absolution is given, for sin cannot be forgiven if there be no sorrow for it. Moreover, as the different parts of the sacrament go to make one moral whole, the penitent's act of sorrow should in some way be referred to the sacrament. For this, however, it will be sufficient if together with the act of sorrow there be the intention to confess the sin. In case, then, a penitent has inadvertently omitted a serious sin from his confession, but remembers it immediately after he has received absolution and mentions it to the confessor, the latter may absolve him at once, nor is it necessary for the penitent to make a fresh act of sorrow for that particular sin.

On account of the necessity of a moral union between the several parts of the sacrament, there must not be too long an interval between the act of sorrow for sin and the reception of absolution for it. Ordinarily, of course, the sorrow is virtually renewed and expressed when the sin is confessed, but if this were not the case, and the act of sorrow preceded the confession by more than one or two days, it would be doubtful whether there was the necessary union between the parts of the sacrament so as to constitute one sacramental sign.

5. There have been heated controversies in the past as to the sufficiency of attrition to remit sin with the sacrament of Penance. Although they are not quite settled even yet, nevertheless, since the Council of Trent the common doctrine is fairly clear and certain. The Council, then, seems to teach[1] that sorrow for sin because of the fear of hell, or its moral turpitude, or on account of the punishment with which God afflicts the sinner even in this life, will be sufficient for the remission of sin in the sacrament of Penance, provided that it destroys all affection for sin in the heart of the penitent and converts him from sin to God. The slavish fear of hell, by which a man refrains from sinful acts while preserving his affection for them, is, of course, insufficient even with the help of the sacrament to forgive sin and reconcile the sinner with God. The fear which is salutary and efficacious must be the filial fear by which the sinner turns to God because he neither wants sin nor its evil consequences any more. Such sorrow has all the elements which, as we saw above, are required in contrition.

6. There is a controversy among theologians as to whether the sacrament of Penance can ever be valid without producing its effects in the soul at the time of its reception on account of some obstacle which is there. We saw above that this may be the case with Baptism and other sacraments. There is a special difficulty with regard to Penance, because the dispositions, whose absence is only an obstacle to grace given by other sacraments, enter into the substance of Penance, and so their absence would seem to destroy the sacrament itself. In spite of this, however, it is a probable opinion that at any rate in two cases the sacrament of Penance may be valid but *unformed*, as theologians say. The first case is when a penitent has forgotten some mortal sin for which he has never elicited an act of sorrow, but confesses other sins for which he is sorry for motives which are special to them and not universal. The second is when, through inculpable ignorance, the penitent thinks that it is not necessary to be sorry for all mortal sins confessed, provided there be the requisite sorrow for some. In these cases there will be all the elements necessary for the validity of the sacrament, which, however, cannot infuse grace into the soul on account of the presence there of grievous sin still unrepented of.

[1] Sess. xiv, c 4.

7. When Penance is received in danger of death with attrition and not contrition, some theologians insist on the necessity of the dying person making an act of perfect love of God, either to make sure before death of the validity of the sacrament of Penance or to satisfy the divine precept, which, according to them, requires all who are in danger of death to make an act of charity. However, when the dying person has made a good confession and been absolved even with attrition, he is certainly in the state of grace, nor is there any valid argument which proves that such a person is obliged to make an act of charity. Neither the dying nor those who assist them are as a rule conscious of any such obligation.

Because the Council of Trent, while describing the process of the sinner's justification, mentions acts of faith, hope, and the beginnings of love toward God, some theologians concluded that explicit acts of those virtues are required for Penance in addition to contrition. Those acts, however, are implicitly contained in the other acts of the penitent, and the fact that the Council explicitly mentions them does not prove that it teaches that they must be explicitly elicited by the penitent sinner in order to receive absolution for his sins.

Section II

The Purpose of Amendment

1. We saw in the preceding section that contrition is essentially a turning away with hatred from sin in order to approach to God, and so all true contrition necessarily implies a purpose not to sin again. If the truly contrite sinner thinks of the future, he can scarcely fail to form an explicit purpose of amendment, and some theologians hold that this explicit purpose is necessary, otherwise why should it find a place in the definition of contrition given by the Council of Trent? On account of its importance, it is well that the purpose of amendment should always be explicit, but still as it is virtually contained in all true sorrow for sin, and the fact that the Council explicitly mentions it does not prove that it must necessarily be explicit, the opinion which denies the absolute necessity of an explicit purpose of amendment for the validity of Penance is safe. A Roman council held in 1725 under Benedict XIII issued an instruction explaining how to make one's confession, and it only insists on an implicit purpose of amendment.

2. Whether it be explicit or implicit, the purpose of amendment must be sincere, efficacious, and universal.

It must be sincere, with a genuine intention to avoid sin in the future; it will not suffice to make profession of good intentions with the lips, without any real determination to carry them into effect.

It must be efficacious, or the sinner must be prepared to take the necessary means to avoid sin. A mere half wish and half resolve will not do. The sinner must be prepared to do and suffer anything rather than fall into sin again. It would, indeed, be unwise to try one's own determination by imagining all kinds of terrible temptations to sin to see if the will would remain constant, but at any rate the will must here and now be so rooted in good that, come what may, it is determined not to be moved.

There must also be a firm resolve to avoid all mortal sins for the future, not merely any that may have been confessed, but all others, or else there can be no friendship with God, whom we must love above all things. He cannot love God above all things who is prepared to offend him mortally. The purpose of amendment need not extend to all venial sins, provided that at least there is the sincere intention of avoiding some sin that is confessed, or at any rate of lessening the number of smaller transgressions.

CHAPTER IV
CONFESSION

1. CONFESSION, or the self-accusation of a penitent made to a priest with a view of obtaining sacramental absolution, is the second material element of Penance. Such confession is necessary because it is an essential element of the sacrament of Penance, which, as we have seen, is a necessary means of salvation for all who have fallen into grave sin after Baptism. The Council of Trent teaches that " From the institution of the sacrament of Penance, as already explained, the universal Church has always understood that the entire confession of sins was also instituted by the Lord, and is of divine law necessary for all who have fallen after Baptism."[1]

2. This confession must be made by word of mouth according to the practice of the Church and the teaching of the Council of Florence.[2] However, oral confession is not absolutely necessary for the validity of the sacrament, for mutes or penitents who know no language known also to the confessor, or those who are dying and are unable to speak, may confess by signs. Moreover, for good reason, anyone may write his confession, hand it to the priest to read, and accuse himself in general terms, such as " I confess all that is written there." Although mutes and other penitents may thus confess in writing, yet there is no obligation to do so, for sacramental confession should be secret and auricular, whereas writing makes it to some extent public, *litera scripta manet*.

Clement VIII, by a decree dated June 20, 1602, condemned the opinion that it is lawful to confess by letter to an absent priest or to receive absolution in the same way from an absent priest, and forbade the opinion ever to be put in practice; whence theologians conclude that such confession or absolution would be invalid by divine law, else the Pope could not have condemned it in such absolute terms. It seems to follow that confession by telephone would also be invalid, for confession would be made by one who is absent, not present with the priest at the time of receiving this sacrament, as is required by the conditions of its valid administration.

[1] Sess. xiv, c. 5. [2] Decretum pro Armenis.

3. A full, entire, and specific confession of all the mortal sins which have been committed after Baptism is prescribed by divine law. According to the Council of Trent,[1] "If anyone saith that in the sacrament of Penance it is not necessary by divine law for the remission of sins to confess all and singular the mortal sins which after due and diligent previous meditation are remembered, even those mortal sins which are secret, and those which are opposed to the two last commandments of the Decalogue, as also the circumstances which change the species of a sin . . . let him be anathema."

Theologians distinguish between the material and the formal integrity of confession. The material integrity consists in making known each and all the mortal sins which have been committed and which have not yet been confessed; the formal integrity consists in confessing all the mortal sins which occur to the mind after a diligent examination of conscience, or at least of all the sins which the penitent is bound under the circumstances to confess to the priest. It is formal integrity which is prescribed by divine law, and to procure it the penitent is bound before confession to make a diligent examination of his conscience. He should not be too anxious in making this examination; it will be sufficient if he employ that diligence which prudent men employ in worldly matters of importance. No general rule can be given to measure the length of time which the examination should occupy. Much depends upon the character of the individual, the length of time which has elapsed since the last confession, whether the penitent is accustomed to commit grave sins or not, and on similar circumstances. If the penitent cannot recollect the number of times that he has fallen into serious sin, he should mention the number as nearly as he can, and if he has fallen very frequently and almost continuously over a long period of time, it will be sufficient to mention the approximate number of times that he has fallen in the day or week, together with the length of time during which the habit has lasted.

4. A number of special questions must here be considered which touch on the integrity which is required in confession.

The Council of Trent, as we have just seen, teaches that those circumstances which change the nature of a sin must be made known; the theft of a consecrated chalice, which is a sacrilege, would not be adequately confessed by simply saying, "I committed theft." Not only circumstances which change the specific nature of a sin must be confessed, but also those

[1] Sess. xiv, c. 7.

which make a venial sin mortal and *vice versa*. The quantity in theft, then, must be indicated sufficiently to enable the priest to judge whether it was a mortal or a venial sin. Divines are not agreed whether circumstances which merely increase the malice of a sin but do not otherwise change its nature or moral quality are necessarily to be confessed. Many, with the Catechism of the Council of Trent, teach that there is an obligation to confess them, but as they give no convincing reason for their opinion and the contrary is held by many approved theologians, we may safely follow the more easy and the more lenient view.

It is not sufficient to confess as an internal sin one which was completed in external act. It would not be sufficient for a penitent to say that he desired to steal when he actually stole. For although the malice of sin is in the internal act of the will, and the external act adds nothing to it *per se*, yet, considered as human actions, an internal is different from an external act, and therefore as sins are bad human actions, an internal sin is specifically different from the same sin completed in external act.

It is a matter of controversy whether the mere effect of a sin must be confessed. If a man wounds another with the intention of killing him, and then repents and confesses unlawful wounding with the intention of killing, but afterward the man dies, will his assailant be obliged to go to confession again and confess homicide? The opinion is more probable that there is no such obligation, for such an effect of sin is not a sin, and we are only bound to confess sins; a sin is a human action, and when the victim dies his assailant does not act; he would now prevent the death if he could, and so he does not sin.

A vicious habit or custom of committing sin is a cause of sin rather than sin itself, and as sins are the matter of confession, *per se* it is not necessary to confess a sinful habit. If, however, the penitent did not use sufficient diligence to correct his bad habit, and this caused him inadvertently to commit sin, to blaspheme, for instance, then although the blasphemy, because inadvertent, is not sinful in itself, it is nevertheless voluntary and sinful in its cause, and so the uncorrected bad habit must be confessed. It is sometimes of importance for the confessor to know whether his penitent has contracted a habit of sin in order to be able to direct him, and so the confessor has a right to ask in confession whether a habit has been contracted, and the penitent is then under an obligation to tell the truth.

If many sins have been committed with others it is usually

immaterial whether they were committed with one and the same or with different persons. However, if a sin against chastity is committed with a married person, that circumstance must be mentioned, as it causes the sin to be against justice as well as against chastity. Similarly, if one or both accomplices in such a sin are bound by a vow of chastity, that must be mentioned. A religious who is a priest, and even if he is solemnly professed, would satisfy his obligation of confessing a sin against chastity by mentioning it, and adding that he is under a vow of chastity. For it is probable that there is no specific difference between the violation of a solemn and a simple and even private vow of chastity, and a priest, like a religious, is bound to chastity by vow.

Sins against chastity committed with relations have the special malice of incest, but with the exception of the first degree in the direct line of consanguinity, it is probable that the several degrees of kindred or affinity do not constitute a specific difference in the sin. There is a special malice and difformity in a sin of impurity committed with parent or child, but among civilized peoples this is happily of rare occurrence. Hatred against relations is not only against general charity, but is also contrary to piety, which binds relations to love each other with a special affection. Grave hatred will be a serious sin also against this virtue of piety if it is indulged in against near relations, not if it is against more remote kindred with regard to whom the obligation is not so strict.

Mere superiority or position of itself does not change the nature of a sin committed by rulers, magistrates, and people in authority. And so if a master sin with his servant, the sin does not of itself differ from ordinary fornication. If, however, the sin is also a violation of a special duty, then of course it will have a special malice, and so if a schoolmaster corrupt a youth committed to his care, he must mention this circumstance in confession.

The time at which a sin was committed does not change its nature, and so even though a sin which has been committed recently be confessed as though it were a sin of one's past life, the confession will be valid, but of course the practice is not to be commended, nor should it be indulged in.

5. Integrity of confession is prescribed by divine law, but as even divine law does not bind to what is impossible, physical or moral impossibility of making a full confession will excuse the penitent from obeying the law. And so danger of death when the dying person has not the strength or time for making

a full confession, or ignorance of any language known to the priest, or danger of violation of the seal of confession, or danger to life from pestilence or other cause, will excuse the penitent from making a full confession of all his sins. Innocent XI condemned the proposition that a large concourse of penitents on some great feast is a sufficient reason for absolving them without requiring a full confession. When a penitent has been absolved without making a full confession on account of the physical or moral impossibility of doing so, there always remains the obligation of supplying the defect in the next confession, unless the impossibility continues. A proposition asserting the contrary was condemned by Alexander VII. Moreover, that a penitent may lawfully ask for absolution without making a full confession, the following conditions must be verified:

(*a*) There must be some sort of necessity for making the confession here and now, as, for instance, the obligation of receiving the sacraments at Easter, or the hardship of remaining long without the sacraments or in a state of mortal sin.

(*b*) There must be no other confessor at hand to whom a full confession could be made without grave inconvenience.

(*c*) All sins must be confessed which can be mentioned without grave inconvenience, extrinsic to confession, which affects the penitent, the confessor, or some third person. The reason of this is because it cannot be supposed that Christ our Lord intended to bind penitents to make a full confession when it would entail such a hardship, whereas we know that he did command a full confession in spite of shame or other difficulties which are the natural accompaniments of confession of sin to a fellow-man.

6. By a general confession is meant a repetition of preceding confessions. Sometimes this is necessary, sometimes it is useful; otherwise it is harmful, likely to beget scruples, and lead the penitent to think about the past when he should be thinking about the present and the future, and so it should not be permitted.

A general confession is necessary when, through want of jurisdiction on the part of the confessor, or of a full confession or of sorrow for sin on the part of the penitent, former confessions were certainly invalid. In these cases all the invalid confessions must be repeated at least as far as the necessary matter is concerned.

A general confession at certain times extending over a certain period is frequently prescribed to religious by rule, which, of course, should be dutifully observed. Moreover, it is useful for most people to make a general confession sometimes, especially when about to enter upon a new state of life, or when, while making a spiritual retreat and meditating upon sin, the grace of God moves the soul to greater sorrow for the past than one ordinarily feels. Sometimes a general confession may be allowed to allay doubts and scruples of conscience with regard to past sins.

Unless some notable spiritual fruit is to be hoped for, a general confession should in other cases besides the above be regarded as harmful, and should not be allowed.

CHAPTER V

SATISFACTION

1. It is part of the law of eternal justice that when we sin by following our own will instead of the will of God we must be brought back again into the right way by suffering what we would not. And so sin brings with it its penalty; when we have sinned we must suffer for it either in this world or the next. It is in keeping with this principle that by the institution of Christ one of the elements of the sacrament of Penance by which sin is forgiven is satisfaction. By satisfaction is understood some action which entails labour and pain, imposed by the priest in confession on the repentant sinner and accepted by him. We have already seen that the Council of Trent teaches that satisfaction is an element in the material part of Penance, and the same council in another place[1] adds: " Therefore the priests of the Lord ought, as far as the Spirit and prudence shall suggest, to enjoin salutary and suitable satisfactions according to the quality of the crimes and the ability of the penitent."

Confessors, then, are under the obligation of giving a penance to their penitents in satisfaction for the sins which they confess. As a general rule, they must give a grave penance for grave sins, otherwise they will sin grievously; but probably only a venial sin would be committed by neglecting to give a suitable penance for light faults.

In the early Church the penances enjoined were very severe, but, according to modern discipline, that is considered a grave penance and suitable for a penitent who has confessed grave sins which would bind under a grave obligation if it were imposed by ecclesiastical law. The Church encourages her children to make up by gaining indulgences for what the justice of God may require in addition to the comparatively light penances which are imposed nowadays.

The natural sequence of judicial acts in the tribunal of Penance requires that a penance should be enjoined by the priest before giving absolution, but it will be valid if imposed after absolution.

[1] Sess. xiv, c. 8.

The Ritual expresses a wish that, as far as possible, penances should be given which are contrary to the sins confessed, as almsgiving for avarice, fasting or other bodily affliction for lust, humiliations for pride, acts of devotion for sloth. For such as but seldom confess more frequent reception of the sacraments may be enjoined. The confessor should never apply to personal objects alms imposed on his penitents, nor enjoin public penance for secret sins.

2. The penitent is bound to accept and to execute a reasonable penance which his confessor has imposed on him. This obligation will be grave when a grave penance has been imposed for serious sins, otherwise it will bind under pain of venial sin. As the penitent is bound to accept the penance, so he is obliged to execute it at the time prescribed, if any time was fixed, or if not, then at a reasonable time. To defer its execution so long as to be in danger of forgetting it would be equivalent to not fulfilling it. It is best to execute the penance as soon as can conveniently be done.

If the penitent forgets the penance which was enjoined, he is excused from fulfilling any penance, as he is not bound to confess the same sins a second time, and he cannot substitute some other of his own choice, as he is not the minister of the sacrament.

3. In order to be sure of obtaining the sacramental effect of fulfilling the penance enjoined by the confessor, the penitent must be in the state of grace when he fulfils it, for God does not remit temporal punishment due to past sins in favour of one who is at enmity with him. However, by fulfilling the penance even in the state of mortal sin, what had been enjoined would have been executed, though it would not then effect its object of remitting temporal punishment due to sin confessed. It is a disputed point among theologians whether fulfilment of penance while in a state of sin would produce its effect when the sinner repented and again recovered the state of grace. Many theologians hold that it does so, and that it revives in the same way as a sacrament revives which has been validly received, but which does not produce grace at the time of its reception on account of the presence of some obstacle in the soul.

Although it is better and safer to execute the penance while in the state of grace, and if it is executed in a state of mortal sin it does not at any rate at once obtain its effect, yet it is not certain that any fault is committed by doing one's penance while in sin, any more than it is sinful to assist at Mass while out of the friendship of God. One who in sin hears Mass on Sunday satisfies the precept, though he does not obtain the full fruit of the sacrifice; in the same way one, who while in sin says his penance, fulfils indeed his obligation, but does not thereby obtain at the time the sacramental fruit of his action.

4. Although a penitent may not of his own authority substitute another penance for that which was imposed by his confessor, yet he may for good reason get this commuted either by the same or by a different confessor. The same confessor may commute the penance which he himself imposed either in or out of confession, provided that so long an interval has not elapsed that the commutation cannot be considered one moral act with the confession and the imposition of the penance which is commuted. If the penitent goes to another confessor and asks for a commutation of a penance which has been enjoined him, the commutation must be granted in confession, otherwise the new confessor will have no jurisdiction over the penitent. The former confession need not be repeated; it is probable that it will be sufficient if the new confessor knows the penance which was given and for which a commutation is asked, together with the difficulty which the penitent feels in executing it.

CHAPTER VI

THE FORM OF PENANCE

1. WE must distinguish the form which is required for the validity of the sacrament from the form which is commonly used according to the Ritual. " I absolve thee from thy sins " is sufficient for the validity of the sacrament, and probably even the mere words " I absolve thee." The Ritual form consists of the four short prayers beginning with *Misereatur*, etc., of which the third is the most important, as it contains the absolution from censures and from sin. The absolution from censures is always given before the absolution from sin for the sake of greater security, because if the penitent were under censure, he could not lawfully receive a sacrament. A rubric of the Ritual expressly lays down that the other three prayers may be omitted in shorter and more frequent confessions, but it is better always to add the last prayer, as it probably gives a special satisfactory efficacy to the good works which the penitent subsequently performs.

We saw above that absolution cannot be given validly by a priest to a penitent who is not morally present at the time. This sacrament is a judicial process, and the priest, who is the judge, pronounces sentence on the culprit who is present in court. The absolution must be pronounced by word of mouth, and the penitent must be within hearing distance, not farther distant than the ordinary tone of voice carries.

2. The priest cannot pass sentence without having a sufficient knowledge of the sins to be absolved and the dispositions of the penitent. It is not necessary, however, nor is it possible to have a distinct knowledge of the subjective malice with which the sins of the penitent were committed. The confessor may presume that the subjective malice of the penitent corresponds with the objective malice of the sin, unless he has special reasons for concluding otherwise. With his habitual knowledge of the malice of different sins the confessor passes a sufficient judgement on them if he quietly listens to the self-accusation of the penitent.

A merely historical account of the sins which a person has committed may suffice for absolution if the penitent resumes them under some brief formula by which he expresses his desire to confess them and receive absolution for them. The priest must in this case, of course, retain at least a general and vague knowledge of the sins which he absolves.

3. A dying person, who through weakness or other causes is unable to make a full confession, may be absolved absolutely if he mentions what sins he can, or even if he asks for the absolution of his sins, for such a confession is formally integral.

The Ritual prescribes that a dying person who has lost the use of his senses is to be absolved even if he previously only expressed a desire himself or through others to receive absolution. In this case, also, it would seem that the absolution should be absolute.

Dying persons who have lost the use of their senses may be absolved conditionally even if they give no certain signs of a desire to confess or of sorrow for their sins. It may be that in such a state the dying person has the requisite dispositions, and is trying his best to give expression to them, and so the movements of the body or his laboured breathing may be indications of a wish to receive absolution. At any rate, in such a case of necessity we may use even a slenderly probable opinion, and it is now the common practice to absolve conditionally in such cases.

CHAPTER VII
THE MINISTER OF PENANCE

CHRIST our Lord gave his Apostles and their successors a twofold spiritual power to enable them to do the work which he commissioned them to do for the sanctification and salvation of souls. This twofold spiritual power is the power of Orders and the power of Jurisdiction.

The power of Orders has reference to the holy Eucharist, and it was conferred on the Apostles at the Last Supper when, after consecrating the blessed Eucharist, our Lord said to them: " Do this for a commemoration of me." The power of Orders has reference not only to the blessed Eucharist but to everything that is required to prepare and dispose men for the worthy and fruitful reception of it. And so, by the disposition of Christ our Lord the power of Orders is necessary for the forgiveness of sins. In other words, only priests can be ministers of the sacrament of Penance (Can. 871).

The power of jurisdiction is the power of ruling subjects, and it was given to the Apostles by Christ our Lord when he said to them: " Amen, I say to you, whatsoever you shall bind upon earth shall be bound also in heaven, and whatsoever you shall loose upon earth shall be loosed also in heaven. Both powers are implied in the institution of the sacrament of Penance when our Lord said to his Apostles: " As the Father hath sent me I also send you. Receive ye the Holy Ghost, whose sins you shall forgive they are forgiven them, and whose sins you shall retain they are retained."

The power of Orders is conferred by the sacrament of Orders. We will treat of the power of jurisdiction in a separate chapter.

CHAPTER VIII

THE JURISDICTION OF THE MINISTER OF PENANCE

1. Priests are judges in the tribunal of Penance, and judges must have jurisdiction if their sentence is to take effect. As the Council of Trent teaches: "Wherefore, since the nature and order of a judgement require this, that sentence be passed only on those subject to that judicature, it has ever been firmly held in the Church of God, and this synod ratifies it as a thing most true, that the absolution which a priest pronounces upon one over whom he has not either an ordinary or a delegated jurisdiction ought to be of no weight whatever."[1]

Jurisdiction in general is the power of ruling subjects. We must distinguish jurisdiction in the internal forum from jurisdiction in the external forum. The latter has reference primarily and directly to the common good, to promote which it makes laws, administers justice, and directs the machinery of government. Jurisdiction in the internal forum refers directly and primarily to the good of the individual soul, whose actions it directs toward God. It is exercised either in the sacrament of Penance, when sins are forgiven, or outside the sacred tribunal, as when a dispensation is granted from ecclesiastical law. Again, jurisdiction is either ordinary or delegated.

Ordinary jurisdiction is that which is annexed to an office by law; delegated jurisdiction is committed to a person.

The Pope and Cardinals have ordinary jurisdiction for hearing confessions throughout the whole Church.

Local Ordinaries and parish priests and those who are in the place of parish priests have ordinary jurisdiction for hearing confessions in their respective territories, as also has the Canon Penitentiary. The superiors of exempt religious have ordinary jurisdiction for their own subjects (Can. 873).

One who has ordinary jurisdiction for hearing confessions can absolve his subjects wherever he finds them.

Ordinary jurisdiction ceases by loss of office, and, after a declaratory or condemnatory sentence, by excommunication, suspension from office, and interdict.

[1] Sess. xiv, c. 7.

The Ordinary of the place in which the confessions are heard grants delegated jurisdiction to hear the confessions of all penitents, whether secular or religious, to all priests, both secular and religious, even though they be exempt; but religious priests may not use the same without at least the presumed leave of their superior (Can. 874).

Local Ordinaries should not habitually grant faculties for hearing confessions to religious who are not presented by their own superior, nor without grave reason deny faculties to those whom he does present.

Local Ordinaries should only grant faculties for hearing confessions to such as have been proved fit for the office by examination, unless there is question of a priest whose theological knowledge they know from other sources (Can. 887).

Delegated jurisdiction can be granted with certain limitations as to time, place, persons, and cases.

Jurisdiction must be granted in writing or expressly by word, and without charge.

Parish priests, vicars of parish priests, and other priests with general delegation cannot delegate jurisdiction for hearing confessions without the faculty or mandate of the Ordinary of the place (*Com. on Canon Law*, October 16, 1919).

By Canon 881 all priests, whether secular or regular, approved for hearing confessions in any place, whether they have ordinary or delegated jurisdiction, can absolve validly and lawfully homeless persons and strangers who come to them from another diocese or parish, as also Catholics of any Oriental rite.

Without grave cause local Ordinaries may not revoke or suspend jurisdiction for hearing confessions, nor without consulting the Holy See can they lawfully take away faculties at one time from all the confessors belonging to a formed house of religious (Can. 880).

Delegated jurisdiction ceases when the mandate has been executed, when the time has elapsed or the number of cases for which it was given is exhausted, when the final cause of the delegation ceases; by the revocation of him who gave it directly intimated to the delegate, by the renunciation of the delegate directly intimated to him who gave it and accepted by him. It does not cease when he who gave it loses his authority, unless a clause was inserted to that effect, or jurisdiction was given as a favour to special persons to hear a confession and nothing has been done in the matter. If the case has been begun it may be finished (Can. 207).

However, if by inadvertence absolution is given after the

lapse of the time for which jurisdiction was granted, or after the number of cases was exhausted, it is valid (Can. 207, sec. 2).

Even when a priest has not jurisdiction habitually, the Church sometimes supplies it for the good of the penitent, so that the absolution given may be valid.

In danger of death all priests, even though not approved for hearing confessions, may validly and lawfully absolve any penitents from any sins or censures, however reserved and notorious they may be, and even though an approved priest be present, but the special law about absolving an accomplice must be observed (Can. 882).

In a case of common mistake when many of the faithful think that a priest has faculties while he has not, the Church supplies jurisdiction, but if a priest knowingly exposes himself to hear confessions without faculties he sins grievously.

The Church supplies jurisdiction in a case of positive doubt and probability as to whether a priest has it (Can. 209).

According to Canon 883 all priests while on a sea voyage, provided that they have received faculties for hearing confessions, either from their own Ordinary or from the Ordinary of the port where they embarked, or from the Ordinary of any intermediate port by which they pass on their journey, can, during the whole voyage, hear the confessions in the ship of any of the faithful on board with them, although the ship on its voyage may pass by or even stay for some time in various places subject to the jurisdiction of different Ordinaries.

Moreover, when the ship stops on the voyage they can hear the confessions both of the faithful who for any reason come on board, and of such as while they chance to be on land ask them to hear their confessions, and validly and lawfully absolve them even from cases which are reserved to the Ordinary of the place.

The Holy See has made special regulations with regard to the faculties of army chaplains (Can. 451, sec. 3).

CHAPTER IX

THE CONFESSORS OF RELIGIOUS

1. THE local Ordinary can give jurisdiction to hear the confessions of the members of a clerical order of exempt religious, as we have seen. Their religious superior, in accordance with the Constitutions, can likewise grant jurisdiction for hearing the confessions of the religious, of the novices, and of others who by day and night live in a house of the religious as servants, scholars, guests, or for the sake of their health. The religious superior can grant jurisdiction for hearing the confessions of all these to secular priests also, and to priests of other religious institutes.

In an exempt institute of laymen the superior proposes a confessor to the local Ordinary from whom he ought to obtain jurisdiction (Can. 875).

In an institute of laymen who are not exempt the local Ordinary designates a priest to hear confessions (Can. 529).

2. In each house of clerical religious it is prescribed that several lawfully approved confessors be appointed according to the number of the inmates, with power to absolve from cases reserved in the order in the case of exempt religious (Can. 518, sec. 1).

In institutes of laymen it is prescribed that an ordinary and an extraordinary confessor be appointed; and if a religious ask for a special confessor the superior should grant the request without in any way inquiring into the reason for the request, or showing displeasure at it (Can. 528).

To hear the confessions of novices in orders of men it is prescribed that one or more ordinary confessors be appointed according to the number of novices. In the case of clerical orders, these ordinary confessors should live in the novitiate; in the case of orders of laymen, they should at least frequently come to the novitiate to hear the confessions of the novices.

Besides the ordinary confessors some other confessors should also be appointed, and free access to them should be allowed the novices.

Moreover, at least four times in the year an extraordinary confessor should be allowed the novices, and all of them should present themselves to him at least to ask for his blessing (Can. 566).

Finally, while the Constitutions which prescribe or advise confession at fixed times to appointed confessors should be observed, if a religious even, though exempt for his peace of conscience, go to a confessor approved by the local Ordinary, even though he is not one of those designated for religious, the confession is lawful and valid, and any privilege to the contrary is revoked; and such confessor can absolve the religious even from sins and censures reserved in the order (Can. 519).

3. To hear the confessions of religious women in their convents lawfully and validly, both secular and religious priests of any degree or office, except Cardinals, require a special jurisdiction which the Ordinary of the place grants where the convent is situated, and any special law or privilege to the contrary is revoked (Can. 876).

To hear the confessions of such religious women one ordinary confessor only is to be appointed for each convent, unless the great number of the religious or some other cause require more (Can. 520).

The ordinary confessor is appointed for three years, but under certain conditions his office may be prolonged for a second or even for a third period of three years (Can. 526).

An extraordinary confessor for each community of religious women should be granted at least four times in the year, and all the religious and novices should present themselves to him at least to ask for his blessing (Can. 521).

The local Ordinary should appoint some special confessors for every house where a religious community lives to whom any nun may easily have recourse in particular cases, and if any religious asks for such a confessor no superioress in any way may inquire into the reason for the request, refuse it, or show displeasure at it (Can. 521).

4. Besides these confessors a religious sister, for the quiet of her conscience and for greater progress in the way of God, may ask for some special confessor or spiritual director, and the Ordinary should readily grant the request, while taking care that abuse does not creep in (Can. 520).

A religious sister may also go to any confessor approved for women by the local Ordinary in any church or oratory, even semi-public, or in a place lawfully set apart for hearing the confessions of women, without being obliged to refer to her superioress; indeed, the superioress is not allowed to forbid her going, or to inquire about it even indirectly (Can. 522).

A religious sister who is seriously ill, though not in danger of death, may call any priest approved for hearing the confessions of women though not designated for religious, and confess to him as often as she wishes during her serious illness, nor can the superioress forbid it, directly or indirectly (Can. 523).

Any priest can absolve anyone in danger of death.

The confessors of religious women should be conspicuous for probity and prudence, forty years of age, unless in the judgement of the Ordinary a good reason otherwise require, and they have no power over the religious in the external forum.

CHAPTER X

RESERVED CASES

1. THE Council of Trent says:[1] " It hath seemed to our most holy Fathers to be of great importance to the discipline of the Christian people that certain more atrocious and more heinous crimes should be absolved not by all priests, but only by the highest priests." And so the absolution of certain graver sins and censures, or *cases* as they are called, is reserved to higher ecclesiastics. Ordinary confessors retain their jurisdiction for other sins, but it is limited, so that they have no authority over reserved cases. The motive for thus reserving sins is the spiritual good of the faithful, so that they may be deterred from committing those sins on account of the difficulty of obtaining absolution for them, and if unfortunately they should fall into them, they may have more skilful guides than ordinary confessors are presumed to be.

2. Reservation is the limitation of jurisdiction, and so in general all those who have ordinary jurisdiction, when they delegate it to others, may reserve some cases for treatment in their own tribunal.

In particular the Pope reserves certain censures and sins of all the faithful throughout the world. In nearly all papal cases both the censure and the sin are reserved, but the sin is reserved on account of the censure, so that if, through any cause, the censure is not incurred, then the sin is not reserved. False accusation of solicitation made against a confessor is an exception, and is reserved to the Holy See on its own account (Can. 894).

The Code of Canon Law divides the censures reserved by the Holy See into four classes. Some are reserved in a most special manner to the Holy See itself, others in a special manner to the Holy See, others are simply reserved to the Holy See, others, again, are reserved by the Holy See to the Ordinary. A fifth class of papal censures are reserved to none, and may be absolved on proper conditions by any priest with ordinary faculties.

Local Ordinaries should not reserve sins except after discussion in Synod or the necessity or usefulness of reservation

[1] Sess. xiv, c. 7.

has been approved out of Synod by the Chapter and some prudent priests who have the cure of souls. Bishops' cases should be few, only three or four, the more atrocious crimes, and not papal cases. The reservation should be withdrawn when it has obtained its effect (Can. 895-898).

In England the First and Fourth Synod of Westminster reserved to the bishop the case of a priest going to the theatre and thereby incurring suspension. In the United States two cases are reserved by provincial law: (*a*) The excommunication incurred by those who attempt to marry again after getting a civil divorce; (*b*) the excommunication incurred by those who marry before any non-Catholic minister.

Besides these cases reserved by law the bishops reserve a few cases to themselves for which the *pagella* of faculties must be consulted. When the bishops reserve a sin with a censure attached to it, it was a disputed point whether the reservation of the censure is the primary object in view, as in papal cases, or whether the reservation of the sin and of the censure are of equal importance and independent of each other. This question is now settled by Canon 2246, sec. 3, which decides that when a censure has been absolved or is not incurred the reservation of the sin ceases.

The superiors of religious orders may also reserve cases of their subjects. Clement VIII issued a list of eleven cases which they might reserve, and forbade them to reserve others except with the consent of a general or provincial chapter of the order (Can. 896).

3. Certain conditions are required in order that any particular sin may be reserved. First of all it must be a grave sin such as forms the necessary matter of confession, for a venial sin which the penitent need not confess cannot be effectually reserved. It is not the practice of the Church to reserve merely internal sins; there must be an external act and as such gravely sinful. So that a slightly indecent word, even if uttered with a seriously bad intention, would not fall under reservation if all sins of indecency were reserved. The sin must be completed and perfect in its kind, not merely attempted, for reservation is to be strictly interpreted. For the same reason it must be certain that the sin is reserved, so that any prudent doubt of law or of fact whether a particular sin is reserved is sufficient to enable the confessor to give absolution without special faculties.

4. Those who are under the age of puberty do not incur papal cases unless they are expressly included in the law. The

only papal cases in which they are so included is the violation of the enclosure of nuns. The same rule may be applied to bishops' cases, unless a bishop has made known his intention to bind even those who have not reached the age of puberty. Ignorance of a censure, unless it be crass or supine, excuses from the censure, as is expressly laid down in the Decretals.[1] As in papal cases the reservation of the sin is on account of the censure annexed to it, and ignorance excuses from incurring this, therefore ignorance will excuse one from incurring papal reserved cases to which a censure is attached. The reservation of false accusation of solicitation is very probably penal, as theologians gather from the words by Benedict XIV in the Constitution *Sacramentum Poenitentiae*, and as ignorance of a penalty excuses one from incurring it, therefore ignorance will excuse one from incurring this reserved case. This opinion, however, which many hold to be still probable, is hardly of practical importance, for the ecclesiastical judge who receives the false accusation will certainly warn the culprit of the penalty incurred by false accusation.

It is a disputed point whether ignorance excuses from incurring bishops' cases or not. It excuses, indeed, from incurring any *censure* inflicted by any ecclesiastical superior, but it certainly does not excuse from incurring a reserved *sin* if the bishop has expressed his intention of reserving it even when committed in ignorance of the reservation. Otherwise it is probable that ignorance excuses in episcopal as well as in papal cases, for reservation is partly penal, and it cannot attain its end of deterring the faithful from committing reserved sins if they are ignorant of the reservation.

According to Canon 900, all reservation ceases:

(1) When either the sick who cannot leave the house make their confession, or those about to be married with a view to marriage.

(2) Whenever either the lawful superior on being asked has refused to grant faculties for absolving a particular case, or in the prudent judgement of the confessor faculties for granting absolution cannot be asked for from the lawful superior without serious detriment to the penitent or without danger of violating the seal of confession.

(3) When the penitent is outside the territory of him who reserved the case, even though he left it only to obtain absolution. But, according to the Commission for the Interpretation of Canon Law a stranger (*peregrinus*) incurs the

[1] C. 2, de const. in 6to; can. 2229, sec. 3, i.

reserved cases of the place where he is staying (A.A.S. xii, 575).

5. In general absolution from reserved cases may be obtained from the person who reserved them, from his successor, his superior who has jurisdiction over the same subjects, and from anyone who has been specially delegated by one of these to grant absolution.

Canon 2237, sec. 2, gives Ordinaries power to absolve from cases simply reserved to the Holy See when they are occult either in person or by their delegate.

The Vicar General and the Canon Penitentiary can absolve from cases reserved to the Ordinary (Can. 401).

Vicars forane have power to absolve from cases which the bishop reserves to himself, and they should be able to delegate the same power to other priests of their district (Can. 899, sec. 2).

By the same canon, sec. 3, parish priests are empowered to absolve from cases which Ordinaries reserve to themselves during the time allowed for making one's Easter duties, and missionaries have the same power during missions.

When the penitent is in danger of death any priest can absolve him from any sins or censures however they may be reserved, but if a penitent in that condition has been absolved from a censure *ab homine* or one most specially reserved to the Holy See by a priest without special faculties, and he recovers, he is bound under pain of falling again under censure to have recourse to him who inflicted the censure if it was *ab homine*, or to the Sacred Penitentiary or to the bishop or someone else with special faculties and submitting to their commands (Can. 2252).

Moreover, when it is necessary for a penitent to receive absolution in order to avoid scandal or loss of reputation, or because he must say Mass or make his Easter Communion, or when he feels it a great hardship to remain in the state of sin during the time required for obtaining special faculties to absolve him, a simple confessor may absolve him from all reserved cases (Can. 2254).

If the penitent does not feel it a hardship already the confessor may induce him to feel it, and then absolve him. But in any case the confessor must impose on the penitent whom he has absolved the obligation of having recourse within a month at least by letter and through the confessor, if it can be done without serious inconvenience, without mentioning the penitent's name, to the Sacred Penitentiary or to the bishop, or to any other superior endowed with faculties for the case, and of obeying his commands. Unless the penitent fulfils this obligation he will again fall under the censure.

The ordinary confessors of exempt religious men of clerical institutes can absolve from cases reserved in the order; as also can confessors approved by the local Ordinary (Can. 518, 519).

If a confessor without special faculties absolves from a reserved case in ignorance of the reservation, the absolution is valid, except in the case of a censure *ab homine* or one most specially reserved to the Holy See (Can. 2247, sec. 3).

CHAPTER XI

DE ABUSU SACRAMENTI POENITENTIAE

1. SANCTISSIMIS institutis abuti hominum malitia valet, nec sacramento Poenitentiae excepto. Ecclesia tamen nihil intentatum reliquit ut abusus hujus sacramenti evitentur vel ut iis si forte occurrant aptum remedium praebeatur. Gregorius XV aliique Romani Pontifices et praesertim Benedictus XIV leges tulerunt contra sollicitationem in sacro tribunali ac absolutionem complicis in peccato turpi. De his in hoc capite agimus ac primo de sollicitatione (Can. 904).

De crimine sollicitationis in sacro tribunali Benedictus XIV Constitutione *Sacramentum Poenitentiae* tria statuit. Primo committit ac mandat omnibus locorum Ordinariis universi orbis christiani in suis respectivis dioecesibus ut diligenter omnique humano respectu postposito inquirant et procedant contra omnes ac singulos sacerdotes, tam seculares quam regulares quomodolibet exemptos, qui sollicitationis sunt rei, eosque graviter puniant. Rei autem sunt sollicitationis qui aliquem poenitentem, quaecumque persona illa sit, vel in actu sacramentalis confessionis, vel ante, vel immediate post confessionem, vel occasione, aut praetextu confessionis vel etiam extra occasionem confessionis in confessionali, sive in alio loco ad confessiones audiendas destinato aut electo, simulatione audiendi ibidem confessionem, ad inhonesta et turpia sollicitare, vel provocare, sive verbis, sive signis, sive nutibus, sive tactu, sive per scripturam aut tunc aut post legendam, tentaverint, aut cum eis illicitos et inhonestos sermones vel tractatus temerario ausu habuerint. Secundo, omnes et singuli sacerdotes ad confessiones audiendas constituti tenentur suos poenitentes quos noverint fuisse ab aliis sollicitatos sedulo monere de obligatione denunciandi locorum ordinariis personam quae sollicitationem commiserit, etiamsi sacerdos sit qui jurisdictione ad absolutionem valide impertiendam careat, aut sollicitatio inter confessarium et poenitentem mutua fuerit, sive sollicitationi poenitens consenserit, sive consensum minime praestiterit, vel longum tempus post ipsam sollicitationem jam effluxerit, aut sollicitatio a confessario non pro seipso sed pro alia persona peracta fuerit. Tertio, potestas absolvendi eos qui sive per se sive per alios apud ecclesiasticos judices falso innoxios sacerdotes sollicitationis accusant reservatur Summo Pontifici, ut tam detestabile facinus metu magnitudinis poenae coerceatur (Can. 894).

2. Ex dictis igitur, quae fere ad verbum in Constitutione Benedicti XIV inveniuntur, constat Ordinarios teneri sub gravi inquirere in sollicitantes ac hujus criminis reos graviter punire. Praxis Sacri Officii est ut post unam alteramve denunciationem sacerdos denunciatus observetur. Post tertiam vero contra suspectum procedi solet. Ad formale examen vocantur parochi aliique spectatae virtutis viri qui de indole et qualitatibus denunciantis et denunciati sub juramento de veritate dicenda et de secreto servando testimonium proferunt. Poenae jure reis infligendae sunt privatio omnium facultatum ad confessiones excipiendas, suspensio ab exercitio ordinis, privatio beneficiorum, privatio vocis activae et passivae si sit regularis, omnes tamen sunt ferendae sententiae (Can. 2368). Termini adhibiti in crimine definiendo strictae sunt interpretationis.

In actu sacramentalis confessionis: hoc intelligendum est de intervallo quod intercedit inter benedictionem et absolutionem etiam si poenitens non fuerit absolutus ob defectum dispositionum vel ob aliam causam.

Ante vel immediate post: ita ut nulla actio non referibilis ad sollicitationem intercesserit.

Occasione vel praetextu confessionis: occasio est quando confessio sequebatur vel sequi debebat juxta intentionem petentis. Praetextus habetur quando confessarius ficte proponit confessionem ut sollicitet. Quare si mulier et sacerdos fingunt confessionem faciendam ad alios decipiendos et ad tutius peccandum non est locus denunciandi, nec probabilius si poenitens praetexat confessionem ad sacerdotem vocandum et sollicitandum. Probabilius non est denunciandus sacerdos qui propter cognitam ex confessione fragilitatem mulieris eam domi sollicitat, quia occasione scientiae ex confessione habitae sollicitat, non occasione confessionis.

In confessionali sive in alio loco ad confessiones audiendas destinato aut electo simulatione audiendi ibidem confessionem: unde non denunciandus est sacerdos qui sollicitat mulierem stantem ante confessionale, deest enim simulatio audiendi ejus confessionem.

Inhonesta et turpia: haec significat gravia peccata contra sextum decalogi praeceptum. Graviter inhonesti sermones vel tractatus quin ulterius procedatur constituunt sollicitationem si ceterae conditiones habeantur. Qui externe consentit poenitenti sollicitanti videtur esse denunciandus.

3. Omnes confessarii monere suos poenitentes, sive feminas sive masculos tenentur quos ab aliis sacerdotibus fuisse sollicitatos noverint de obligatione denunciandi sacerdotes sollicitantes locorum ordinariis vel Sanctae Sedi per Sacrum Officium vel per Poenitentiariam. Infra mensem ab accepta cognitione denunciationis faciendae obligatio est implenda, aliter poenitens sollicitatus incurrit excommunicationem nemini reservatam ex Constitutione Pii IX, *Apostolicae Sedis*, et Can. 2368, sec. 2. Omnes etiam qui certo sciant casum sollicitationis sacerdotem reum denunciare tenentur, non tamen sub censura. Confessarii monere poenitentes de obligatione denunciandi sollicitantes tenentur, etiamsi praevideant eos obligationem non impleturos, nisi sint in articulo mortis, tunc enim dissimulare ob salutem animae licet. Nec capax est absolutionis qui onus implere recusat vel saltem nisi promittat se onus impleturum quum primum poterit. Confessarius audiens poenitentem qui sollicitatus fuisse videtur, circumstantias casus investigare debet ut moralem certitudinem de crimine patrato acquirat antequam obligationem denunciandi sollicitantem imponat. Denunciatio juridice est facienda, ac proinde qui denunciat personaliter adire debet ordinarium loci ubi crimen patrabatur, ac sub juramento testimonium dare. Qui ordinarium adire nequit, ad eum scribat, ut delegatum sibi substituere valeat ad denunciationem accipiendam. Scriptae denunciationes anonymae nullius sunt momenti, nec sufficiunt ad obligationi satisfaciendum.

Qui falso juridice accusat sacerdotem sollicitationis gravissimum committit peccatum et incurrit in excommunicationem cujus absolutio speciali modo Romano Pontifici reservatur a qua nequit ullo in casu absolvi nisi falsam denunciationem formaliter retractaverit, et damna reparaverit. Peccatum etiam ratione sui reservatur Sanctae Sedi (Can. 2363, 894).

4. Ex eadem Constitutione Benedicti XIV, *Sacramentum Poenitentiae*, confessarius poenitentem quocum peccatum grave contra castitatem commiserit a peccato complicem absolvere nequit; qui autem talem complicem absolvere attentat in casum incidit specialissimo modo reservatum Romano Pontifici. Eandem poenam incurrit qui se absolvere fingit vel, sive directe sive indirecte, complicem inducit ad peccatum complicitatis tacendum quum ad confessionem venit. Si vero poenitens bona fide vel inadvertenter peccatum complicitatis omiserit dum complici confitetur valide ab eo absolvitur. Idem videtur dicendum si complex ab alio sacerdote directe a peccato complicitatis jam absolutus idem peccatum postea tamquam

materiam liberam sacerdoti complici confitetur. Praestat autem ut sacerdos complex nunquam confessionem complicis excipiat nisi in casu necessitatis (Can. 884, 2367).

Complex vero in peccato turpi hic intelligitur qui interne et externe grave peccatum contra castitatem sive verbis sive aspectu sive facto cum sacerdote etiam ante sacerdotium susceptum commiserit. Ut incurratur censura absolutio debet esse formalis ita ut sacerdos sciat se absolvere poenitentem complicem, vel saltem ut ejus ignorantia sit crassa et supina. Requiritur etiam ut poenitens cognoverit se peccasse cum hoc sacerdote sive in actu peccati sive saltem ante absolutionem acceptam, quamvis non sit necessarium ut poenitens confessarium in actu confessionis agnoscat. Sacerdos igitur qui larvatus et incognitus cum muliere peccavit eam adhuc ignorantem suum complicem absolvere valide potest, nam aliter sese proderet poenitenti ac alii confessario ad quem poenitens absolutionis causa accederet.

5. In articulo seu periculo mortis absolutio complicis data a complice sacerdote semper est valida ne anima pereat, ait Benedictus XIV. Praeterea complex moribundus qui nequit aut non vult alteri sacerdoti confiteri licite etiam a complice sacerdote absolvitur. Si vero alius sacerdos etiam non approbatus adsit, vel sine infamia et scandalo advocari possit ad confessionem accipiendam, sacerdos qui complicem in periculo mortis constitutum absolvat excommunicationem non evitat.

In locis remotis ubi complex alium confessarium habere nequit, et in periculo est ne sine absolutione discedat e vita, potest probabiliter a complice absolvi ne anima pereat. Poterit etiam sacerdos facultatem obtinere ut complicem in tanta necessitate absolvat.

CHAPTER XII

THE DUTIES OF A CONFESSOR IN THE CONFESSIONAL

THE confessor does not satisfy his obligations merely by absolving the penitents who come to him, and refusing absolution to those who are not properly disposed. In the confessional he holds the place of Christ for the reconciliation of sinners with God; he is also the minister of the sacrament, and as such he is bound to see that it is validly and lawfully received by the penitent. In other words, as theologians say, the confessor is the spiritual father, doctor, counsellor, and judge of his penitents. Something must be said on each of these heads (Can. 888, sec. 1).

SECTION I

The Confessor as Spiritual Father

The confessor should remember how our Lord used to act toward sinners during his mortal life; with what charity, forbearance, and patience he dealt with them, and he should strive to imitate his divine model. Like him he should be interested in the souls of men, not in their social position, age, or sex. Whoever they may be, he should receive all sympathetically and kindly. This does not mean that he should treat all precisely in the same way. Just because of his interest in his penitents and of his sympathy for them, he will treat them as their various needs demand; not expecting the same degree of virtue in all, nor attempting to raise all to the same height of sanctity. He should try to discover what God designs for each soul and be content to second the inspirations of the Holy Spirit.

In dealing with pious penitents, especially of the other sex, he should be brief and austere, otherwise he will lose much time with little or no fruit, and expose himself to no little danger. With these penitents, especially, he should treat of nothing in the confessional except what concerns their consciences, and that in a fatherly way, but briefly. Even if he recognizes his penitents, it will be better as a rule not to show that he knows them for what they are outside the confessional. He will thus be able to deal with them for the good of their souls with more freedom and detachment.

Section II

The Confessor as Physician of Souls

1. It is the confessor's duty not merely to reconcile the sinner with God by absolving him from sin, but by suggesting to him means and remedies against relapse to enable the penitent to lead a good life in future. The confessor is the spiritual physician of souls, and he should be skilled in diagnosing the diseases of the soul and in applying the proper remedy. Catholic literature is very rich in ascetical books whose special province it is to map out the way of spiritual progress, to point out and describe the many vices and other obstacles to be overcome by the Christian wayfarer, and the means to be taken for the purpose. Among the best known of such works are: Rodriguez' *On the Practice of Christian Perfection*, *The Devout Life* of St Francis de Sales, *The Spiritual Exercises* of St Ignatius, *The Spiritual Combat*, by Scupoli, etc. The confessor should make himself as familiar as possible with one or two such treatises, and he should have tested their worth by applying the lessons which they give to the conduct of his own life. Here it will be sufficient briefly to indicate some general remedies which may be usefully prescribed in most cases where there is a sincere desire to amend. Frequent and fervent prayer, frequent reception of the sacraments of Penance and the Eucharist, pious meditation on the end of life and on the presence of God, avoiding evil company and the occasions of sin, avoiding idleness by constant occupation of mind and body, as far as is possible. Besides these general remedies, the confessor may suggest special ones for the correction of particular vices. The selfish and thoughtless should be told to practise kindness to those about them; the proud, acts of humility; the voluptuous, mortification of their passions; the envious, praising the good deeds of others; and so on. There is special difficulty as to the best method of treating recidivists and those who are placed in an occasion of sin, and something must now be said on each of these classes.

2. A recidivist is one who after many confessions has fallen into the same sin without any or with scarcely any amendment. There is a controversy among theologians as to whether and on what conditions such a one may be absolved. Certain

rigorists maintained that a recidivist could not be absolved until, by abstaining from sin for a considerable time, he had proved the sincerity of his conversion. According to the judgement of St Alphonsus, there is intolerable rigour in this opinion. On the other hand, laxists held that a penitent who has contracted a habit of sin should be absolved at once without delay even though there be no hope of amendment, provided that he make verbal profession of his sorrow and purpose of amendment. The foregoing proposition was condemned by Innocent XI, and if it were put in practice it would lead to grave abuses. For a confessor cannot give absolution to one whom he cannot reasonably judge to be truly sorry for his sins. There are cases where in spite of verbal protestations the confessor cannot form even a probable judgement that the recidivist is truly sorry for his sins. And sometimes it will benefit the penitent to defer absolution for a short time even if it might absolutely be given at once. The common opinion lies between these two extremes, and we cannot do better than explain it in the words of Lugo, for the lengthy discussions of subsequent authors on this question have added nothing of substantial value to the older doctrine.

(a) If a confessor judge a penitent, notwithstanding a past habit of sin, to have here and now a true sorrow and a firm resolve not to sin again, he can absolve him; because present sorrow and a purpose of amendment are sufficient, and future amendment is not required. And so he may absolve him even though he thinks he will fall again.

(b) But in the second place it is certain that when a priest, considering the past habit of sin, the propensity to it, and other circumstances, cannot judge the penitent to be sufficiently averse from the sin, he cannot absolve him, however much the penitent asserts that he is sorry, because if the priest does not believe him he has not the requisite ground for giving absolution.

(c) It will help toward forming a judgement about the present dispositions of the penitent if he show special signs of sorrow, or if he has already tried to correct his habit, or if, having never before been told what means to employ to correct his habit, now, on being told, he willingly accepts and proposes to employ them.

(d) Finally, it will sometimes be useful, with the penitent's leave, to put off absolution for some days so as to excite the penitent to make greater efforts to overcome himself and show signs of real amendment.[1]

[1] Lugo, *De poenit.*, xiv, n. 166; can. 886.

3. An occasion of sin is an external circumstance which leads one to commit sin. It is a proximate occasion if, when a person is placed in it, it leads him to commit sin oftener than not; otherwise it is remote. It is a necessary occasion if he cannot avoid it by using ordinary diligence; otherwise it is voluntary.

(*a*) There is no necessity to avoid remote occasions of sin, for it is not possible to do so, and in spite of them sin may be avoided by using the proper means.

(*b*) We are bound to avoid proximate and voluntary occasions of sin, for we cannot remain in them without exposing ourselves to the proximate danger of committing sin, and if we voluntarily choose to remain in a proximate occasion we voluntarily choose the sin. As we are bound to avoid sin we are bound to take the necessary means for that end. This doctrine is confirmed by the 61st, 62nd, and 63rd propositions, condemned by Innocent XI.

(*c*) A necessary occasion is one which we cannot avoid. It is physically necessary if we cannot physically get away from it; it is morally necessary if it is more difficult to avoid it than to keep from sin while in it by using proper means and precautions.

There is no obligation to avoid necessary occasions of sin, for we cannot be obliged to do what is impossible; but we are bound to take the necessary means to avoid sin in spite of being in the occasion, and such means are always at hand if we have the good will to use them, for God's goodness will never permit us to be tried above our strength. By using the means to avoid sin while placed in an occasion of sin, we make the proximate occasion remote, as theologians say.

It follows from this that one who finds his ordinary avocation in life, which is supposed to be an honest one, a proximate occasion of sin to him is seldom bound to give it up; he is only bound to make the occasion remote, which is generally possible with a good will and the help of God's grace.

Section III

The Confessor as Counsellor

1. The duties of the confessor require considerable expert knowledge in one who aspires to the office. He must in the first place have a competent knowledge of Christian morals and of all that belongs to the valid and lawful adminstration and reception of the sacraments. St Alphonsus teaches us

that it is not sufficient merely to know the general principles of Christian morality; the confessor must have considerable skill in applying those principles correctly, according to the infinite variety which is found in human actions. The confessor should have received a thorough grounding in moral theology during the course of his priestly studies, and he should continue to keep it up during the rest of his life, for it is quickly lost unless means are taken to keep it fresh in the mind. The Church shows that she is conscious of this danger by insisting that all who have the cure of souls should at certain times every year be present at the conferences of the clergy, where moral questions are discussed. Every confessor is not called upon to be an authority in moral questions, but at least he should be able to decide correctly ordinary doubts and difficulties, and know when to doubt about more serious questions.

2. The confessor is bound to instruct a penitent before he can give him absolution when he finds that he is ignorant of what he must know in order to receive the sacrament of Penance validly and lawfully. And so if the penitent does not know how to make an integral confession, or how to make an act of contrition, the confessor must instruct him. In the same way, he must teach one who is ignorant of those truths which must be believed in order to be saved. Innocent XI condemned the proposition that a man is capable of receiving absolution however great may be his ignorance of the mysteries of the Faith, and even if through culpable negligence he does not know of the mystery of the most blessed Trinity and of the Incarnation of our Lord Jesus Christ. Ignorance of those Christian truths whose knowledge is required by precept, and of the obligations of one's state of life, is not a bar to valid absolution, and in spite of it absolution may lawfully be given on condition that the penitent undertake to learn what he should know, if the confessor cannot give the necessary instruction at once.

3. No general rule can be laid down as to whether the confessor should instruct a penitent whom he finds to be ignorant on other matters. Various cases must be distinguished. If the ignorance of the penitent is morally hurtful to him, as is an erroneous conscience which thinks that a perfectly harmless act is sinful, the confessor should put his conscience right. Again, if the penitent asks whether an action is lawful or not, the confessor should instruct him. In other cases, if the penitent is ignorant of his obligation, and he would not fulfil it even if he were told, as a general rule the confessor may and

should abstain from telling him under the circumstances. For the information would do no good, but only harm, inasmuch as the sins which hitherto were only material would henceforth be formal. There is, however, an exception to this rule when what is done in ignorance and good faith is a cause of public scandal, for then the public good requires that the penitent should be told even to his temporary private loss.

On these principles authors agree that if a confessor detect a diriment impediment between parties who think that they are validly married, he should not inform them of it, at any rate until he has obtained the necessary dispensation, so that he can at once proceed to set the matter right.

Section IV

The Confessor as Judge

1. As judge in the tribunal of Penance the confessor passes sentence and imposes satisfaction proportionate to the sins confessed. If the penitent makes a full confession, is truly sorry for his sins, and is ready to fulfil to the best of his ability all his grave obligations at least, there is nothing to prevent the confessor giving a penance and absolution at once. There is no necessity for putting questions to well-instructed penitents who make their confession with care and diligence, or to those who have only light matter to confess. If, however, the penitent does not fully declare the number and species of his grave sins, or if the confessor is not satisfied about his dispositions, he is bound to question him to procure a full confession and the necessary dispositions before giving absolution.[1]

If the confessor knows that the penitent has committed some serious sin, but says nothing about it in confession, he should question him as to whether there is anything else on his conscience. If the penitent denies that there is, he should as a rule be absolved; it is a received maxim that " the penitent must be believed in his own favour as well as against himself." Even if the sin was known to the confessor from the confession of someone else, he must not, of course, put any question which would amount to a violation of the seal, but he may put a general question as to whether there is anything else, and if the penitent denies that there is, he may as a rule absolve even then. It may be that the penitent did not commit formal sin, or that he has forgotten it, or thinks that he is not bound

[1] 4 Lat., c. 21; Ritual.

to mention it to this confessor, or there may be some mistake on the part of the confessor or the informant. Still, if it is quite evident to the confessor that the penitent is making a bad confession, and so is not disposed for absolution, he cannot, of course, absolve him.

2. The confessor's obligation of putting questions to the penitent in order to supply any defect on the part of the latter is a grave one. Still it is only secondary; the obligation lies with the penitent in the first place, and so the confessor may be excused from grave sin if occasionally he does not put questions even to obtain what is necessary matter for confession. We may allow this especially when the confessor is weary after hearing a great many confessions, and, partly through weariness, partly through some slight negligence, fails to ask questions which are *per se* necessary.

3. The Ritual and theologians warn the confessor against putting unnecessary and indiscreet questions to the penitent. By doing so he may easily scandalize him or even teach him to commit sin. This is especially the case with regard to the young. In the matter of chastity it is a maxim that it is better to fail in putting many questions than to put one which is not necessary.

The confessor should be moderate in questioning the penitent, and only put questions about matter in which it is probable that he has committed sin. He should remember that the penitent is only bound to confess what his own conscience accuses him of; he does not sin nor is he bound to confess according to the conscience of his confessor.

CHAPTER XIII

MISTAKES MADE IN HEARING CONFESSIONS

1. ONE who culpably causes unjust harm to another is bound in justice to repair that harm as far as he can. Even if the action which causes harm to another is done innocently, there will nevertheless arise an obligation to prevent the harm as far as possible as soon as the danger is noticed, and if there is grave negligence in doing this without reasonable excuse, injustice will be committed and the obligation of making restitution incurred. A confessor who admits a penitent to confession is bound in justice to absolve him if he is properly disposed for absolution. And so if he has neglected to do so, he must repair the error afterward, especially if the penitent were in danger of death and may die in sin without sacramental absolution.

Similarly, if the confessor gave his penitent false instruction in faith or morals, or bad advice, or bound him to make restitution when he was under no obligation to do so by the law of God, or released him from such an obligation when he was really under it, the confessor must afterward correct his mistake, taking the precaution to ask the penitent's leave to say something to him about his confession if an opportunity is afforded him only out of confession. When the penitent was wrongfully compelled to make restitution with grave fault on the part of the confessor, the latter is bound in justice to make him restitution for the loss that he has suffered, if he cannot otherwise recover his money. The confessor is in the same way bound to make restitution to the defrauded creditor when, with grave fault, he released a penitent from the obligation of paying a just debt, if in consequence the penitent is now unwilling or unable to fulfil his obligation.

2. If the confessor merely neglected to impose a penance, or supply for the deficiency of the penitent's confession by questioning him, or failed to correct some mistake that he was labouring under, or to warn him of the obligation of making restitution, he did not thereby sin against justice, and he is not bound to make restitution, unless indeed in the circumstances his silence was equivalent to positive approval. Still,

if knowingly and wilfully he did any of these things, he committed sin, and in as far as harm to his penitent or to others ensued he violated charity, which obliges every man to do what he can to prevent loss and damage to others. Even out of confession if he can prevent harm being caused by his failure to do his duty in the confessional, he should with the penitent's leave do his best to prevent it.

CHAPTER XIV

THE SEAL OF CONFESSION

1. By the seal of confession is understood the religious obligation to keep secret anything that is manifested in sacramental confession.

This obligation is imposed by the natural, the divine, and by positive ecclesiastical law. For the very fact that a penitent makes known his sins in secret to the confessor, with a view to obtaining absolution, lays upon the confessor the strictest obligation in justice and in charity not to violate the trust placed in him, much as a doctor or a lawyer when consulted about private matters is bound to observe secrecy with respect to what has been confided to him. Our Lord, who commanded all who fall into grave sin after Baptism to go to confession, could not have imposed such an obligation without requiring confessors to observe the strictest secrecy about what they hear in confession.

The Church, too, in the Fourth Council of Lateran (c. 21) forbids the confessor under grave penalties ever to betray by word, sign, or in any other way, what he has heard in sacramental confession. The Code punishes the confessor who presumes directly to violate the seal of confession with excommunication most specially reserved to the Holy See, if indirectly, with severe penalties. Others who violate the seal are to be severely punished (Can. 2369).

The obligation of the seal of confession differs from all other secrets in that it is never lawful under any circumstances to make known the least thing that has been manifested by a penitent in confession. If questioned about confessional matter, even in a court of justice, the priest must always answer that he knows nothing about it, as with perfect truth he may do, for what he knows as a confessor, he knows as the vicegerent of God, not as man. Not even to save his life or the lives of others may a priest violate the seal; like Fr. Henry Garnett, or St John of Nepomuk, he must be prepared to lay down his life rather than break the seal. He is never released from his obligation even by the death of the penitent, for people are unwilling that their secret sins should be mentioned even after their death.

A grave sacrilege would be committed by the direct manifestation of the least fault known from sacramental confession, but theologians allow that if the danger of confessional matter becoming known is very remote there may be only venial sin in indirect violation of the seal.

2. The person who hears the sacramental confession of another made with a view to obtaining absolution is primarily bound by the seal. Even if such a person were not a true priest, but merely represented himself to be one, he would, nevertheless, be bound by the obligation of the seal, for he could not violate the trust placed in him without such violation injuring the penitent and turning people away from the sacrament.

Not only the priest, but all others, who mediately or immediately come to know anything confessed to a priest with a view to absolution, are bound by the obligation of the seal. Superiors, then, who are asked for faculties to absolve from reserved cases, other confessors whose advice is asked about cases of conscience, anyone who by design or by accident overhears what is said in confession, are bound equally with the confessor.[1] The obligation of the seal is imposed in favour of the penitent; it is the penitent's secret, but he himself is not bound by it. It does not follow, however, that penitents may without let or hindrance talk to others about what the confessor has said or done to them in the confessional. They are at least bound by a natural obligation to reveal nothing which would tend in any way to injure or aggrieve the confessor. A confessor may speak with the penitent in the confessional about past confessions in as far as this is necessary for the present guidance and instruction of the penitent; but outside of confession he may not speak of confessional matter even to the penitent without the latter's express leave freely given. There is a question discussed among theologians as to whether one who finds and reads the written confession of another violates the seal or is bound by it. It is better to distinguish various cases. If the circumstances in which the paper is found show that it has been used for the purpose of making a sacramental confession, as when it is found in the confessional, then the written confession is a sort of continuous confession, and knowledge derived from it comes under the seal. The same must be said of a letter written to an ecclesiastical superior for faculties to absolve from a reserved case. Otherwise, inasmuch as the writing down of one's sins

[1] Can. 889.

is not sacramental confession, knowledge gained from such a source without reference to actual confession does not seem to come under the seal.

Similarly, there is a difficulty about giving or refusing to the penitent an attestation that he has been to confession. If the penitent is unworthy of absolution and has not been absolved, but asks for the confessor's attestation that he has been to confession, what is the latter to do? If the refusal of the attestation would in the circumstances show that the penitent was not absolved, it is clear that it cannot be refused without a violation of the seal; in other circumstances the confessor will be free to give or refuse it.

3. Not only all sins mentioned in confession are the matter of the seal, but everything which was mentioned because it was thought to be a sin, and every circumstance which was mentioned in order to make a full confession and whose manifestation would tend to injure the penitent or make confession odious, comes under the seal. And so if one who is under a vow of chastity mentions the fact in order to make a full confession of a sin of impurity, the fact that the person is under vow is protected by the seal. In the same way moral and social defects, such as scrupulosity and illegitimacy, come under the seal if they were made known with reference to confession, and if their manifestation would be to the injury of the penitent or make confession odious.

The virtues of a penitent are not the matter of the seal, nor does a confessor seem to violate his obligation if he merely says that he has heard the confession of such a one, unless on account of special circumstances it would cause injury to the penitent or make confession odious. Nor does a confessor whose watch was stolen by a penitent while making his confession break the seal by giving information of the theft to the police.

4. The seal may be broken directly or indirectly. It is broken directly when the confessor says that such a penitent told him such a sin in confession. It is broken indirectly when the confessor says or does anything or abstains from saying or doing anything from which others may come to the knowledge of confessional matter, or by which the penitent may be aggrieved or confession made odious. A confessor, then, indirectly violates the seal by changing his conduct to the detriment of the penitent in consequence of what he has heard in confession; by saying that a certain sin is rife in a place in which he has heard few confessions; by talking

with another confessor about the sins of a penitent of both of them.

It used to be a common view among theologians that ecclesiastical superiors might use knowledge gained in hearing confessions for external government, provided that in such use there was no direct or indirect revelation of confessional matter. After the decree of Clement VIII, May 26, 1593, and that of the Holy Office, November 18, 1682, this opinion has become obsolete, and now it is universally held that no knowledge gained in the confessional can be used by the priest for external government if such use aggrieves the penitent, or makes the sacrament odious, or otherwise directly or indirectly violates the seal (Can. 890).

In spite of the strictness of the seal the confessor may make use of knowledge gained in the confessional to correct his own faults, to treat his penitents and others with more kindness, to learn by experience how better to fulfil his duties as confessor, how to preach more fruitfully, but always with prudence and without giving any just cause of complaint to his penitents.

BOOK VII
EXTREME UNCTION

CHAPTER I
THE NATURE OF EXTREME UNCTION

1. THE Council of Trent defined that Extreme Unction is a true sacrament of the New Law insinuated by St Mark and promulgated and recommended to the faithful by St James when he wrote: " Is any man sick among you ? Let him bring in the priests of the Church, and let them pray over him, anointing him with oil in the name of the Lord: and the prayer of faith shall save the sick man; and the Lord shall raise him up; and if he be in sins they shall be forgiven him."[1]

This sacrament, as the Council of Trent also teaches, is the complement or completion of Penance. As we have seen, Penance was specially instituted for the remission of post-baptismal sin, and its reception is necessary for all Christians who have fallen into grave sin after Baptism. Penance, then, ordinarily precedes Extreme Unction, which is properly a sacrament of the living; its primary effect is to infuse sanctifying grace into the soul for the salvation of the sick man. If any sins still remain on the soul, provided that there be at least attrition for them, they will be remitted together with the remains of sin. By the remains of sin are undertsood the temporal punishment due to them, spiritual weakness and inclination to evil, lethargy in the doing of good. The sacrament removes these wholly or in part, according to the dispositions of the recipient, and, moreover, if it be for the good of the sick person and in keeping with the providence of God, it restores him to bodily health. This last effect is not produced by miracle, but by means of natural causes; the sacrament consoles and soothes the sick person, dispels his mental anxieties, and the resultant state, with the blessing of God, sometimes brings about a recovery. In order to produce this effect with more certainty the administration of the sacrament should not be too long deferred.

[1] Jas. v 14, 15.

2. The remote matter of Extreme Unction is olive oil blessed by a bishop for the purpose, or by a priest who has received power to bless it from the Holy See (Can. 945). Ecclesiastical law requires that priests obtain the oil of the sick from their own ordinary, not from any other Bishop.

The proximate matter is the anointing with oil of the principal organs of the senses, and where the organs are double both are anointed, the right one first. In England, according to the Ritual, the eyes, ears, nostrils, mouth, hands, and feet, are anointed; but when the recipient is a woman in a public infirmary or hospital, the priest has special leave to omit the anointing of the feet if he thinks that it would excite scandal or comment. According to Canon 947, sec. 3, the anointing of the feet may be omitted for any reasonable cause.

If some sense-organ is wanting, the part of the body nearest to where it should be is anointed. Each anointing has its own special form, that for the eyes being: " By this holy anointing and through his most sweet mercy may the Lord forgive whatever sins thou hast committed through thy sight. Amen." The form for the other senses is similar. If the near approach of death will not allow of all the senses being anointed with their appropriate forms, the forehead may be anointed with the following general form: " By this holy anointing may the Lord forgive whatever sins thou hast committed. Amen."[1] As, however, Extreme Unction is only probably valid when administered with such a single anointing under one general form, if there is time it should be repeated immediately in the form prescribed by the Ritual.

[1] S.O., April 25, 1906; can. 947, sec. 1.

CHAPTER II

THE MINISTER OF EXTREME UNCTION

ONLY a bishop or a priest can validly administer this sacrament, and the only lawful minister is the bishop or priest who has the cure of souls in the place where the sick man dwells, or another priest with his express or at least reasonably presumed leave.

In the Latin Church one priest performs all the unctions, but the sacrament is valid if different priests perform the several unctions, as is done in the Greek Church. The organs should not merely be touched with the holy oil, but anointed, and the Ritual prescribes that this should be done by making the sign of the Cross on the organ with the thumb after dipping it in the oil. Care should be taken not to finish the form before both organs have been anointed when they are double, and the several anointings should be done continuously, as it is probable that all together constitute the sacrament by which grace is not given until the last anointing is finished.

The priest who has the cure of souls in the place is bound to administer this sacrament to the sick in justice in person or through another priest; in case of necessity any priest is bound to administer it out of charity (Can. 939).

CHAPTER III

THE RECIPIENT OF EXTREME UNCTION

1. In order to be able to receive Extreme Unction validly a man must be baptized, must have attained the use of reason, and must be in probable danger of death from sickness. Extreme Unction, then, may be administered to those adults who are in danger of death from disease, from the pains of childbirth, from a wound, from poison, and from old age, even though they be no longer in their right senses. It cannot be validly given to soldiers before going into battle, to criminals who are going to be executed, to imbeciles who have never had the use of reason, to children who have not yet come to the use of reason, nor to unbaptized persons.[1]

2. This sacrament may only be given once in the same sickness and in the same danger, but if the sickness be prolonged and after partial recovery the sick person again becomes dangerously ill, Extreme Unction may be repeated. According to some good authors, it may be repeated after a month's interval, for as a general rule the danger may be considered a new one after such a period of time.

No good Catholic would wish to depart this life without the help of this and the other sacraments; still there is no obligation under grave sin to receive Extreme Unction. But although the faithful who, without despising it, neglect to receive this sacrament do not thereby commit grave sin, yet a priest who has the cure of souls would sin grievously if he neglected to give those under his charge the opportunity of receiving this sacrament in their last sickness. As soon as there is probable danger of death the last sacraments may be given in the following order: Penance, Viaticum, Extreme Unction, and finally the papal blessing for the moment of death.

Canon 941 prescribes that when it is doubtful whether a sick person has attained the use of reason, whether he is really in danger of death, or whether he is dead, this sacrament should be administered conditionally.

[1] Ritual.

BOOK VIII

THE SACRAMENT OF ORDERS

CHAPTER I

THE NATURE OF ORDERS

1. THE priesthood of the New Law is not a mere office and bare ministry of preaching the Gospel: Our Lord instituted it and gave it the power of offering the sacrifice of his Body and Blood and of forgiving sins.[1] This power is conferred on priests by the sacrament of Orders, which also gives the grace to those who are rightly ordained to perform their sacred functions worthily. Those functions are various, and partly by divine institution, partly by ecclesiastical, they have been divided and assigned to separate grades of a spiritual hierarchy. The perfection of the priesthood and the whole of its powers reside in the episcopate; some portion of what bishops possess is communicated to the inferior ranks of the clergy by a special rite for each grade. Thus Orders is one sacrament, but the different ranks of the clergy participate in it in different degrees, or in other words, there are several Orders. There are three major or sacred Orders, to which by ecclesiastical law is annexed a solemn vow of chastity, and there are four minor Orders. The sacred Orders are the priesthood, the diaconate, and the subdiaconate; by the minor Orders are ordained acolytes, exorcists, lectors, and door-keepers.

It is a moot point among theologians whether all these Orders are sacraments or not; more probably only the episcopate, priesthood, and diaconate are sacraments and of immediate divine institution, the rest being of ecclesiastical institution. Those Orders which are sacraments impress a character on the soul.

The first tonsure, by which a lay person is made a cleric, is certainly of ecclesiastical institution and is not a sacrament.

2. The matter of the minor Orders is the handing to the cleric the symbols of the office to which he is ordained, and the words which accompany this act constitute the form. There is a controversy whether the handing to the subdeacon

---

[1] Trent, sess. xxiii, c. 1.

of an empty chalice with the paten alone, or also the giving to him of the book of epistles, is the matter of the subdiaconate, and similarly with regard to the form. It is also a matter of controversy whether the imposition of hands alone is the matter of the diaconate, priesthood, and episcopate, or the handing to the ordinand the symbols of his office, or whether both together constitute the matter. There is the same difference of opinion with regard to the form, but these questions belong to dogmatic theology.

3. In practice, the rite prescribed for ordination in the Pontifical must be observed, and if anything be omitted which even probably belongs to the essence of the sacrament, the whole must be repeated again, at least conditionally. Thus, if in the ordination of a priest the chalice with wine and the paten were not handed to the ordinand to touch while the bishop pronounced the appropriate form of words, the whole ordination would have to be repeated before one thus ordained could be allowed to say Mass. Similarly, if the imposition of hands is omitted which precedes and accompanies the prayer and preface which are said by the bishop and which contain the form, the whole rite must be repeated. On the contrary, if the third imposition of hands which accompanies the prayer, " Receive the Holy Ghost, etc.," is omitted, this portion of the rite alone need be supplied afterward, as it is certain that it only belongs to the integrity of the sacrament, not to its essence.

Although previous reception of the priesthood is more probably necessary for the valid ordination of a bishop, the inferior Orders do not seem necessary for the valid ordination to the priesthood.

Whether three co-consecrators are necessary for the validity of an episcopal consecration is disputed, but at least the Pope can give faculties to have only one consecrating bishop.

The functions of those who are in minor Orders, with the exception of exorcists, may, according to modern discipline, be exercised by laymen.

CHAPTER II

THE MINISTER OF ORDERS

1. THE ordinary minister of Orders is a bishop, who is the only valid minister of the episcopate and priesthood. A priest may receive delegated authority from the Pope to confer minor Orders, and the subdiaconate, and probably also the diaconate. Thus Abbots have power to give minor Order to their own subjects, and Cardinals, if they be priests, may give them to clerics belonging to their titular churches in Rome.

Ecclesiastical law requires that Orders be received only from one's own bishop, or from another bishop with his leave, which is granted by giving the subject dismissorial letters.

The Code bids a bishop ordain his own subjects unless he is prevented by some good reason.

One's own bishop, as far as Orders are concerned, is only the bishop of the diocese in which the ordinand has a domicile, together with origin therein, or simply a domicile without origin; but in this latter case the ordinand ought to affirm on oath his intention perpetually to remain in the diocese, unless there is question of promoting a cleric to Orders who has already been incardinated in the diocese by the first tonsure, or of promoting a student who is destined for the service of another diocese in accordance with Canon 969, sec. 2, or of promoting a professed religious, of whom there is question in Canon 964, n. 4 (Can. 956).

2. By the common law, regulars must be ordained by the bishop in whose diocese their convent is situated, but some have a special privilege of giving dismissorials to their members for ordination by any bishop who is in union with the Holy See. Whenever a bishop holds an ordination outside his own diocese he requires the leave of the bishop of the place to exercise pontifical functions.

CHAPTER III

THE SUBJECT OF ORDERS

1. To be able to receive Orders validly, the subject must be of the male sex and baptized (Can. 968). It has always been understood in the Church that women cannot receive Christian Orders. Moreover, an adult must have at least an habitual and express intention to receive ordination (unless indeed he is an imbecile and has never had the use of reason).

2. Many qualities and conditions are requisite for the lawful reception of Orders about which something must here be said; the fuller treatment of this matter belongs to canon law.

As we saw when treating of the clerical state, one who aspires to Orders must be of good life and must be called by God.

At least the Orders which are sacraments should be received in the state of grace, and Canon 1001 prescribes that before receiving the first tonsure and minor Orders the ordinand should devote at least three whole days to spiritual exercises, and before receiving sacred Orders he should devote at least six whole days to them.

In order that one may be lawfully ordained Canon 974 requires: (1) The reception of the sacrament of Confirmation; (2) moral conduct agreeably to the Order to be received; (3) the canonical age; (4) the required knowledge; (5) the reception of the lower Orders; (6) the observance of the interstices; (7) a canonical title if there is question of major Orders.

The subdiaconate may not be conferred before the completion of the twenty-first year of age, the diaconate before the completion of the twenty-second, and the priesthood before the completion of the twenty-fourth (Can. 975).

No one, whether secular or religious, is to receive the first tonsure before beginning his course of theology (Can. 976).

The subdiaconate may not be given except at the end of the third year of the course of theology, the diaconate only at the beginning of the fourth year, and the priesthood only after the middle of the fourth year (Can. 976, sec. 2).

Orders should be conferred by degrees, so that ordinations by leaps and bounds are altogether prohibited (Can. 977).

THE SUBJECT OF ORDERS

Canon 978 prescribes that the interstices are to be observed, and during them those who have been promoted should exercise themselves in the Orders received according to the directions of the bishop.

The interstices between the first tonsure and the Order of door-keepers and between the minor Orders are left to the prudent judgement of the bishop; one year should elapse between the Order of acolytes and the subdiaconate; three months between the subdiaconate and the diaconate.

Without special leave of the Roman Pontiff minor Orders may never be given with the subdiaconate or two sacred Orders on one and the same day, and any custom to the contrary is reprobated; it is also forbidden to give the first tonsure together with one of the minor Orders, or all the minor Orders at once.

A bishop must have completed his thirtieth year.

By common law sacred Orders should be conferred during Mass on the Saturdays in Ember Week, or before Passion Sunday, or before Easter Sunday. For grave reason a bishop can confer them on any Sunday or holiday of obligation.

The first tonsure may be conferred on any day and at any time; minor Orders on Sundays and on doubles, in the morning (Can. 1006).

Those who receive sacred Orders must communicate in the Mass of ordination (Can. 1005).

The Church does not wish her clergy to have to beg or to exercise some unbecoming trade in order to gain a livelihood, so she requires that to be admitted to sacred Orders a cleric must have a title, as it is called, or a certain guarantee of decent support. Various titles are recognized by ecclesiastical law, such as a benefice, pension, patrimony, poverty for religious, a common table, the Mission, and others. If a cleric already ordained loses the title of his ordination he should find another, unless in the bishop's judgement his decent support is otherwise provided for (Can. 980).

Before ordination regulars must be solemnly professed, unless they have a special privilege by which simple profession suffices.

After ordination a priest pays homage to the bishop and solemnly promises obedience to his ordinary. He undertakes no new burden by this promise; he simply binds himself anew to pay canonical obedience to the bishop in all matters subject to his authority; and a secular priest obliges himself not to leave the diocese for which he was ordained without the leave of his bishop.

BOOK IX

MARRIAGE

CHAPTER I

BETROTHAL

1. THE seventh sacrament of the Christian Church is Marriage, and because it is usually preceded by an engagement to marry, we will first treat of betrothal. Betrothal may be defined as a mutual promise of future marriage between persons who may marry lawfully.

It is a mutual promise or a bilateral contract between a man and a woman, and the conditions which are required for the validity of any bilateral contract are requisite for betrothal. There must be a serious, voluntary, and deliberate intention to enter into the agreement. Mere unmeaning flirtation, or the expression of a wish by the man that he could make the woman his wife, does not make a betrothal. Anything which destroys the voluntariness of the act will prevent it from being a valid contract. Substantial mistake about its nature or about the identity of the other party to the contract, and probably even mistake about some unessential quality in the other party, if it were the motive for entering into the contract, would make it null and void. As grave and unjustly caused fear is a diriment impediment to marriage, so, too, it prevents a valid engagement to marry.

The promise must be deliberate, made with full knowledge and advertence to the serious step which is being taken. There must be, as divines say, the deliberateness about the act which is necessary to commit a grave sin. The mutual consent of the parties must be expressed by words, writing, or other suitable sign. The acceptance by a woman of a ring from a man who has asked her to be his wife is a sufficient expression of consent and concludes the contract.

For many years past a special law has existed in Spain by virtue of which no betrothal is valid unless attested by a formal document in writing. In the year 1900 this law was extended to the whole of Spanish America, and by the decree of the Sacred Congregation of the Council, August 2, 1907, no betrothal between Catholics or in which one of the parties is a Catholic is valid in conscience or in law or has any canonical effects unless it is contracted in writing and is signed by the parties, and also signed either by the parish priest, or by the local ordinary, or at least by two witnesses. If either of the parties or both of them are unable to write, the fact should be noted in the document, and another witness must be added who will sign the document together with the priest, or the local ordinary, or the two witnesses mentioned above. This decree binds all Catholics of the Latin rite throughout the world, and takes effect from Easter Sunday, April 19, 1908 (Can. 1017).

The term *parish priest* in this decree is used to designate not only him who is lawfully placed in charge of a canonically erected parish, but in countries where there are no canonically erected parishes the priest to whom the cure of souls in a definite district is lawfully entrusted, and who is equivalent to a parish priest, and in missions where as yet the districts are not definitely marked out all priests who in any place have the general cure of souls assigned them by the superior of the mission.

The parties must be capable of entering into a lawful marriage at any rate at the time contemplated when the engagement is made. For a promise to do something which is impossible or unlawful has no binding force, and so if at the time contemplated there will still be some diriment or prohibitory impediment between the parties, an engagement to marry is void.

A valid contract to marry at a future time when the parties will be free to do so may be entered into by those who are now hindered by some impediment. And so children under age, though incapable of marrying, may enter into a valid betrothal. According to the old canon law, even their parents might make a valid engagement for them, if they were present and did not express dissent; or, if absent, afterward ratified the contract. The decree of August 2, 1907, abolishes this rule, as also the presumption of law by which marriage attempted by children under age was presumed to be a valid engagement to marry.

Some authors applied that presumption to the case of clandestine civil marriages contracted in places subject to the decree *Tametsi* of the Council of Trent. They held that although such a marriage was null and void, yet it had the effects of a betrothal, as in the case of those under age. Leo XIII, however, by a decree dated March 17, 1879, decided that a clandestine marriage has not the effects of a betrothal even if the parties intended that it should have.

Betrothal of children under seven is presumed to be invalid for want of the use of reason, but if it is proved that the parties to the contract had sufficient use of reason in spite of their tender age, the engagement will be valid; malice is then said to supply for the want of age.

2. Betrothal under condition, as, "I will marry you if I can earn £200 a year," is lawful, and follows *per se* the ordinary rules of conditional contracts. Such a betrothal will impose on the party who enters into it an obligation to do what he can to fulfil the condition, and when the condition is fulfilled the engagement will become valid and binding without any renewal of consent. Similarly, an engagement in this form, "I will marry you if I reach the age of twenty-one," will become a binding engagement on attaining that age. On the contrary, an engagement under an impossible condition is null and void from the commencement. And so, if two parties between whom there is a diriment impediment, which either cannot be dispensed or for which a dispensation is not usually given, enter into an engagement under the form, "I will marry you if we can get a dispensation," there will be no valid contract. It is much controverted among canonists and divines whether the same is to be said when the impediment is one for which a dispensation can be, and usually is, granted. If cousins, for example, entered into an engagement under the form, "I will marry you if I can get a dispensation," what would be the effect of such an engagement? There would, of course, be an obligation to ask for a dispensation; but if it were got, would there be a valid betrothal by virtue of the conditional engagement, or would the parties have to renew their consent? Many authors maintain that in this case there is no valid betrothal without a renewal of consent. For proof of their view they point out that the parties were not free to enter on an engagement to marry on account of the diriment impediment between them; that it is unbecoming to contract on condition that the superior grant a dispensation from the law which should be observed by all; and that when the question has been submitted to Rome the decision has uniformly been in favour of this view. On the other hand, many good authors hold that there is nothing in these reasons to prohibit us from applying to such cases the ordinary doctrine concerning conditional contracts, and so the general question remains undecided and uncertain. Both opinions are theologically probable.

CHAPTER II

THE EFFECTS OF BETROTHAL

1. As betrothal is a contract and the matter is serious, the betrothed are under a grave obligation in justice to fulfil their engagement. If a special time was agreed upon, they must keep to the appointed time, otherwise they must marry at a reasonable time after the engagement has been concluded. As grave inconveniences are likely to arise from a too prolonged betrothal, it is the duty of those who have the cure of souls to admonish those engaged that they should marry if without just cause they defer doing so too long. A delay of over a year without good reason seems excessive.

2. After betrothal the parties are under a special obligation to live chastely, and if either commit a sin of impurity with a third person the sin has a special malice on account of his violation of the fidelity which he owes to his betrothed. It is a disputed point whether the circumstance of betrothal changes the species of the sin so that mention of it must be made in confession, or whether it merely aggravates its malice. It is probable that it does not change the species of the sin, for betrothal does not, like marriage, give one party a right in the other, but gives only a right to have the other when the engagement is executed.

3. Betrothal to one prevents valid betrothal to another as long as the former tie lasts, for a promise to do what is unlawful has no binding force. If, however, in spite of betrothal to one the party marries someone else, the marriage will be valid but illicit, just as the sale of a house to one person is valid in spite of a previous promise to sell it to someone else. Betrothal, in other words, is a prohibitory, not a diriment impediment of marriage with third persons.

4. The consent of the parents of the parties is certainly not necessary for the validity of marriage. The Council of Trent teaches this.[1] Nor is it necessary *per se* for the lawfulness and the validity of betrothal, because in the choice of a state of life every man is his own master. It does not follow, however, from this doctrine, that children need not consult their parents

---

[1] Sess. xxiv, c. 1, de ref. Matr.

about marriage and about a partner for life. In a matter of such importance for the future happiness of the child, and because the marriage of a member of the family concerns not merely the individual, but the whole family, and especially the head of it, a dutiful child will ordinarily consult his parents before entering on an engagement to marry. If a child wishes to contract an unsuitable marriage, as if the heir of an honoured house wishes to marry an actress of doubtful reputation, the parents have a right to object to such a marriage; and if they forbid it, the son is bound to obey, and he commits sin if he goes against his parents' commands. An engagement contrary to the reasonable commands of one's parents is unlawful and therefore invalid. Mere inequality of rank between the parties of itself is not a sufficient reason why parents should forbid a marriage, but a difficulty arises when inequality of rank will be the cause of dissension and ill-feeling in the family. Even in this case a son who wishes to marry someone of inferior rank is not always bound in conscience to submit to the wishes of his parents. If he is satisfied that the woman he loves will make him a good wife, and he is not prepared to take anybody else, he is not bound to sacrifice his own happiness in deference to the wishes of his parents, especially when these originate in social prejudice rather than in a desire for the welfare of their child.

English civil law requires the consent of the father or guardian for the lawfulness of the marriage of a minor. In most of the United States of America the law is similar.

Canon 1034 bids parish priests seriously to warn minors against contracting marriage without their parents' knowledge and consent. If minors insist on doing this, parish priests should not assist at the marriage without consulting the Ordinary.

CHAPTER III

DISSOLUTION OF BETROTHAL

1. BETROTHAL, like other contracts, can be dissolved in various ways. The parties may both agree to release each other and then they will be free, for by a rule of law all things are dissolved by the same causes which gave them birth. If children under age have been betrothed, they cannot release the contract even by mutual consent until the age of puberty, and then within three days either may resile from the contract without waiting for the consent of the other party; but if they do not use this privilege granted by canon law they are presumed to ratify the contract.

2. One of the betrothed may resile if a circumstance of importance be detected or happen which if it had been known before would have prevented the contract being entered into. This rule is commonly admitted by divines, who explain it by saying that betrothal is of its nature conditional, and has such a condition as the above annexed to it. If, then, one of the parties finds that the other has an ungovernable temper, or great debts, or is given to drink, or if the other becomes afflicted with a disease like consumption or paralysis, he will be free to rescind the contract. The innocent party may resile if the other commit fornication with someone else, and certainly the man is free if he find out that the woman was corrupted even before betrothal. The same rule may be applied in favour of the woman when she finds out that the man committed fornication before betrothal, at least if in the particular case it is a sign of inconstancy or is very much resented.

Betrothal is annulled if an impediment of marriage come to exist between the parties unless it had its origin in the culpable fraud of one of them, for then he must do what he can to obtain a dispensation or at least compensate the other, as no one should reap advantage from his own fraud.

3. One who is betrothed may resile in order to enter a religious order, or to take sacred orders, or even with a view of living in the world under a perpetual vow of chastity, for in all these cases a higher life is embraced, and betrothal has also the condition annexed, "Unless afterward I am called to a higher life."

4. The Pope may for a just cause grant a dispensation from betrothal. Some authors maintained that the Pope had not the power to grant such a dispensation, inasmuch as it would violate the rights of the other party. However, if an individual is unreasonably obstinate in the maintenance of his rights, the head of the society to which he belongs should have the power of granting relief to others whom that obstinacy places in difficulties. This is what the Pope sometimes does; when a civil marriage contracted in violation of betrothal to another, though null and void in the eyes of the Church, makes it impossible for the married party to return to his former betrothed, the Pope will grant a dispensation even if the other party refuses to forego his rights.

5. When one of the parties labours under a secret defect which, if known, would furnish sufficient ground for resiling from the engagement, there is no strict obligation to make it known to the other party, unless it will be to his detriment. Past sin, then, need not be declared, but if the woman has undergone an operation which makes her incapable of bearing children, she should not contract marriage with a man who is ignorant of the defect and hopes to have children.

Whether marriage with a woman contracted in violation of a promise of marriage made to another annuls the former betrothal altogether, or whether the obligation to marry the first is only suspended and revives again if the wife die before the husband, is a disputed question among divines. Of course, such a breach of faith makes the other party free to marry someone else if she choose, and the opinion is at least probable that by such a radical change in circumstances as marriage with another the former engagement is altogether dissolved and cannot revive. There is something incongruous in the idea of a person who is married to one, being nevertheless still under the obligation to marry someone else.

6. If a man after betrothal without the knowledge or consent of his betrothed goes to live elsewhere at a distance so that personal intercourse between them is impossible, the woman may consider herself free to break off the engagement. A short absence makes no difference in the mutual obligations of the parties. If it is uncertain with what intention and for how long a time a betrothed person has absented himself, information as to his intentions should be sought by letter before breaking off the engagement. If a time was fixed for the marriage, the obligation is not extinguished by failure to keep to the time, unless it is certain that the intention of the

parties was to break off the engagement if the marriage were not contracted at the appointed time. Presents made to the betrothed in view of marriage are forfeited if the engagement is broken off through the fault of him who made the presents, otherwise, if the fault is on the other side.

If it is certain that there is good cause for breaking off an engagement, this may be done by private authority; it will only be necessary to have recourse to the ecclesiastical judge when the cause is doubtful, or when scandal would arise if the engagement were broken off by private authority on account of the cause being unknown.

When valid betrothal has been broken off by one of the parties without good reason, the other has no right of action in the ecclesiastical court to compel the defaulting party to fulfil the contract, he has only a right to an action for damages (Can. 1017, sec. 3). This action is *mixti fori* (A.A.S., x, 345).

7. People who are only engaged to be married have not the rights of married people, and if they attempt to use them they are guilty of sin against the sixth commandment. It is, however, as a rule, morally necessary for them to become acquainted with each other, and they are justified in showing to each other those marks of affection which are not wrong in themselves and which are usual in the circumstances. It is to be desired that they should not be much together alone, especially at night, and if they are left alone they should not show greater familiarity toward each other than they do when a mother or sister is with them.

CHAPTER IV

BANNS OF MARRIAGE

1. BEFORE publishing the banns of marriage the priest who has the cure of souls must have at least a general knowledge of those who wish to marry. The Ritual prescribes that he should inquire whether there is between them any impediment of kindred or affinity, or any other; whether they wish to marry freely and of their own accord; whether they be of age, and know the rudiments of the Faith so as to be able to teach it to their children (Can. 1020).

With regard to people with no fixed abode, strangers, the wives of soldiers, sailors, and others, who are said to have died in foreign parts, the Ritual admonishes the priest not to admit them readily to marriage before making all needful inquiries about them, and referring their case to the bishop, so as to have his leave for the marriage.

Canon 1021 prescribes that the parish priest demand the certificate of baptism of the parties unless they were baptized in his parish, and their reception of Confirmation, as far as possible.

2. If no impediment has been discovered by examining the parties, the priest publishes the banns in accordance with the decree of the Council of Trent.[1] "It ordains that for the future before a marriage is contracted the proper parish priest of the contracting parties shall three times announce publicly in the Church, during the solemnization of Mass, on three continuous festival days, between whom marriage is to be celebrated; after which publication of banns, if there be no lawful impediment opposed, the marriage shall be proceeded with, in the face of the Church."

The reasons for this law are: the avoidance of clandestine marriages, so that it being known who are married, there may be less danger of bigamous marriages; the discovery of impediments of marriage; and the protection of the rights of others arising from former betrothal. The banns must be published by the parish priest in the church of the parish or district where the parties have their domicile or quasi-domicile.

[1] Sess. xxiv, c. 1, de ref. Matr.; can. 1024.

If they live in different parishes, the banns must be published in both; and if either or both have lived six months in another place after the age of puberty, the parish priest should inform the bishop, who will prescribe what is to be done (Can. 1023). They must be published during the principal Mass on three successive days of obligation; but if the publication has been omitted at Mass, the omission may be made good in the evening if there be a considerable concourse of people at the evening service.

3. The very form which is commonly made use of in publishing banns shows that by them the Church intends to impose a serious obligation on all who know of any impediment between the parties who wish to marry to communicate their knowledge to the parish priest. This precept of the Church will bind even when the impediment is matter of a natural or promised secret, for such a secret cannot avail against the just commands of a superior. A professional secret binds more strictly, but it does not excuse one who knows it from doing what he can without betraying the secret to procure the removal of the impediment.

4. The obligation of publishing banns is a serious one, but for good reason the bishop or his Vicar-General may dispense with them either wholly or in part. According to approved theologians, the bishop is even obliged sometimes to dispense with banns, when charity toward his flock requires it. Thus a dispensation should be given when it is probable that otherwise the marriage will be maliciously prevented, when it is a necessary means to preserve the reputation of the parties who are thought to be man and wife already, and when the parties are obliged to depart at once to foreign countries. For lighter reasons the bishop may dispense, but he is not obliged to do so.

A parish priest has no jurisdiction in the external forum, and so he cannot dispense of his own authority from banns. In some special case, however, it might be necessary to marry the parties without delay, and then if there were no time to have recourse to the bishop, a simple priest might declare that under the circumstances the law with regard to banns ceased to be of obligation.

Sec. i. According to Canon 1031, when a doubt has arisen about the existence of an impediment between the parties—

(1) The parish priest should investigate the matter more carefully, interrogating at least two witnesses under oath, who are worthy of credence, provided that there is no question of an impediment from the knowledge of which the reputation

of the parties will suffer, and interrogating also the parties themselves if it be necessary.

(2) Let him proceed with or finish the publication of the banns if the doubt arose before they were begun or before they were finished.

(3) Let him not assist at the marriage without consulting the Ordinary if he prudently judge that the doubt still remains.

Sec. ii. When a certain impediment has been discovered—

(1) If the impediment be secret, let the parish priest proceed with and finish the banns, and without mentioning names let him report the matter to the local Ordinary or to the Sacred Penitentiary.

(2) If it is public and is discovered before the publication of the banns is begun, let the parish priest not proceed further until the impediment is removed, although he may know that a dispensation has been obtained only for the forum of conscience; if it is discovered after the first or second publication of banns, let the parish priest finish the banns and report the matter to the Ordinary.

Sec. iii. Finally, if no impediment, doubtful or certain, has been discovered, let the parish priest, after the banns are published, admit the parties to the celebration of marriage.

Canon 1030 lays it down that this should not be done until the parish priest has received all the necessary documents and three days have elapsed after the last publication of the banns, unless there be some good reason to the contrary.

Canon 1026 forbids banns to be published of a marriage which is contracted by dispensation from the impediment of mixed religion or difference of worship, unless the local Ordinary deems it proper to permit them with prudence and the removal of scandal, provided that the apostolic dispensation has been granted and no mention be made of the religion of the non-Catholic party.

The Ritual prescribes that the parties should be diligently instructed how they should live in a pious and Christian way in the state of wedlock. This is done partly in the confessional, partly outside. The parish priest may make a brief discourse to them at the end of the ceremony, or if he prefer he may read to them the instruction which is inserted in the Ritual for the purpose (Can. 1033).

Canon 1034 bids parish priests seriously to warn minors not to contract marriage without the knowledge of their parents or against their reasonable wish. In case of disobedience parish priests should not assist at the marriage without consulting the local Ordinary.

CHAPTER V

THE MARRIAGE CONTRACT

1. MARRIAGE may be defined as a contract between a man and a woman by which they give each other the right to exercise the acts requisite for the procreation of children, and bind themselves to live indissolubly together. Living in accordance with this contract constitutes the state of marriage.

The primary end of marriage is the procreation of children for the preservation and increase of the race; besides this there are also the secondary ends of mutual society and help, and a lawful outlet for concupiscence. The Fathers and councils mention a threefold good in marriage: that of children, that of mutual fidelity, and that of the sacrament, or an indissoluble and holy union, typified by the union between Christ and his Spouse the Church.

It is the teaching of the Church, defined by the Council of Trent, that marriage between baptized Christians is a sacrament, and so Christ our Lord, though he did not institute marriage, yet raised it to the dignity of a sacrament of the New Law, causing the marriage contract to be productive of grace *ex opere operato* whenever it is worthily entered into by baptized Christians. Between these the contract is the sacrament, there is no real distinction between them, and among Christians a marriage cannot be valid without being also a sacrament (Can. 1012, 1013).

2. There are certain technical terms used by theologians to designate different kinds of marriage, and it will be well to give them here.

A valid marriage between non-baptized persons is called *legitimate;* when it is perfected by the use of marital rights it becomes *consummated;* a valid marriage between Christians not yet consummated is said to be a *ratified* marriage.

A *true* marriage is one that has been validly contracted and which can be proved by suitable arguments; a *presumptive* marriage is one presumed by law; a *putative* marriage is one thought to have been validly contracted by at least one of the parties, until both parties become certain of its invalidity (Can. 1015).

A *canonical* marriage is one celebrated according to the laws of the Church; a *civil* marriage is contracted according to the laws of the State; a *secret* marriage, or a marriage of conscience, is one celebrated without banns by the bishop's leave before the parish priest and witnesses who are bound to secrecy; a *morganatic* marriage is contracted by a person of rank with one of inferior position in life on condition that she and her children are excluded from the rank of the father.

3. Marriage is rooted in human nature; it was instituted by God and raised by our Lord to the dignity of a Christian sacrament; and so of course it is honourable and its use is lawful. The marital rights, or the *debt* as St Paul calls it,[1] is the matter of the matrimonial contract, and therefore the right to use marriage is of its essence, and without it marriage cannot exist. However, marriage does not necessarily imply the exercise of the right which it gives, any more than the ownership of a house implies the use of it. Our Lady and St Joseph were really married though our Lady always remained a virgin.

Although marriage is lawful and honourable, yet all are not commanded to marry. A man may remain a bachelor if he please, and many women remain single without their having the option of being married. The Church, following St Paul, teaches that the state of celibacy, or virginity, voluntarily chosen in order to render a more whole-hearted service to God, is more perfect than the state of marriage. Our Lord himself said that there are some who refrain from marriage for the sake of the kingdom of heaven, and he added, "He that can take, let him take it." At the same time he said, "All men take not this word, but they to whom it is given."[2] And certainly for some who are strongly inclined by nature to the pleasures of the flesh, or who have fostered their passions by indulgence, the word of St Paul remains true: "It is better to marry than to be burnt."

4. The efficient cause of marriage, as of all contracts, is the consent of the parties lawfully expressed outwardly by sensible signs. That consent must be mutual, referring to the present, not to the future; it must be deliberate and voluntary, and expressed by suitable signs; not only because it is a bilateral contract, but also because it is a sacrament, which is essentially an outward sign of invisible grace.

For the validity of the contract any suitable signs by word, or writing, or nods, would suffice. The contract is valid when entered into by proxy, by letter, or by other means of com-

---

[1] 1 Cor. vii 3. [2] Matt. xix 11.

munication between the absent. Ordinarily, for the lawful celebration of marriage the parties must be present with each other, and all must be done in accordance with what is laid down in the Ritual and in law.

Anyone who having entered into the contract of marriage afterward asserted that he had only feigned consent would not be listened to in the external forum. In the forum of conscience he should be told that he must give a real and internal consent, as that is practically the only way to repair the injury which by his fraud he has inflicted on the other party. If such a case occurred, it would not be necessary to go through the form of marriage again; all that would be required would be for the defaulting party to make good the expression of his consent (Can. 1135).

5. Marriage should be contracted absolutely, but if in any particular case it is contracted under condition, we must distinguish various cases to see how the condition will affect its validity.

(a) A marriage contracted under a condition which has reference to the past or to the present and is verified, as, " I agree to marry you if you are a maid," is valid, but it will not be lawful to use marital rights until it is known whether the condition is verified or not. If the condition is not verified, the contract is invalid.

(b) An explicit condition against the essence of marriage which has reference to the future makes it null and void for want of true consent to marriage. Thus the conditions, " I marry you if you agree to have no offspring," or, " Until I find a more suitable partner," or, " If you will sell yourself for money," make the marriage null and void; for such conditions destroy the perpetual and exclusive right, the transference of which is of the essence of the contract of marriage.

(c) If nothing against the substance of marriage is expressed in the contract, but one or both of the parties intends to do something which is against the essence of marriage, such an intention will vitiate the contract or not, according as it excludes marital rights or only implies a determination to abuse them. Thus if a man intended to have two wives on a footing of perfect equality, he would be married to neither of them; but if he intended really to be married to one and was also bent on keeping a concubine, his marriage with the first would be valid. Similarly, if two were to marry with the intention of living together in virginity, the marriage would be null and void if there was no transference of marital rights; if their intention excluded only the use of marital rights, the marriage would be valid.

The validity of marriage contracted with mutually opposed intentions will depend on which is predominant, or on which would be chosen if their mutually destructive character were known and realized. And so, if a baptized person wants to be married but does not want the sacrament of matrimony, he will be married if that is the predominant intention; he will not be married if the intention to exclude the sacrament is predominant (Can. 1092).

CHAPTER VI

THE MINISTER, MATTER, AND FORM OF MATRIMONY

1. We have seen that according to the teaching of the Church the contract of marriage was raised by our Lord to the dignity of a sacrament, so that the marriage contract constitutes the sacrament, and as such confers grace on baptized and worthy recipients to enable them to perform the duties of their state of life like true Christians. The efficient cause of the contract is the mutual consent of the parties, who thereby confect the sacrament, and who are, therefore, its ministers to each other. The remote matter would seem to be the marital rights which are the matter of the contract; the proximate matter is the mutual offer, and the form the mutual acceptance of those rights. It is uncertain whether a Christian who by dispensation marries a non-baptized person receives the sacrament or not, as the other party is certainly incapable of receiving a sacrament. It is also disputed whether the marriage of unbaptized persons who are converted to the Faith becomes a sacrament on the reception of Baptism.

2. The civil authority probably has power over the marriages of non-baptized subjects, so that it can make diriment and prohibitory impediments to such marriages for the common good. Christian marriage is a sacrament, and the administration of the sacraments belongs exclusively to the Church, so that the State has no power to make diriment or prohibitory impediments for Christian marriage. The regulations which the civil authority makes concerning marriages of soldiers and others should, of course, be observed if they are reasonable and just, but they are not impediments in the strict sense. There is nothing to prevent the State from making laws concerning the civil effects of marriage, such as the property rights of married people, rights of inheritance and succession, titles of nobility, and similar matters; these things are within the competence of the State. But questions which affect the bond of marriage and the capacity of parties to contract marriage belong exclusively to the Church, and so laws of divorce made by the civil authority are of no validity in the

forum of conscience, except in so far as they sanction and apply the laws of the Church (Can. 1016).

3. Marriage is a sacrament of the living, and should be received in the state of grace. The priest should endeavour to get the parties to go to confession and Communion when they are married, so that they may enter on their new state of life with the blessing of God. The rite in Catholic marriages should be performed in the Church, and if the wife has not received the nuptial blessing before, it is the wish of the Church that, whenever the rubrics permit, the Mass *Pro Sponso et Sponsa* should be said, and the nuptial blessing given as therein laid down. This Mass may be said on all days outside close time except on feasts of the first and second class, and on days of obligation. On these days, however, a commemoration may be made of the Mass *Pro Sponso et Sponsa* and the prayers after the *Pater* and Communion may be added.

The common law of the Church prescribes that the nuptial blessing shall not be given out of Mass, and in England, by a special indult of the Holy See, when the nuptial Mass is not said, a special blessing is given by the priest according to the Ritual.

In England the State does not acknowledge Catholic marriages unless they are celebrated in presence of a registrar and in a building registered for marriages. A priest who solemnized marriage otherwise would be liable to severe punishment as a felon. Due notice of a marriage must also be given to the superintendent registrar of the district or districts in which the parties reside. The marriage cannot take place without the registrar's certificate, which cannot be granted before the expiration of twenty-one days after the notice has been entered if the marriage is to be without *licence*, or of one day if it is to be with *licence*. These and other laws which the civil authority has imposed on Catholic marriages should be observed in order that the marriages of Catholics may be recognized by the law of the land, and to avoid greater evil. The Nonconformist Marriage Act of 1899 enabled Nonconformists to dispense with the presence of the registrar, but its onerous conditions prevented the Catholic Bishops from accepting it except in some parishes.

CHAPTER VII

THE PROPERTIES OF MARRIAGE

1. Unity and indissolubility are the properties or peculiar qualities of marriage which we have to discuss in this chapter. Its unity consists in its being a contract in which the parties are necessarily one man and one woman. If several men have one and the same wife at the same time, we have polyandry, which is contrary to the law of nature, for it prevents the natural increase of the human race, makes domestic life almost impossible, and on account of the uncertainty of paternity renders the proper education of the children who are born very difficult. If one man has several wives at the same time, there is polygamy, which is certainly less in keeping with man's nature than monogamy. Polygamy degrades woman, destroys that equality which in regard to marriage rights should exist between the sexes, and makes it difficult for peace and harmony to reign in the family. It is certainly against the positive divine law, promulgated anew by Christ our Lord, and obligatory on all men after the preaching of the Gospel. The Council of Trent anathematized him who should say that it is lawful for Christians to have several wives and that this is not forbidden by divine law.[1]

2. Marriage is also indissoluble, at least by divine law, so that no human power can dissolve a marriage once validly contracted; "What God hath joined together let no man put asunder."[2] This text has the strictest application to the consummated marriage of baptized Christians which can only be dissolved by divine authority. The Pope can for a grave reason dispense in the ratified but not consummated marriage of a Christian; ratified marriage is also dissolved by religious profession of solemn vows; and there is the case of the Pauline privilege.

(a) The Pope not unfrequently uses the power given to him by our Lord to dissolve the merely ratified marriage of Catholics for some grave reason. A probable suspicion of impotence in one of the parties, and a serious quarrel which leaves no hope of reconciliation, have been held sufficient causes for granting

---

[1] Sess. xxiv, c. 2.   [2] Matt. xix 6.

a dispensation from a ratified marriage. As the Pope has no jurisdiction over non-baptized persons, he cannot exercise his authority to dissolve their marriages. But if a non-baptized married couple were converted to the Faith, the Pope would have power to dissolve their marriage if it had not been consummated after baptism, for even if it had been consummated before baptism it would only rank as a ratified marriage. By authority of the Holy See a baptized pagan who had several wives is sometimes permitted to keep any one of them who may be converted with him, if the first is unwilling to become a Christian. Similarly, a married pagan converted in circumstances which render it impossible to interpellate the other party is sometimes allowed by papal dispensation to contract another marriage with a Catholic.

(b) Solemn profession in a religious order with solemn vows annuls a previously existing ratified marriage by ecclesiastical law. Mere entrance into religion and even profession of simple vows in orders that have solemn vows is not sufficient. By ecclesiastical law a period of two months is granted after marriage, during which there is no obligation to render the debt, in order that either of the parties may use his privilege of entering religion (Can. 1119).

(c) The consummated marriage of two pagans may be dissolved by the Pauline privilege if one of them is converted to the Faith, and the other will neither be converted nor live at peace without trying to draw the convert to sin. It is in this sense that the Church interprets the words of St Paul: " But if the unbeliever depart, let him depart. For a brother or sister is not under servitude in such cases. But God hath called us in peace."[1]

The marriage is not dissolved by the Baptism of one of the parties, but if the conditions mentioned above are verified, the convert after Baptism may contract a second marriage with a Christian, and by this marriage the former is dissolved. In order that it may be known whether the other party is willing to be converted or at least to live at peace with the convert, he must be interpellated by the bishop or by his authority. Both interpellations are required, and more probably they are necessary for the validity of the second marriage, unless a dispensation from them is obtained from the Holy See. Thus in a case of insanity of the other party, a dispensation from the interpellations was granted, and in countries where Christians were forbidden to live with Jews, only one interpellation was

[1] 1 Cor. vii 15.

put, " Whether the other party was willing to be converted to the Faith," and if a negative answer was given, the convert was free to marry again (Can. 1120 *ff.*).

3. Married people ought to live together as man and wife unless there is some good reason to the contrary.

If one of the parties commits adultery, the other has the right to separate from him altogether as to bed and board, unless he consented to the crime, or was the cause of it, or expressly or tacitly condoned it, or he himself has committed the same crime.

When an innocent spouse has separated from the adulterer by his own authority or that of a judge, he is under no obligation to admit him again to marital cohabitation; but he may admit him or recall him, unless with his consent he has adopted a life incompatible with marriage.

If a spouse has joined a non-Catholic sect, if he is educating a child as a non-Catholic, if he is leading a criminal and shameful life, if he is the cause of grave danger to the soul or body of the other, if by his cruelty he makes cohabitation too difficult for the other, these and similar causes are so many lawful reasons of separation for the other party, by the authority of the local Ordinary and also by his own authority if the causes are certain and there is danger in delay.

In all these cases when the cause of separation ceases cohabitation should be restored; but if separation was decreed by the Ordinary for a certain or uncertain time the innocent party is not obliged to cohabit unless the time fixed has elapsed or by the decree of the Ordinary (Can. 1128-1131).

4. Although questions concerning divorce and the separation of married people belong of right to the ecclesiastical court, in most modern States the civil authority claims and exercises jurisdiction in these matters. May Catholics take their marriage cases to the civil courts, and may Catholic judges and Catholic lawyers lend their aid in deciding them? No answer can be given to these questions which will apply to all countries and circumstances. In some countries Catholics can still have their rights safeguarded by recurring to the ecclesiastical courts, and there is no reason why they should carry their matrimonial suits to the civil tribunals. In England and in the United States the Church tacitly or explicitly permits Catholics to apply to the civil courts at least for a judicial separation. Before doing so they should put their case before the ecclesiastical authorities, and this is prescribed under liability to penalties by the Third Plenary Council of Baltimore.[1]

[1] N. 126; S.O., December 19, 1860.

With regard to divorce cases, Catholics in England and in the United States may have recourse to the civil courts in order to obtain a declaration of nullity when a marriage has already been declared invalid or annulled by the ecclesiastical authorities. They may not go to the civil courts in order to obtain dissolution of a valid marriage with the intention of marrying again. This is obvious from what has been said above. There is a difficulty as to whether a Catholic may petition for a divorce in the civil courts, not with the intention of considering the marriage dissolved and marrying again, but in order to obtain the civil advantages annexed to divorce, such as a change of marriage settlements or release from the obligation of supporting his wife's child by another man. The question is disputed among theologians, but as the law in English-speaking countries does not express hostility to religion and does not affect to touch the conscience but only the external relations of the citizens, the better opinion is that Catholics for good cause may petition even for divorce in the civil courts, with the intention of using only the civil advantages that follow from it. A consequence of this is that Catholic lawyers and judges may for grave reasons undertake these cases in the civil courts. For greater safety and to show their submission to the Church they should ask the leave of the Bishop.

CHAPTER VIII

THE IMPEDIMENTS OF MARRIAGE IN GENERAL

1. THE impediments of marriage are certain conditions or circumstances which prevent marriage between the persons whom they affect. Some have their origin in natural and divine law, as the impediment of previous marriage, which as long as it lasts prevents a second marriage; others have their origin in ecclesiastical law, like that of public decency. Some prevent marriage being lawfully contracted and are called prohibitory, though a marriage contracted in spite of them is valid; others are diriment impediments and where they exist prevent marriage being validly contracted; but if they arise after marriage has already been contracted they cannot make it null and void.

Diriment impediments are, in general, annulling laws which for the common good make the parties affected incapable of contracting a valid marriage, and render the act null and void if marriage is attempted in spite of them. Such laws remain in force in spite of ignorance or fear, and so as a general rule a marriage contracted in ignorance of a diriment impediment which exists between the parties is null and void in spite of the ignorance. In the same way private inconvenience does not make a diriment impediment cease to bind, but if the law cannot be observed without causing public harm and inconvenience, then it ceases to be of obligation. Thus, if illness prevents one of the parties from going to be married in the Church on the day appointed, he is not justified in contracting marriage privately at home; but if all the priests of a country are driven out, as were those of France in the Revolution, marriage may be contracted without the presence of the parish priest.

2. The impediments of natural and divine law bind all men, whether infidels or Christians, and so a marriage between parent and child is always and everywhere null and void. The civil authority more probably has power to make impediments of marriage which will bind its non-baptized subjects, but the Church alone has power to make impediments for Christians who have been baptized.[1] All baptized persons, whether

[1] Leo XIII, *Encyc. Arcanum,* February 10, 1880.

Catholics or heretics or schismatics, are subject to the diriment impediments of marriage unless they have been specially exempted from them. For all who are baptized thereby become members of the Church of Christ and subject to the jurisdiction of the divinely constituted head of that Church. The Supreme Pontiff, then, has power to bind all who are baptized by those impediments of marriage which are of ecclesiastical origin. Neither the practice of Rome nor the express declarations of the Popes afford any ground for the opinion that it is not the Church's intention to bind heretics and schismatics by the diriment impediments of marriage. Especially since the time of Benedict XIV many cases have been decided of marriage contracted between non-Catholics being declared null and void on account of some impediment of ecclesiastical origin. The general principle is clearly stated in the answer of the Sacred Congregation of the Council to the Bishop of Rosenau, August 20, 1780: " But, you say, because heretics in Hungary marry among themselves even within the prohibited degrees in virtue only of royal permission, I may well be asked what is to be said about the validity of such marriages. The answer is that unless a lawful dispensation of the Church by whose authority those impediments were introduced is obtained for them, the declaration of Benedict XIV clearly decides that those marriages are invalid. For it lays down that in Holland marriages between heretics are to be held as valid, even though the form prescribed by the Council of Trent was not observed in solemnizing them, provided that no other canonical impediment stood in the way; and this exception shows clearly that if there be any other canonical impediment, such as exists within the forbidden degrees of kindred, those marriages are not valid."

According to the common opinion, then, marriages contracted by baptized heretics and schismatics, when there is a diriment impediment of ecclesiastical origin between the parties, are invalid, though the impediment may not be recognized in the sect to which they belong. Such marriages, however, inasmuch as they are contracted in good faith, are putative, and the children are legitimate.

CHAPTER IX

THE PROHIBITORY IMPEDIMENTS

THERE are four prohibitory impediments of marriage according to modern ecclesiastical law: the prohibition of the Church, close time, betrothal, and simple vows. Something must be said on each of these.

1. The impediment called the Church's prohibition is either special or general. A special prohibition of marriage is issued by the parish priest, or the Bishop, or the Pope, when it has been found out that the proposed marriage will violate the rights of a third party, or when a well-founded suspicion arises that there is some impediment between the parties (Can. 1023, sec. 3). By a general prohibition is understood a law of the Church which forbids marriage in the circumstances but does not make it null and void if in spite of the prohibition it is contracted. Thus the Church forbids marriage without banns and mixed marriages. We have already treated of the law concerning banns, and it will be more convenient to treat of mixed marriages under the diriment impediment of disparity of worship. Clandestinity, or marriage without the presence of the parish priest and witnesses, is now a diriment impediment, to be treated of below. In Great Britain and in the greater part of the United States of America the decree *Tametsi* was never published, but clandestinity is now a diriment impediment of marriage in Great Britain and in the United States, as well as throughout the Western Church, by virtue of the decree *Ne temere*, August 2, 1907, and Canon 1094.

2. During close time, or the periods between the first Sunday of Advent and Christmas Day, and from Ash Wednesday to Easter Sunday, the solemnization of marriage is forbidden by the common law of the Church. The solemnization of marriage consists especially of the Mass *Pro Sponso et Sponsa*, the nuptial blessing, and outward pomp and feasting in connection with the marriage. A simple and private marriage without these solemnities during close time is not against the common law (Can. 1108).

3. Betrothal between two persons prevents the parties from lawfully marrying any third party unless the betrothal is legiti-

mately broken off. In other words, betrothal is a prohibitory impediment of marriage with any other person than the betrothed, as we saw above.

4. There are several simple vows which are so many prohibitory impediments of marriage (Can. 1058).

A vow of chastity hinders marriage, for he who has taken such a vow exposes himself to the danger of violating it if he marries, or of depriving the other party of his marital rights. Even after marriage has been contracted the obligation of the vow remains, unless a dispensation is obtained or the obligation of the vow is indirectly annulled by the other party.

By a vow of virginity he who takes the vow promises God that he will not commit a consummated sin against chastity. He will sin, therefore, by marrying, because he exposes himself to the danger of breaking his vow or of defrauding the other party of his rights. If by a consummated sin against chastity his virginity has been destroyed, the vow can no longer be observed, and ceases.

The same rules hold with regard to a vow of celibacy which is violated by marriage, but after marriage has been contracted no further obligation remains.

Chastity, virginity, and celibacy are loosely used one for the other, and if a case arose in the confessional the intention of the penitent would have to be inquired into in order to discover what obligation he wished to take upon himself by his vow.

One who has vowed to receive sacred orders would commit sin by marrying, for by marriage the other party obtains rights which are incompatible with the observance of the vow. Canon 987 lays down that marriage is an impediment to the reception of orders, and so the obligation of the vow will ordinarily cease as being impossible of fulfilment, though *per se* it is only suspended, and revives on the death of the other party.

Similarly, one who has taken a vow to enter religion commits sin by marrying, as he makes the observance of his vow difficult or impossible. Before consummating marriage he is still bound by his vow if it bound him to enter a religious order in the strict sense. After marriage has been consummated he may use his marital rights, and the vow usually ceases on account of impossibility of observance.

5. The power of dispensing from the impediments of an absolute and perpetual vow of perfect chastity taken after

completing the eighteenth year of age, the vow of entering religion with solemn vows, and the proof of *liber status* when it is not altogether certain, are reserved to the Holy See.

Bishops can dispense in banns and in vows that hinder marriage and are not reserved to the Pope. Regular and secular confessors have specially delegated faculties for dispensing in vows that are not reserved.

CHAPTER X

THE DIRIMENT IMPEDIMENTS

ARTICLE I
Impotence

1. IMPOTENCE is the incapacity to have carnal intercourse such as is required for the procreation of children. It is *absolute* if the incapacity extends to all persons of the other sex, otherwise it is *relative*. *Temporary* impotence exists only for a time, and may be cured by lapse of time or by some lawful operation which does not endanger life; *perpetual* impotence lasts for life. It is *antecedent* if it precedes marriage, otherwise it is *subsequent*.

2. Antecedent and perpetual impotence annuls marriage by the law of nature, for the matter of the marriage contract is in that case impossible. This is true whether the impotence be absolute or only relative, but in the former case marriage is out of the question, while in the latter a valid marriage may be contracted with someone else, though it is impossible with a person with respect to whom the party is impotent. Subsequent impotence, which has supervened on marriage, cannot, of course, annul the marriage already contracted, but if it is altogether certain it makes the use of marriage unlawful (Can. 1068).

This, however, is not to be lightly presumed, for the right is in possession, and for its lawful exercise it suffices if there be any probability of its not being impossible.

Neither does antecedent but temporary impotence annul marriage, for a contract is valid if the matter is possible or by using ordinary means can be made possible.

When it is doubtful whether a spouse is impotent or not the decision must be in favour of the validity of the marriage, and since all such questions belong to the *forum externum*, they fall under the cognizance of the bishop, nor can they be settled by the confessor.

3. Mere barrenness or sterility is not impotence, nor does it make marriage impossible or unlawful. There is a controversy among experts as to whether removal of the ovaries

or of the womb or of both organs makes a woman impotent or only sterile. The decisions which have been given by the Roman Congregations in particular cases are quoted in defence of both opinions, and as yet no general solution of the question has been given. Until this happens, a woman who has undergone such operations should not marry without consulting the bishop, but if she is already married the more favourable opinion should be followed. This impediment is recognzied by English law.

Article II

Age

Males under sixteen years of age and females under fourteen are presumed not to have that maturity of judgement which is requisite for entering the married state. The Church has made them incapable of marrying by requiring the age of sixteen complete in males and fourteen complete in females for the validity of marriage (Can. 1067). The age of puberty varies according to race and climate; in northern latitudes it is not reached till the age of about fifteen in girls and seventeen or eighteen in boys. Even though the parties may not yet be capable of having children, they may marry validly if they are of the age required by the Church, though it is desirable not to marry before full maturity. Those who are not baptized are not subject to the ecclesiastical impediment of age, but in this matter English law agrees with the old canon law, which fixed the age of valid marriage at fourteen and twelve respectively.

Article III

Previous Marriage

1. One who is already married cannot validly contract a second marriage unless the former bond is dissolved by one of the means described above, or by the death of the other spouse. Previous marriage, then, is a diriment impediment of a second marriage as long as it subsists, by the law of nature and by positive divine law. This impediment, therefore, binds all men, whether Christian or heathen.

It is not lawful for one who has been married before to contract a second marriage, unless there is certain proof that the first marriage has been dissolved by lawful authority or by the death of the former spouse (Can. 1069).

If the decease is proved by a certificate of death or some similar authentic document, or by two witnesses who are above suspicion, or by any other legitimate means, the parish priest may allow the second marriage. If, however, there is no certain proof to be had, and it is doubtful whether the party in question is free to marry, the case must be referred to the bishop, who will investigate the circumstances, and if any prudent doubt remain he will not allow the second marriage without consulting the Holy See. Sometimes in special circumstances the Pope allows a second marriage, even when strict proof of the death of the former spouse is not obtainable, as he did in the case of the wives of the Italian soldiers who perished in the battle of Adoua.[1]

2. If a person has unlawfully contracted a second marriage without the necessary certainty concerning the death of a former spouse, it does not follow that the second marriage is invalid, and that the parties must separate. If there is only slight doubt about the death of the former spouse, after making fruitless inquiries, the parties may live together as man and wife. If only one of the parties is in bad faith and is not certain of the death of a former spouse, while the other knows nothing of the difficulty, he should render the marriage debt, but he has no right to ask it as long as he remains in bad faith. If both parties are in bad faith, they cannot lawfully use marriage as long as they are in that state. Inquiries should be made, and if probable reasons can be discovered for thinking that the former partner is dead, they may use marriage, according to a probable opinion. For even in this case the marriage has been contracted, it is probably valid, and it is not certain that anyone else has a prior right, so the parties should be allowed to use it. If the second marriage was contracted in good faith, and a doubt about the death of a former spouse arises subsequently, inquiries should be made, and if they are fruitless the parties may live as man and wife. Of course, in all cases when it is found out for certain that a former spouse is alive, the second marriage is invalid, and the parties must separate, or at any rate must not live as man and wife together.

English law enforces this impediment, but if a former spouse has not been heard of for seven years or more, it will not punish the other party as guilty of bigamy if he marries a second time, although he must separate if the former spouse appear subsequently.

[1] S.O., July 20, 1898.

Article IV
Consanguinity

1. Consanguinity is the bond of relationship by blood existing between those who are descended by carnal generation from one and the same near stock. The relationship, therefore, arises from community of blood derived from a common and not too remote ancestor. That common ancestor is called the *stock;* the distance in descent between one person and the other is called the *degree* of relationship; and the series of persons who descend from the same stock is called the *line*, which is *direct* if they descend from one another, otherwise it is *collateral*. The degrees are equal in the collateral line if the persons are equally distant from the common stock; otherwise they are unequal.

It is immaterial whether both parents of the common stock are the same or only one, and whether the birth be legitimate or not.

The method of computing the degrees differs somewhat in canon law from that adopted by modern English civil law, which here follows the Roman civil law. The following are the rules for reckoning the degree of relationship according to canon law, which is followed in moral theology:

(*a*) To find the degree of relationship in the direct line, count the persons, leaving out the common stock.

(*b*) In the collateral line, when the degrees are equal, count the persons in one of the lines of descent, leaving out the common stock.

(*c*) When the degrees are unequal, count the longer line, leaving out the common stock in the same way, and add the number of persons in the shorter line. Thus, an uncle and niece are related in the second degree, touching the first, or mixed with the first (Can. 96).

According to the English method of computation, which is also followed in most States of the Union, all the persons are counted both in the direct and collateral lines, leaving out the common stock. According to this method, an uncle and niece are in the third degree.

Consanguinity in the first degree of the direct line annuls marriage by the natural law; and in further degrees indefinitely, but more probably only by ecclesiastical law. In the collateral line it is disputed whether consanguinity in the first degree annuls marriage by the law of nature or not; it certainly does so to the third degree by ecclesiastical law.[1]

This impediment, therefore, is partly of natural, partly of ecclesiastical law, and although in the more remote degrees of both the direct and collateral line it does not bind those who are not baptized, yet even among them there is a natural bond in blood relationship which after Baptism becomes a diriment impediment of marriage within the prohibited degrees. One who is baptized is subject to the laws of the Church, and cannot, without the necessary dispensation, marry a relation within the forbidden degrees, even if the latter is not baptized.

English law follows in this matter that of Leviticus, and according to its method of computation consanguinity is a diriment impediment of marriage to the third degree inclusive, but not beyond. Thus an uncle cannot marry a niece, but two cousins may marry, by English law.

2. The impediment of consanguinity may be multiple from various causes, but it is only multiplied as often as the common stock is multiplied (Can. 1076, sec. 2).

(a) If two near relations marry, their offspring will be related in several different ways:

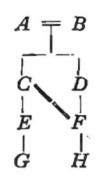

$$\begin{array}{c} A = B \\ | \quad | \\ C \quad D \\ | \quad | \\ E \quad F \\ | \quad | \\ G \quad H \end{array}$$

In this scheme G and H are descended from the common stock $C=F$, and so they are in the second degree mixed with the first in the collateral line. Both G and H are also descended from $A=B$ through C and through F. On this account they are in the third degree of relationship. Thus there is a double relationship between them, and if a dispensation were required for G to marry H, mention should be made of this fact.

(b) Similar results will follow if two relatives marry two relatives:

$$\begin{array}{c} A \qquad\qquad B \\ C \diagup \diagdown D = E \diagup \diagdown F = C \\ \qquad\qquad | \qquad\quad | \\ \qquad\qquad G \qquad\quad H \end{array}$$

---

[1] Council of Lat. 4 (1215); can. 1076.

In this scheme G and H are descended from both A and B, and they are in double second degree of relationship.

(c) Similarly, if one man successively marries two who are related to each other:

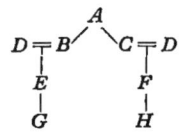

$$D \mathrel{\top} B \overset{A}{\diagup} \quad \diagdown C \mathrel{\top} D$$
$$\phantom{D \mathrel{\top}} E F$$
$$\phantom{D \mathrel{\top}} G H$$

G and H are in the second degree from the common stock D, and in the third from the common stock A. D is supposed to marry his deceased wife's sister.

Article V
Affinity

1. Affinity is the relationship which one contracts with the relatives by blood of a person with whom he has contracted a ratified marriage only or a ratified and consummated marriage (Can. 97, sec. 1).

It has its origin in positive ecclesiastical law with regard to the collateral line and more probably also in the direct line. Affinity annuls marriage in the direct line in every degree, in the collateral line to the second degree inclusively (Can. 1077). The degrees in affinity with the husband are the same as the degrees of consanguinity with the wife and *vice versa*.

2. As this impediment is of ecclesiastical origin, the Church can dispense from it, but she does not dispense in affinity in the first degree in the direct line.

The impediment of affinity is multiplied as often as the impediment of consanguinity from which it proceeds is multiplied, and by marriage with a relative of a dead spouse (Can. 1077, sec. 2).

Affinity, however, does not generate affinity, so that two brothers may marry two sisters, and a father and son may marry a mother and daughter.

English law only acknowledges affinity arising between those who are married, and it extends only to the same degrees, computed in the same way, as does consanguinity.

Article VI

Spiritual Relationship

1. Spiritual relationship arises by ecclesiastical law from the administration of Baptism and Confirmation, but only that which arises from Baptism is a diriment impediment of marriage (Can. 1079). According to modern discipline, it annuls marriage between the minister of the sacrament and the recipient, and also between the sponsors and the recipient. As it has its origin in ecclesiastical law, it does not affect those who are not baptized, and the impediment is doubtful and consequently non-existent when Baptism is doubtful or only probable. The impediment, as far as it affects sponsors, does not arise if Baptism was administered privately without sponsors and afterward the ceremonies with sponsors are supplied in the Church.

Article VII

Adoption

By adoption a person becomes in law the child of another, though he is not such by nature. Legal adoption, according to Roman law, was a diriment impediment of marriage between certain parties, and in this matter the civil law was *canonized* by the law of the Church.

(a) It annulled marriage between the adopter and the adopted and those descendants of the latter who were under his authority at the time of the adoption.

(b) It annulled marriage between the adopted and the children of the adopter as long as they were under his authority.

(c) Finally, it annulled marriage between the adopter and the widow of the adopted, and between the adopted and the widow of the adopter.

Roman law, as such, is nowhere in force at present, and the Code has made new provisions for the circumstances.

Canon 1059 prescribes that in those countries where by the civil law legal relationship arising from adoption makes marriage unlawful, marriage is also unlawful by canon law. Moreover, Canon 1080 prescribes that those who are held incapable of marrying each other by the civil law on account of legal relationship arising from adoption, cannot validly contract marriage and this by force of canon law.

In England adoption exists as a private contract between

the parties, but it is not otherwise recognized by law, and so in England there is no room for the impediment of marriage arising from legal adoption. In most of the States of the Union there seems to be a form of adoption recognized by law sufficient to make it the basis of the ecclesiastical impediment.[1]

Article VIII
Public Propriety

Before the issue of the new Code the impediment of public propriety arose by ecclesiastical law from valid and certain betrothal, and from ratified, not consummated, marriage.

The Code has made a great change in this impediment. According to Canon 1078, the impediment of public propriety arises from invalid marriage, whether consummated or not, and from public and notorious concubinage; and it annuls marriage in the first and second degree of the direct line between the man and the relations by blood of the woman and *vice versa*. Merely civil marriage by itself will not produce this impediment since it produces no canonical effects. But the impediment of public propriety will arise from the public and notorious concubinage which will be associated with merely civil marriage.

Article IX
Solemn Vows and Sacred Orders

1. A solemn vow of chastity, taken in a religious order, strictly so called, or taken implicitly when sacred Orders are received in the Latin Church, is a diriment impediment of marriage by ecclesiastical law. This has long been the practice of the Western Church, and it was solemnly enunciated by the Council of Trent: " If anyone saith that clerics constituted in sacred Orders, or regulars who have solemnly professed chastity, are able to contract marriage, and that being contracted it is valid, notwithstanding the ecclesiastical law or vow; and that the contrary is nothing else than to condemn marriage; and that all who do not feel that they have the gift of chastity, even though they have made a vow thereof, may contract marriage; let him be anathema: seeing that God refuses not

---

[1] Smith, *Marriage Process*, n. 263.

that gift to those who ask for it rightly, neither does he suffer us to be tempted above that which we are able."[1]

In the Eastern Church marriage may be contracted before receiving sacred Orders, and those who have married may use their marital rights after receiving sacred Orders, but sacred Orders are a bar to contracting a new marriage. This shows that sacred Orders, apart from the vow, which in the Latin Church is taken when they are received, are a diriment impediment of marriage. By a special privilege, the simple vow of chastity taken by members of the Society of Jesus at their first profession is also a diriment impediment of marriage.

2. As this impediment owes its origin to ecclesiastical law, the Church can dispense in it, but she seldom does so except for grave reasons which concern the public weal. Leo XIII granted bishops the faculty of dispensing, by themselves or through some trusty ecclesiastic, the sick who are in great danger of death so that there is not time to have recourse to the Holy See, from all, even public, impediments which annul marriage by ecclesiastical law, except the priesthood and affinity in the direct line arising out of the lawful use of marriage.[2] This was confirmed and extended by Canons 1043, 1044.

Article X

Difference of Religion

When a man and woman marry, they enter upon the closest possible union for mutual help and for the rearing and education of a family. Religion should be at the base of that union, and should furnish the fundamental principles for the education of their offspring. This, however, is hardly possible if husband and wife profess different religions, so that the very nature of marriage excludes difference of religion in husband and wife. If both the parties are baptized Christians, but only one is a Catholic, difference of religion is only a prohibitory impediment; if one of the parties is not baptized, and the other has been baptized in the Catholic Church or has been converted to it, it constitutes a diriment impediment. The first is commonly called a mixed marriage, and we will devote to it the following section.

[1] Sess. xxiv, c. 9; can. 1072, 1073.
[2] S.O., February 20, 1888.

Section I

Mixed Marriages

1. Mixed marriages are forbidden by the natural, divine, and ecclesiastical law. For the parties are ministers to each other of the sacrament of Marriage; but it is unlawful for a Catholic without grave necessity to communicate in religious rites with a non-Catholic, and to receive a sacrament from him. Besides, it usually happens that in marrying a non-Catholic the Catholic party exposes himself to the danger of either losing his faith altogether, or at least of suffering its purity and brightness to be tarnished. The Church has forbidden mixed marriages from the earliest ages, and the Popes and bishops have issued innumerable instructions and warnings against them. It is without doubt a grave sin to contract a mixed marriage without a dispensation, and the Church shows her detestation of it by prohibiting any religious function at the marriage, even when a dispensation for it has been obtained (Can. 1060, 1102).

2. However, in countries where Catholics and non-Catholics live together, and especially if the latter greatly outnumber the former, as they do in Great Britain and in the United States, it is almost impossible to avoid mixed marriages sometimes, and the Holy See grants the necessary dispensation. Certain conditions must be fulfilled before the dispensation for a mixed marriage is granted. In the first place, there must be a grave canonical cause, or a good reason such as the Church recognizes to be sufficient for a dispensation in this matter. In order to remove as far as possible the danger connected with mixed marriages, the Church requires that the non-Catholic party shall promise to leave the Catholic the free exercise of his religion, and that both parties promise to bring up all the children in the Catholic faith. Moreover, the Catholic party must undertake to do his best to bring about the conversion of his spouse to the Catholic religion. The necessity of these promises is founded in the natural and divine law, and the common law of the Church requires that there should be moral certainty that they will be fulfilled and that as a rule they should be in writing (Can. 1061).

If one of the parties be a baptized Catholic, but one who has given up the practice of his religion without going over to any heretical sect, there is no strict impediment to his marrying a Catholic, but of course efforts should be made for his conversion, and if he remain indifferent the bishop should be consulted (Can. 1066).

In England, when a dispensation has been obtained for a mixed marriage, the bishops allow the priest to assist at it at the altar rails vested in surplice and stole.

The banns should not be published unless the local Ordinary judge that they may be permitted, taking the necessary precautions to avoid scandal, and omitting all mention of the difference of religion (Can. 1026).

A sermon before or after the function is not prohibited. Mass, however, should never be said nor the nuptial blessing given at a mixed marriage.

The Church does not allow the Catholic party to go through any marriage rite before a non-Catholic minister acting as such. If the non-Catholic minister acts as a civil magistrate, and Catholics are obliged to go through the marriage ceremony in his presence in order to have their marriages recognized by the State, it is permitted (Can. 1063).

Section II

Difference of Religion

According to Canon 1070, sec. 1, marriage contracted by a person not baptized with a person baptized in the Catholic Church or converted to the same from heresy or schism is null.

Sec. 2. If one party at the time of contracting marriage was commonly regarded as a baptized person, or if his baptism was doubtful, in accordance with the rule of law that doubtful marriage is to be deemed valid until the contrary be proved, such marriages are to be held valid until it is proved for certain that one of the parties was baptized and the other was not baptized.

Such a marriage, as is clear from St Paul,[1] has been unlawful from apostolic times, but in the first centuries of the Christian era it was not invalid, and there are several well-known instances of saints being married to pagans. Gradually, however, a marriage between a baptized Christian and a pagan came to be looked upon as invalid, unless contracted in virtue of the Church's dispensation, and this has been the settled rule from about the beginning of the twelfth century. As the impediment is of positive law it can, of course, for grave reason be dispensed with, and then even the apostolic prohibition will cease

[1] 2 Cor. vi 14.

if the dangers which are common to mixed marriages and to difference of religion can be avoided.

Before the new Code came into force the impediment of difference of religion affected baptized non-Catholics as well as Catholics. By the common consent of commentators the effect of Section 1 is to restrict the impediment to those who have been baptized in the Catholic Church or converted to it from heresy or schism. Those are baptized in the Catholic Church who are baptized with the intention of incorporating them as members into the bodily communion of the Catholic Church. So that an infant who in danger of death was secretly baptized to procure its eternal salvation only, would not be baptized in the Catholic Church in the sense of this Canon.

Article XI

Crime

By ecclesiastical law certain crimes committed by married people which are specially opposed to the sanctity of marriage constitute a diriment impediment of a second marriage. These crimes are: adultery together with a promise of marriage or attempted marriage with the adulterer, murder of a spouse with the machination of the other party, adultery and murder of a spouse. In order that these crimes may constitute a diriment impediment of another marriage, certain conditions explicitly or implicitly contained in canon law must be fulfilled. These will be described in the following sections (Can. 1075).

Section I

Adultery with Promise of Marriage

1. When husband or wife commits adultery with a third person and promises to marry that person after the death of the other spouse, the Church makes the adulterers incapable of contracting a valid marriage even after the first has been dissolved by death. The aim of the Church is to protect married people, to guard the sanctity of marriage, and to punish crime. A law, however, which restricts the liberty of marriage must be strictly interpreted, and so Doctors require the following conditions in the adultery and in the promise in order that the impediment may arise:

(a) The adultery must be real, formal on both sides, and complete. It must be real, or one at least of the parties must be united in a true, valid marriage. That fact must be known to both the adulterers, or else they are not guilty of formal but merely material adultery. If each party knows that the other is married and the other conditions are verified, there will be a double impediment between them. The adultery must be complete, so that it would be possible for it to produce its natural result in offspring.

(*b*) The promise, too, must be real, not fictitious, accepted by the promisee, absolute, not conditional, made with knowledge of the present marriage, and undertaking to contract marriage after the death of the other spouse. For one of the objects of the law is to remove the temptation to plot against the life of husband or wife.

Both the adultery and the promise must have place during the continuance of the same marriage, but it is immaterial whether the promise be made before, after, or at the same time as the adultery is committed.

2. This impediment of crime also exists between parties who have committed adultery with each other and attempted to marry during the lifetime of the spouse of one of them. The adultery must have the same qualities as in the preceding case, and the marriage must be really and truly attempted, not merely feigned. It is immaterial whether the attempted marriage precede or succeed the adultery. It is obvious that those will lie under this impediment who, after a civil divorce from a spouse, marry again and consummate the attempted marriage.

Section II

Murder of a Consort

Murder by a man and a woman of the spouse of one of them constitutes a diriment impediment to their marriage. This impediment does not arise unless death really ensues; attempted murder is not sufficient. Moreover, the murder must be committed not by one of them alone, even if the other afterward approve of it, but by both, either by mutual physical help, or by moral persuasion of some sort. Death must also be inflicted with the intention of marrying the other when free, as Doctors gather from the end of the law, which is to prevent murder of a consort with a view to marrying someone else. This intention must at least be manifested in some way to the other party, though it is not necessary that it should openly actuate both of them to the perpetration of the crime.

Section III
Adultery and Murder

1. When a man and a woman commit adultery and one of them murders his consort in order to marry his accomplice in adultery, the third impediment of crime arises between them and hinders the marriage. In this case there need be no promise of future marriage, nor any attempt at marriage, nor need the death be the result of the plotting of both of the parties. It will be sufficient if the adultery have the qualifications mentioned above in the first section, and murder really be committed with the intention of marriage manifested in some way, as by presents or by love letters to the other party.

2. If to adultery and murder as just described there be joined the promise of future marriage, and the plotting of the death of the consort of one of the parties with the conditions laid down in the previous sections, there will be not one but three impediments, and if marriage were actually attempted during the murdered consort's life, there will be four. The impediment is purely of ecclesiastical law, and therefore it does not bind those who are not baptized. If, however, one of the parties is baptized, it will indirectly affect the other.

3. Since the issue of the new Code ignorance of this impediment is no reason why it should not be incurred (Can. 16).

Article XII
Error, Slavery, Imbecility

1. By error is understood a mistaken judgement by which one person or thing is taken for another. It differs from ignorance, which is merely the absence of knowledge. Error, if it is substantial, annuls marriage as it does other contracts, by the law of nature itself. For a contract is not valid unless there be an agreement of wills between the contracting parties, and there cannot be that agreement if one of the parties is in error about the substance of the contract. There will be such a substantial error when there is a mistake about the person with whom marriage is contracted. If *A* thinks he is marrying *B* and intends to marry *B*, the marriage will be invalid if the other party to the contract is *C*, not *B*. Sometimes a mistake about the quality or rank of the other party may be substantial and invalidate the marriage. Thus, if a

woman thinks she is marrying the eldest son of a peer, and only intends to marry the eldest son, who she thinks is present, the marriage will be null and void if the bridegroom is not the eldest son of a peer. Ordinarily, however, a mistake about the quality or condition of the other party will not be substantial, and will not invalidate the contract. If the lady intends to marry the person present who she wrongly thinks is the eldest son, the marriage will be valid. It is possible that there should be a substantial mistake about the subject-matter of the contract of marriage. Thus, if a woman thinks that marriage is a mere union of friendship between the parties, and when she marries does not intend to give her husband any right to have children by her, the marriage is invalid. Mere ignorance as to the way in which children are brought into the world does not invalidate marriage (Can. 1083, 1082).

2. If a freeman married a slave under the mistaken belief that she was free, the marriage was null and void by ecclesiastical law; if he married knowing the servile condition of the other party, the marriage was valid. To this extent the Church received the Roman legislation on the marriage of slaves, according to which they could not validly marry one that was free, and their marriages among themselves were merely at the good will of their masters. The law of the Church corrected what was inhuman in the Roman civil law, and adopted its provisions as far as they were in harmony with Christian principles. Nowadays, of course, this impediment can scarcely be of practical importance in any part of the world (Can. 1083, sec. 2, ii).

3. Imbeciles who have not the use of reason are incapable by the law of nature of contracting a valid marriage, unless it is contracted in a lucid interval. If the loss of reason supervenes on marriage which has been validly contracted already, it cannot of course annul the marriage.

Article XIII

Violence and Fear

1. Violence is the onset of force too great to be resisted, and fear is a perturbation of mind arising from present or future danger. Here we treat of fear caused by extrinsic violence, inasmuch as it is a diriment impediment of marriage.

When marriage is contracted through grave fear, caused unjustly by a free agent with a view to extorting marriage, ecclesiastical law makes it null and void. Whether such a marriage is invalid by natural law is a moot point among Doctors. Fear may, indeed, sometimes be so excessive that it takes away the use of reason, so that a man under its influence does not know what he is doing. If a man married under the influence of such terror, the marriage would of course be invalid for want of consent. But commonly even grave fear does not produce such effects; a man in danger of shipwreck or death knows as a rule what he is doing, and if he marries in such circumstances, though induced by fear to do so, the marriage will be valid. But when he is unjustly forced by someone to marry against his will, the injury done to him is a sufficient reason for the Church to make the marriage null and void, even though he knew what he was doing and consented to the marriage. The only difference between this case and the former lies in the injury inflicted by the fear caused by a free agent. This however, does not seem sufficient ground for asserting the nullity of the contract by natural law, though it affords a just reason why positive law should make it invalid. The better opinion, then, seems to be that grave fear is a diriment impediment of marriage by ecclesiastical law when the fear is caused unjustly by someone with a view to compelling the party to marry against his will. Hence, if one who had violated a woman was threatened with a beating and married her in order to escape it, the marriage would be valid. Fear arising from reverence for parents and superiors is in general not sufficiently serious to make marriage contracted under its influence null and void. In certain circumstances, however, such a fear may become grave and sufficient to annul marriage. Much depends on the character of the party who was influenced by fear and on the means employed to compel acquiescence to the wishes of harsh and severe parents or guardians. The question as to whether in any particular case there was grave fear is a question of fact to be determined by the ecclesiastical judge after weighing all the circumstances of the case (Can. 1087).

2. Although marriage has been contracted under the influence of grave fear sufficient to render it invalid, the marriage may afterward become valid if fear disappears, and the party who was under its influence freely cohabits with the other and expresses matrimonial consent. In this case it will not be necessary to repeat the external solemnization of the marriage unless the impediment was publicly known. It will be sufficient if the parties manifest their consent to be man and wife privately when freed from the influence of grave fear.

As may be gathered from what has already been said, slight fear, such as any ordinarily constituted person can despise, does not invalidate marriage, even when it is caused unjustly with a view to extort marriage.

Article XIV

Abduction

The Council of Trent[1] made the following law: "The Holy Synod ordains that no marriage can subsist between the abductor and her who is abducted so long as she shall remain in the power of the abductor. But if she that has been abducted, being separated from the abductor and being in a safe and free place, shall consent to have him for her husband, the abductor may have her for his wife." This decree made abduction a diriment impediment of marriage, and in keeping with its tenor the impediment may be defined as the violent abduction of a woman from a place of safety to another place where she is detained in the power of the abductor for the purpose of marriage. In order to constitute the impediment the abduction must be against the will of the woman, whether it be effected by open violence, or threats, or fraud; for if she freely consent both to the abduction and to marriage, we have elopement, not abduction. Consent to both abduction and marriage is required, for the Council made an abducted woman incapable of contracting a valid marriage, as long as she is in the power of the abductor. The woman, too, must be the abducted party; if a man were forcibly carried off by the orders of a woman who wished to marry him, this impediment would not arise. It is a disputed point among Doctors as to whether the impediment would arise if a man carried off his betrothed by violence in order to marry her. The better opinion is that the impediment would hinder the marriage, for although betrothal gave the man a right to marry the woman at the proper time, still it gave him no right to use violence for the purpose.

The words in the definition "from a place of safety" signify a place where the woman is not in the power of the abductor, so that to give rise to the impediment the woman must be taken from one place to another which is morally distinct, and where she is under the control of the abductor. The forcible detention of a woman in a place where she is in the man's

[1] Sess. xxiv, c. 6, de ref. Matr.

power but to which she came of her own accord is equivalent to abduction (Can. 1074, sec. 3). The abductor's aim must be to contract marriage, not merely to satisfy his lust.

The impediment is of ecclesiastical law and lasts as long as the person abducted remains in the power of the abductor, for, as the Council says, if the woman be restored to her liberty and then freely chooses to have the abductor for her husband, the impediment ceases (Can. 1074, sec. 2).

The Council imposed the penalty of excommunication on the abductor and on all who aid and abet him, besides obliging him to give the woman a sufficient dower whether he marry her or not. Other penalties are assigned by Canon 2353.

Article XV

Clandestinity

1. A clandestine marriage is one that is contracted without the solemnities which are prescribed by the Church, so that a civil marriage before the registrar, a marriage in private, and a marriage before a priest not duly authorized to assist at it, are all clandestine marriages. Such a marriage always was and is gravely sinful, because it is forbidden by the Church on account of the great evils which frequently are the consequence, and because marriage is a sacrament and it should be received with fitting solemnity in the Church. Moreover, the Council of Trent by the decree *Tametsi*[1] made clandestine marriages invalid in all places where the decree has been published according to the directions therein laid down. These will be best set forth in the words of the Council itself. The Council says:

"And that these so wholesome injunctions may not be unknown to any, it enjoins on all ordinaries that they as soon as possible make it their care that this decree be published and explained to the people in every parish church of their respective dioceses; and that this be done as often as may be during the first year, and afterwards as often as they shall judge it expedient. It ordains, moreover, that this decree shall begin to be in force in each parish at the expiration of thirty days, to be counted from the day of its first publication made in the said parish."

This decree was duly published in the parishes of Catholic countries like Italy, France, and Spain, and consequently in

[1] Sess. xxiv, c. 1, de ref. Matr.

those countries it bound all baptized persons, Protestant as well as Catholic. In Protestant countries like England, Scotland, and Norway it was not published at all, and bound neither Catholics nor Protestants. In countries like Ireland and Holland it bound Catholics but not Protestants. In these latter countries mixed marriages were declared to be exempt from the decree. This varying discipline led to inextricable confusion, and more marriages were invalid on account of clandestinity than from any other cause. To remedy these evils the Sacred Congregation of the Council issued its decree *Ne temere* on August 2, 1907, and it began to have the force of law for Catholics in the Western Church on Easter Sunday, April 19, 1908. With a few changes the Code has adopted the provisions of the *Ne temere* decree, and so now the impediment of clandestinity may be described as follows:

Only those marriages are valid which are contracted before the parish priest of the place or the local Ordinary or a priest delegated by either of them and at least two witnesses.

The parish priest and the Ordinary of the place validly assist at a marriage:

(*a*) Only from the day of taking canonical possession of their benefice or entering upon their office, unless by sentence they have been excommunicated, interdicted, or suspended from office, or declared to be such.

(*b*) Only within the limits of their territory; and within the limits of their territory they assist validly not only at the marriages of their subjects, but also of such as are not their subjects.

(*c*) Provided that not being compelled by violence or grave fear they demand and receive the consent of the contracting parties.

The parish priest and the local Ordinary who can validly assist at a marriage can also grant leave to another priest so that within the limits of their own territory he may validly assist at the marriage (Can. 1094, 1095).

This leave to assist at a marriage ought to be given expressly to a particular priest for a particular marriage, otherwise it is invalid; so that all general delegations are excluded, unless there is question of curates (*vicarii cooperatores*) for the parish which they serve.

The parish priest or the local Ordinary should not grant this leave unless everything has been done which the law requires for the proof of the freedom of the parties to marry (Can. 1096).

Moreover, the parish priest or the local Ordinary assist lawfully at a marriage:

(*a*) When they are satisfied according to law as to the freedom of the parties to marry.

(*b*) When, moreover, they are satisfied as to the domicile or quasi-domicile or of a month's stay, or, if there is question of a homeless person, of the actual staying of one of the contracting parties in the place of marriage.

(*c*) If the conditions just mentioned be wanting, the priest must have the leave of the parish priest or of the local Ordinary of the domicile or quasi-domicile or month's stay of one of the contracting parties, unless there is question of homeless persons who are moving about and staying nowhere, or there is a grave necessity which excuses from asking leave.

In all cases let it be the rule that marriage be celebrated before the parish priest of the bride unless there be some good reason to the contrary.

A parish priest who assists at a marriage without the required leave has no right to the stole fee, and he should send it to the proper parish priest of the contracting parties (Can. 1097).

If a parish priest or a local Ordinary or a priest delegated by one of them cannot be had or approached without serious inconvenience to assist at marriage:

(*a*) In danger of death marriage contracted before witnesses alone is valid and lawful; and also at other times provided that a prudent judgement be formed that the same state of things will last for a month.

(*b*) In both cases if there is another priest who can assist he ought to be called and assist at the marriage, but if this is not done the marriage before witnesses alone is valid (Can. 1098).

All who have been baptized in the Catholic Church are bound to observe this form of marriage, as well as all converts to it from heresy or schism; even though they afterwards fall away from it. All these are bound to observe the form laid down even when they contract marriage with non-Catholics, or with Catholics of the Oriental rites. But non-Catholics, whether baptized or not, are nowhere bound to observe it when they marry among themselves, nor are those born of non-Catholic parents but baptized in the Catholic Church, who from the age of infancy have grown up in heresy, schism, or infidelity, or without any religion at all, when they contract marriage with a non-Catholic (Can. 1099).

Canon 1103 prescribes that when marriage has been celebrated the parish priest or one who takes his place should enter the marriage in the Marriage book as soon as possible. He should also make the proper entry in the Baptism book if either or both of the parties were baptized in his parish, otherwise he must send notice of the marriage to the parish priest of Baptism in order that he may make the entry in the Baptism book.

When marriage has been contracted in case of necessity without the presence of the parish priest or his delegate, if another priest was present, he and the witnesses are jointly and severally bound with the contracting parties to see that the entries of the marriage are made in the proper books as soon as possible.

CHAPTER XI

DOUBTFUL IMPEDIMENTS

1. When there is a doubt as to the existence of a diriment impediment which annuls marriage by natural or divine law, marriage must not be contracted, for as there would always be a doubt as to whether it was valid, the parties would be exposed to the continual danger of sinning against the natural law. Theologians make an exception to this general rule in favour of those who labour under probable impotence, for these may marry on account of the strong presumption that all men are potent unless the contrary is certain, and because it would be an intolerable hardship to prohibit a person from marrying because of such a doubt (Can. 1068, sec. 2). In the case of a doubtful impediment of positive law, we must distinguish between a doubt of law and a doubt of fact. When there is a doubt whether the positive law extends to the particular case, as whether spiritual relationship arises between the sponsors in a private Baptism and the child, the impediment practically does not exist, as the law is of strict interpretation and the Church dispenses as far as is necessary in such a case of doubt.

When the doubt is about a fact, as whether the parties are related within the prohibited degrees of kindred, the Church does not supply if the impediment really exists, and a dispensation should be asked for to make sure. The Bishop has power to dispense in such cases of doubt (Can. 15).

When marriage is contracted with a supposed impediment which in reality does not exist, the marriage will of course be null and void if the parties thought that it was altogether impossible, and merely intended to go through the external form. On the other hand, it would seem to be valid if they intended to marry as far as they could, though they were afraid they could not do so. And so if one whose consort has been absent for a long time and who is not known to be dead, as in fact he is, marries again, giving her consent to the marriage as far as possible, it would seem that the marriage is valid though unlawful.

2. When a marriage has been contracted and a doubt subsequently arises as to the validity on account of the probable

existence of a diriment impediment, inquiry must be made with a view to settling the doubt, and in the meanwhile the party in doubt must abstain from asking for the marriage debt, though he is not precluded from rendering it to a consort who asks for it in good faith without any suspicion about the validity of the marriage. If the doubt still remains after ordinary diligence has been used in making inquiries, the doubt may be put aside, and the marriage may be presumed to be valid. The rules of law may be applied to such a case, " In doubt we must presume the validity of the act," and " In doubt the condition of him who is in possession is the stronger." These rules apply with all the greater force inasmuch as marriage is favoured, and the decision must always be given in its favour in case of doubt (Can. 1014).

If it becomes certain that a marriage which has been contracted is invalid by reason of a diriment impediment existing between the parties, and the invalidity is publicly known, the parties must separate. Otherwise there would be danger of sin and public scandal. If the impediment is secret and the parties are in good faith without any knowledge of its existence, they should be left in their ignorance until a dispensation from the impediment has been obtained. The dispensation should be executed in one of the ways to be described in a subsequent chapter.

If the parties know of the existence of the impediment and of the consequent nullity of their marriage, they must separate, at least from bed, until a dispensation can be procured. Whether they can be permitted to live together as brother and sister in the same house depends on whether they can thus avoid all proximate occasion of sin. If they cannot, some excuse to avoid scandal and awaking suspicion must be found for a temporary separation.

CHAPTER XII
DISPENSATIONS FROM DIRIMENT IMPEDIMENTS

1. THE Church cannot grant a dispensation from those impediments which belong to the natural and divine law. She cannot, for example, allow a Christian to marry again while a former wife is still alive, nor dispense in a case of certain impotence. Although she can dispense in all impediments which have their origin in ecclesiastical law, yet as a matter of fact she but seldom does so in some of them, such as the priesthood, and affinity in the first degree arising from consummated marriage. The Council of Trent decreed universally that " as regards marriages to be contracted, either no dispensation at all shall be granted, or rarely, and then for a cause, and gratuitously."[1] Still, according to modern discipline it is not uncommon for dispensations to be granted in the more remote degrees of consanguinity and affinity, in spiritual relationship, in occult crime, and in some other impediments.

2. As the diriment impediments of marriage belong to the common law of the Church, *per se* only the Holy See can lawfully dispense in them.

However, in certain cases, whether by law or by special indult, bishops and others have power to dispense.

(*a*) A bishop can dispense a doubtful impediment when the doubt is about a fact (Can. 15).

(*b*) In pressing danger of death, local Ordinaries, to appease conscience, and, if the case admit of it, for the legitimation of offspring, can dispense both in the form to be observed in the celebration of marriage, and in each and all impediments of ecclesiastical law, whether public or occult, even though they are manifold, except the impediments arising from the sacred order of priesthood, and of affinity in the direct line when marriage has been consummated (they can dispense) their own subjects wherever they be, and all who are actually staying in their territory, but scandal must be avoided, and if the dispensation is granted for difference of religion or for a mixed marriage, the usual promises must be given (Can. 1043).

[1] Sess. xxiv, c. 5, de ref. Matr.

DISPENSATIONS FROM DIRIMENT IMPEDIMENTS 239

(c) In the same circumstances, and only for cases in which not even the local Ordinary can be approached, both the parish priest has the same power of dispensing, and the priest who assists at marriage contracted in danger of death in accordance with Canon 1098, n. 2, and a confessor, but the latter for the internal forum in the act of sacramental confession only (Can. 1044).

(d) Subject to the clauses laid down at the end of Canon 1043, local Ordinaries can dispense in all the impediments mentioned in that same canon, whenever the impediment is discovered when everything is ready for the marriage, and without probable danger of grave harm the marriage cannot be put off until a dispensation is obtained from the Holy See (Can. 1045).

(e) This same faculty avails also for the convalidation of marriage already contracted, if there is the same danger in delay, and there is no time to have recourse to the Holy See (*ibid.*, sec. 2).

(f) In the same circumstances, the parish priest and other priests mentioned in Canon 1044 have the same faculty, but only for occult cases in which not even the local Ordinary can be approached or not without danger of violating the seal of confession (*ibid.*, sec. 3).

The parish priest or the priest mentioned in Canon 1044 should at once notify the local Ordinary of the dispensation granted for the external forum; and enter it in the book of marriages (Can. 1046).

The above special faculties for particular cases are granted by law; sometimes Bishops receive other faculties for granting dispensations by indult from the Holy See. The Code lays down the following rules which govern the exercise of such faculties:

In marriages already contracted or to be contracted, he who has a general indult for dispensing in a certain impediment can dispense in it even though it is manifold, unless the indult expressly prescribes otherwise (Can. 1049, sec. 1).

One who has a general indult for dispensing in several impediments of different kinds, whether diriment or prohibitory, can dispense in those same impediments even if they are public, when they occur in one and the same case (*ibid.*, sec. 2).

If ever together with a public impediment or impediments, in which one can dispense by indult, there is another impediment in which he cannot dispense, the Holy See ought to be approached for all of them; but he can use his faculties if the impediment or impediments in which he can dispense are discovered after a dispensation has been asked for from the Holy See (Can. 1050).

By a dispensation in a diriment impediment granted either by ordinary authority or by authority delegated by general indult, but not by rescript in particular cases, legitimation of offspring is thereby also granted if any was born or conceived of those who were dispensed, with the exception of adulterous or sacrilegious offspring (Can. 1051).

A dispensation from an impediment of consanguinity or affinity granted in any degree of the impediment is valid notwithstanding a mistake about the degree in the petition or in the grant, provided that the true degree is lower, or although another impediment of the same kind in an equal or lower degree was not mentioned (Can. 1052).

A dispensation granted from a minor impediment is annulled by no defect of obreption or subreption, although the only motive cause mentioned in the petition was false (Can. 1054).

The impediments of minor degree are:
(a) Consanguinity in the third degree of the collateral line.
(b) Affinity in the second degree of the collateral line.
(c) Public propriety in the second degree.
(d) Spiritual relationship.
(e) Crime arising from adultery with a promise of marriage, or with attempted marriage even though it be only civil. All the other impediments are of greater degree (Can. 1042).

The Pope grants matrimonial dispensations through various Roman Congregations. The Congregation of the Holy Office grants dispensations in mixed marriages and in the impediment of difference of religion. The Congregation on the Discipline of the Sacraments grants dispensations from public impediments and for the external forum. The Sacred Penitentiary grants dispensations only for the internal forum. If a case occur in which there is both a public and an occult impediment, the petition for dispensation from the public impediment should be sent to the Sacred Congregation on the Discipline of the Sacraments in the ordinary way, and another petition without mentioning the real names of the parties should be sent to the Sacred Penitentiary, mentioning the public impediment in the case as well as the occult.

Dispensations are granted gratuitously by the Sacred Penitentiary, but for dispensations from public impediments granted by the Roman Congregations besides the expenses of agency a small tax is imposed on those who can afford to pay. This is lowered or altogether remitted in favour of the poor.

3. Matrimonial dispensations cannot be granted lawfully even by the Pope without good cause. A cause is motive or final when it is ordinarily deemed sufficient for granting a dispensation; when it only induces the superior to grant a dispensation more readily, it is said to be impulsive. When the petition for a dispensation omits to mention what should be mentioned, it has the defect of *subreption;* when it alleges what is false, there is *obreption.* When subreption or obreption occurs in the motive cause, the dispensation from the impediments of greater degree, not from those of minor degree, is invalid at least if the cause alleged was the sole cause, and even if it was not the validity of the dispensation is doubtful. Supreption or obreption in an impulsive cause does not affect the validity of the dispensation. In doubt as to whether a cause falsely alleged for a dispensation was motive or impulsive, the presumption will be in favour of the validity of the dispensation, *In dubio standum est pro valore actus.* If the motive for granting a dispensation from an impediment of greater degree ceases before the dispensation is executed, the dispensation will lapse; if, however, the motive cause ceases to exist after the dispensation has been executed, though before the marriage has been contracted, the impediment has been removed, and the parties may marry.

Propaganda, May 9, 1877, issued an instruction on matrimonial dispensations, which sets forth and explains the ordinary canonical causes which are accepted as sufficient for granting a dispensation. The same causes, however, are not sufficient for a dispensation from all impediments, and the party interested should put down in his petition all the grounds that he can find for granting the favour he requests. We cannot do better than give here the chief portion of this important document in Fr. Guy's translation:

"(1) *Smallness of the place,* either absolute or relative (as regards the female petitioner alone), seeing that in the place of her birth or even domicile a woman's relationship is so widely spread that she is unable to meet with anyone to be married to of an equal position with her own, save a relative by blood or by marriage, without leaving her country, which would be a hardship to her.

"(2) *The advancing age of the woman.* If, for instance, she is over twenty-four and has not hitherto met with one of her own position to whom she might be married. But this reason does not hold good in the case of a widow wishing to marry again.

"(3) *Deficiency or absence of dowry.* If a woman has not actually a dowry large enough to enable her to marry another of her own position, unconnected by blood or marriage, in her own place of abode. And this reason becomes all the more weighty when the woman has no dowry at all and a relation by blood or by marriage is willing to marry her, or even to make a suitable settlement upon her.

"(4) *Contentions about inheritance* that have already arisen or serious or imminent danger of the same. If a woman has on hand an important suit in reference to her inheriting wealth of great amount, and there is no one else to undertake a contention of this kind and carry it on at his own expense save the person who is desirous of marrying her, a dispensation is usually granted, for it is of benefit to the community at large that an end should be put to the contention. A reason of this nature, however, suffices only in cases of remote grades of relationship.

"(5) *Poverty* on the part of a widow with a numerous family which some man promises to support. But at times a widow obtains the benefit of a dispensation owing to her youth and the danger of incontinence.

"(6) *The blessing of peace;* and under this head come not only treaties between realms and princes, but the cessation of serious enmities, disturbances, and ill-will between citizens.

"(7) *Too great, suspicious, or dangerous familiarity,* as well as having, almost unavoidably, to dwell together under the same roof.

"(8) *Previous connection* with a relation by blood or by marriage, or with any other party under an impediment, and *pregnancy, with consequent legitimization of the offspring,* in order to provide for the well-being of the offspring and the good name of the mother, who would otherwise remain unmarried.

"(9) *Disgrace* coming upon the woman arising from a suspicion that through over-familiarity with a relative or connection she had been seduced by him, although the suspicion should be false, in a case when unless she marries, a woman seriously defamed would either remain unmarried, or must marry beneath her, or serious loss would ensue.

"(10) *Revalidating a marriage* which has been contracted in good faith, and publicly in the way prescribed by the Council of Trent, because its dissolution could hardly be brought about without grave public scandal and heavy loss, especially on the woman's part. But if the parties have got married in bad faith, they by no means deserve the favour of a dispensation as the Council of Trent decides.

"(11) *Danger of a mixed marriage,* or of its being celebrated before a non-Catholic minister. When there is danger of those wishful of being married, though connected in one of the closer degrees, going before a non-Catholic minister for the marriage in defiance of the authority of the Church, by reason of the refusal of a dispensation, there are just grounds for dispensing; for there is imminent danger not only of a most serious scandal to the faithful, but also of apostasy and loss of faith on the part of those so doing and disregarding the impediment to matrimony, especially in countries where heresy flourishes unchecked. The same must be said in the case of a Catholic woman who ventures upon marriage with a non-Catholic man.

"(12) *Danger of incestuous concubinage.*

"(13) *Danger of a civil marriage.* From what has been said, it follows that probable danger of those who are petitioning for the dispensation having only a civil marriage, as it is called, if they cannot get the dispensation, is a lawful reason for dispensing.

"(14) *The removal of grave scandal.*

"(15) *Putting a stop to open concubinage.*

"(16) *Merit,* that is in the case of one who has by resisting the enemies of the Catholic faith, or by generosity toward the Church, or by his learning, virtue, or some other means, deserved well of religion.

"Such are the more common and strong grounds which are usually brought forward when matrimonial dispensations are to be petitioned for; and theologians and canonists treat of them exhaustively.

"But this instruction now turns to those points which, in addition to the grounds for obtaining the dispensation, must, whether by law, custom, or the practice of the curia, be expressed in the petition, or the dispensation becomes null if the truth be kept back or what is untrue is advanced even in ignorance. These are:

"(1) *The name* and *surname* of the petitioners must both be written down distinctly and clearly, without any abbreviation.

"(2) *The diocese* of birth or of actual domicile. When petitioners have a domicile out of the diocese of their birth they can ask, if they please, that the dispensation should be sent to the Ordinary of the diocese in which they are actually residing.

" (3) *The species* (in its most determinate form) of the impediment, whether it is consanguinity or affinity, public morality (*honestas*); in the case of an impediment by reason of crime, whether it arose from murder of the party's spouse with the promise of marriage, or from such murder with adultery, or from adultery alone with the promise of marriage.

" (4) *The degree of consanguinity or affinity* or morality (*honestas*) arising from a marriage ceremony, and whether it is a simple or mixed degree, the more remote as well as the less, together with the line, and whether it is direct or collateral; likewise, whether the petitioners are related by a double tie of consanguinity, both on the father's and mother's side.

" (5) *The number of impediments;* for instance, is the consanguinity or affinity twofold or manifold; or is there affinity as well as relationship; or any other kind of impediment, diriment or prohibitory?

" (6) *Various circumstances*, such as whether the marriage is to be or has been contracted; if contracted, it must be stated whether this was done in good faith at least on one side, or with a knowledge of the impediment; likewise, whether it was after proclamation of banns and in accordance with the prescriptions of the Council of Trent, or whether with the view of more easily obtaining a dispensation; finally, whether it has been consummated, if in bad faith, at least on one side, or with knowledge of the impediment."[1]

The instruction required that mention be made of incest, if this crime had been committed between the parties who asked for the dispensation, but this obligation was abolished by a decree of the Holy Office, June 25, 1885.

If a mistake occurs in the names of the petitioners, or of the diocese or parish, it does not invalidate the dispensation, provided that in the judgement of the Ordinary there is no doubt about the truth of the matter (Can. 47).

If a lower degree is put for a higher, the mistake invalidates the dispensation as a rule, otherwise if a higher or equal degree is put for a lower (Can. 1052).

4. As a rule the Holy See grants dispensations *in forma commissoria*. When the impediment is occult the commission to dispense the party labouring under the impediment is issued to the confessor. It will therefore be the confessor's duty to verify the allegations as far as possible and faithfully to observe all the conditions laid down in the papal rescript. The ob-

[1] *Synods in English*, p. 78.

servance of the conditions expressed by such terms as, *provided that*, *if*, or the *ablative absolute*, is necessary for the validity of the dispensation. Besides the conditions, certain things are also prescribed, such as the destruction of the rescript after it has been executed; but these matters do not affect the validity of the dispensation. One of the usual conditions is previous sacramental confession, which requires the hearing of the confession of the party, but not necessarily his absolution. If this clause is not in the rescript, it may be executed outside the confessional. No special form is prescribed for granting the dispensation, which may be done by word of mouth.

Notice of the dispensation if it was given for the internal but non-sacramental forum should be entered in the secret book (Can. 1047).

When the impediment is public the commission is issued to the Ordinary of the parties or to the Ordinary of the place where they live. After the Ordinary has received the rescript he may delegate the verification of the clauses to the parish priest of the parties, and after this has been done he may grant the dispensation according to the terms of the rescript, and on being signed by the Ordinary the dispensation will at once take its effect. The document or a copy of it should be sent to the parish priest, who will inform the parties that the dispensation has been duly granted (*cf.* Can. 1055, 1046, 1047, 1057).

When the bishop is able to grant the necessary dispensation, he ordinarily does so *in forma gratiosa*. This signifies that on receipt of the petition and having satisfied himself of the truth of the allegations contained in it, he grants the dispensation forthwith by signing a document drawn up in due form, and sends it to the parish priest, who will inform the parties of the terms on which it has been granted.

CHAPTER XIII

REVALIDATION OF MARRIAGE

1. WHEN marriage has been contracted invalidly the ordinary thing to do is to secure its being contracted validly, if this is possible. It may have been invalid on account of clandestinity, or for want of consent, or because there was some diriment impediment between the parties.

When the marriage was invalid on account of clandestinity, it must be revalidated by supplying the defect and contracting marriage anew before the parish priest and two witnesses. If the invalidity of the first marriage was known publicly, the second must be publicly solemnized; otherwise it will be sufficient to contract it in private (Can. 1137).

2. When the first marriage was invalid for want of consent of both the contracting parties, the only way of revalidating it is by both renewing their consent. This, again, should be done publicly if the invalidity of the former marriage was matter of public knowledge; in other cases it will be sufficient to renew consent in private. When the former marriage was invalid for want of consent of only one of the parties, it will be sufficient if this party after becoming acquainted with its invalidity freely renews his consent if the consent of the other party still persists. This may be done validly not only by express word of mouth, but by living together as man and wife, and exhibiting the ordinary signs of matrimonial union (Can. 1136).

3. When the first marriage was invalid on account of some diriment impediment between the parties, the first thing to do is to remove the obstacle to marriage by obtaining a dispensation from the impediment and duly executing it. If both the parties were aware of the impediment, they must renew their consent either in public or in private, according as the nullity of the marriage was publicly known or not (Can. 1135).

This renewal of consent is a new act of the will consenting to the marriage, with knowledge of its previous invalidity, and is necessary for validity by ecclesiastical law (Can. 1133, 1134).

If the impediment is occult and not known to one of the parties, it is sufficient for the party who knows of the impediment to renew his consent privately and in secret, provided that the consent given by the other party still persists (Can. 1135, sec. 3).

Sometimes not even this can be done, and in such cases of special difficulty recourse may be had to a dispensation *in radice*, as it is called, by which the Holy See sometimes revalidates a marriage without any renewal of consent by the parties. By a dispensation *in radice* the diriment impediment which existed is removed, the marriage is validly contracted by the consent which was given in the former marriage and which still subsists, and the children, if any have been born, are legitimized as if the former marriage had been valid. By a fiction of law, the former marriage is held to be valid and to have all the effects of a valid marriage.

It is obvious that to enable the Church to do this the impediment must be merely of ecclesiastical origin, and so capable of being removed by the Church; the consent given in the former marriage must of itself be valid and capable of effecting a real marriage except for the impediment, and, moreover, the consent of the parties must still persist at the time when the dispensation is given, otherwise true marriage can never exist between the parties. If these conditions are fulfilled by a dispensation *in radice* without any renewal of consent, the parties will be truly married, and the effects of marriage will date from the first contract, though it was invalid (Can. 1138-1141).

CHAPTER XIV

DE DEBITO CONJUGALI

1. VERBA S Pauli prooemii locum teneant nobis hanc foedam materiam breviter tractaturis: "Uxori," inquit Apostolus, "vir debitum reddat, similiter autem et uxor viro. Mulier sui corporis potestatem non habet, sed vir; similiter autem et vir sui corporis potestatem non habet, sed mulier. Nolite fraudare invicem, nisi forte ex consensu ad tempus, ut vacetis orationi; et iterum revertimini in idipsum, ne tentet vos Satanas propter incontinentiam vestram."[1]

Proinde non tantum licitus est usus conjugii sed alteri parti serio et rationabiliter petenti est ex justitia debitum sub gravi reddendum.

Quod quamvis sit certissimum admittuntur tamen causae excusantes ab hac obligatione, ita ut nulla sit obligatio reddendi debitum quando reddi non possit sine periculo vitae, morbi gravis, vel quando non rationabiliter petatur, ut ab amente aut ebrio, vel petatur nimis frequenter, ut si pluries in eadem nocte. Etiam semi-ebrio petenti videtur licitum, praesertim propter periculum gravium defectuum tum corporalium tum moralium in prole forte gignenda, debitum denegare nisi propterea timeantur rixae, discordiae, et incontinentia ex parte petentis.

Dictum est in his circumstantiis nullam adesse obligationem debitum reddendi, imo per se illicitum esset debitum reddere cum proximo periculo vitae vel sanitatis. Attamen si morbus esset diuturnus nec proxime tendens ad mortem, qualis est syphilis, permittitur sano debitum reddere cum periculo infectionis ad incontinentiam vitandam vel ad amorem conjugalem fovendum. Major difficultas habetur quando judicio medici proles gignenda morti esset matri. Tales vero casus non sunt facile admittendi, et quidem medici judicium de periculo vitae facilius pronunciant eo quod mulieres illud aucupantes videant. Nisi igitur casus sit omnino specialis, tuto confessarius consilium mulieri tale judicium medici alleganti dabit ut viro placere studeat ac cum magna fiducia Deo se committat.

[1] 1 Cor. vii 3-5.

Quum conjuges sibi invicem debitum reddere teneantur, patet eos ad simul cohabitandum regulariter etiam teneri, nisi quando necessitas id non patitur vel quando ex mutuo consensu sine periculo incontinentiae et sine scandalo aliter fit.

Conjugibus senibus vel debilibus qui saepius copulam nonnisi imperfecte exercent non est denegandus usus matrimonii dummodo aliqua sit spes eos posse rite actum perficere.

2. Quid liceat quid non liceat conjugibus sequenti regula generali continetur: Quod utile est ad actum conjugalem exercendum licet; quod est contra prolis generationem vel tendit ad illam impediendam est graviter illicitum; quod non est contra prolis generationem, quamvis sit praeter illam, saltem non est graviter illicitum.

Unde resolves: Licet conjugi tactibus et aspectibus impudicis sese ad copulam excitare, et post vir se retractavit licet uxori tactibus se excitare ad delectationem veneream completam. Copula sodomitica et copula incoepta sed abrupta cum effusione seminis extra vas mulieris graviter illicita est. Si autem experientia constat conjugibus se posse sine proximo periculo pollutionis copulam incoeptam abrumpere, non videtur hoc esse mortale si uterque consentiat. A fortiori alii tactus et aspectus turpes sine proximo periculo pollutionis a conjugibus admissi non videntur mortalia, et ab omni peccato excusantur si ex justa causa exercentur, ut ad affectum conjugalem fovendum.

3. Peccatum grave contra naturam et finem matrimonii committit vir qui copula imperfecta sese voluntarie ab uxore retrahit et extra vas seminat. Ex facto Onan vocatur peccatum onanismus.[1]

Constat autem esse peccatum grave ex Sacra Scriptura ex eo quod frustratur finem principalem matrimonii, et tendit in ruinam generis humani. Constat etiam ex pluribus responsis SS Congregationum. Moraliter nil refert quo medio peccatum hoc frustratae naturae committatur, sive instrumento quodam, sive involucro, sive lotione vasis mulieris post copulam, sive mere retractione viri ante seminationem. Si mutuo consilio et consensu conjugum tale quid fiat uterque graviter peccat.

Si tamen actus viri onanisticus uxori displiceat, quae etiam eum inducere ad rem honeste perficiendam frustra tentavit, haec non videtur prohibenda quominus debitum viro petenti reddat vel etiam ex gravi causa postulet. Ipsa enim materialiter

[1] Gen. xxxviii 9.

tantum cum peccato viri cooperatur, quae cooperatio ex gravi causa est licita. Habetur vero gravis causa tum ex parte viri ne offendatur, tum ex parte uxoris quae cum periculo incontinentiae non est privanda juribus suis maritalibus. Licet igitur mulieri etiamsi vir onanistice agat, venereae delectari in usu matrimonii, imo licet ei postquam vir sese retractavit excitare sese tactibus ad completam satisfactionem si hanc nondum sit experta.

Confessarii regulariter conjuges interrogare non debent de modo quo jura maritalia exerceant. Si tamen conjux dubia proponat de liceitate onanismi confessarius doctrinam Catholicam breviter ei declarare debet. Imo si suspicionem fundatam habet conjuges sive bona sive mala fide onanistice agere eos monere debet, cum de gravi peccato valde nocivo ipsis conjugibus et societati humanae agatur. Conjux qui doctrinae Catholicae de hac re acquiescere nolit per se absolutionis est incapax.

4. Dummodo copula rite perfici possit nullus situs in ea exercenda graviter est illicitus, et situs non naturalis cohonestatur ita ut ne venialiter quidem sit illicitus dummodo justa aliqua causa habeatur.

Vetere lege accessus ad uxorem prohibebatur menstruorum et purgationis tempore, imo antiqua lege ecclesiastica similis vigebat prohibitio. Videtur dicendum illas leges esse positivas nec amplius Christianos obligare. Variae sunt Doctorum sententiae circa liceitatem talis accessus. Rationes quas afferebant plures ut actus illiceitatem demonstrarent fabulis nitebantur, attamen scientia physiologica comprobat sententiam juxta quam ob statum nerveum mulieris menstruorum et purgationis tempore sub veniali saltem est viro abstinendum nisi justa causa excusat. Idem dicendum videtur de tempore praegnationis, imo si esset copula periculo proximo abortus sub gravi tunc esset abstinendum. Vix tamen constare potest de tali periculo unde obligatio abstinendi urgeri non valet.

Probabilis videtur sententia plurium juxta quam tactus impudici quos conjux secum exercet altera parte absente dummodo nullum sit periculum proximum pollutionis non sunt peccata mortalia. Ipse status matrimonialis, aiunt, reddit tales actus minus indecentes, ita ut quod apud solutos sit grave, apud conjugatos sit tantum veniale.

Nec delectatio morosa de copula habita vel habenda, secluso iterum periculo proximo pollutionis, videtur sub gravi conjugibus prohibita. Imo delectatio mere rationalis de objecto licito, qualis est copula conjugibus, ne veniale quidem esset; attamen practice delectatio de actu conjugali vix mere rationalis esse poterit, quatenus naturaliter excitat sensus et membra. Unde delectatio morosa de copula habita vel habenda sub veniali saltem regulariter etiam conjugibus prohibetur.

Copulam cum conjuge exercere cum mente adulterina, cogitando de alia persona praeter conjugem, grave est peccatum propter mentem adulterinam.

BOOK X
CENSURES

Part I
CENSURES IN GENERAL

CHAPTER I
THE NATURE OF AN ECCLESIASTICAL CENSURE

1. We here understand by a censure a spiritual and remedial penalty by which a baptized and contumacious delinquent is deprived by ecclesiastical authority of the use of certain spiritual advantages. It differs from other penalties, such as degradation, which are also spiritual and inflicted by the Church, in that a censure has in view the correction and amendment of the delinquent, while other penalties have chiefly in view the common good to be procured by the punishment and repression of crime. The Church has jurisdiction only over those who are baptized, and she punishes by censures only those of her children who have done wrong with their eyes open, with knowledge of the wrongfulness of their action and of the spiritual censure by which the Church punishes it.

A censure does not and cannot deprive a man of all the spiritual advantages which he may possess. There are some spiritual gifts in man's possession which depend only on his personal relations with God, such as sanctifying grace, and the supernatural virtues and gifts which accompany it. These may adorn the soul of one who is not baptized, and they are not possessed by all members of the Church. There are, however, other spiritual privileges which a Christian enjoys through membership with the Church of God. Among these theologians distinguish those that are internal, external, and mixed. Internal comprise the special providence and helps which God grants to the members of his Church because they belong to his Spouse who is continually interceding for them. External are the society and special charity which binds the members of the Church to each other. Mixed are the participation in the same sacraments and sacrifice, the common suffrages, satisfactions, and indulgences, which the children of the Church in communion with her enjoy. According to the common opinion, excommunication deprives the delinquent of all these privileges, it puts him outside the communion of the faithful, and consequently leaves him without the benefits of union. The other two censures, suspension and interdict, deprive him at least of some of those benefits, as of their nature they are limited in their effect. There are, however, some theologians who with Suarez deny that a censure deprives a man of the merely internal advantages which membership with the Church confers.

2. With reference to the effects produced by them, censures are of three kinds: excommunication, suspension, and interdict. With reference to the manner in which they are inflicted, they are said to be *a jure*, or *ab homine*. The former are imposed by a stable and permanent law, the latter by way of particular precept or sentence. Sometimes a censure is incurred by the very fact of committing a crime, without any declaratory sentence of a judge; it is then said to be *latae sententiae*. Sometimes it needs the intervention of a judge, and is said to be *ferendae sententiae*.

3. Certain conditions must be fulfilled in order that a censure may be incurred:

(*a*) As it is a serious penalty, and a serious penalty can only be inflicted for a grave fault, a censure can only be incurred by one who has committed a mortal sin.

(*b*) The Church does not judge of what is merely internal, and so the fault which is punished by censure must be grave externally as well as internally. A slight blow given to a cleric, which does not constitute a serious injury, does not involve excommunication incurred by those who violate the privilege of the canon, even though the act were accompanied with mortal hatred.

(*c*) Penalties must be interpreted strictly, and therefore the crime which is punished by censures must be completed, not merely attempted.

(*d*) Inasmuch as a censure is remedial and inflicted on the delinquent for his correction and amendment, it cannot be incurred for a crime which is altogether past, and which has left no traces behind it. Sometimes suspension or interdict may be inflicted in punishment of such crimes, but then they are inflicted for a definite period, or for ever, and become pure penalties, not censures.

(*e*) There must be contumacy in order that a censure may be incurred, or, in other words, the delinquent must be conscious at the time that he is committing a crime which is punished by the Church by censure. It follows from this that a censure cannot be inflicted *ab homine* by a particular sentence without previous admonition, and this should ordinarily be in writing so as to be capable of proof. In censures inflicted *a jure* or *ab homine* by a general precept which is of the nature of a law, no special admonition is required, as the law itself is a sufficient admonition. Nor is an admonition necessary when suspension or interdict are inflicted by way of mere penalty (Can. 2242).

4. It is of faith that the Church has the power of inflicting censures. It is contained in the general power of binding and loosing granted to the Church by her divine Founder. This power is exercised by all ecclesiastical prelates who have jurisdiction in the external forum, unless their authority has been restricted. The Pope and a general council have jurisdiction over the whole Church, and they can bind all the faithful by their laws and censures. A bishop can inflict censures on his subjects, as can regular prelates on theirs. A parish priest has no jurisdiction in the external forum, and cannot as such impose censures, nor can laymen, nor women.

A bishop cannot lawfully exercise contentious jurisdiction outside his diocese, and consequently he cannot inflict censures outside his diocese when the case requires a judicial process. If the case does not require any judicial process, he may impose a censure on a guilty subject even when he is outside his diocese.

A bishop within his diocese may punish with censure a subject who is now outside the diocese on account of a crime which was committed within the diocese, and even on account of a crime which has been committed outside if it had reference to the diocese. And so a parish priest who is absent from the diocese and refuses to come to synod, or who is taking too long a holiday, may be punished by censure. The more probable opinion holds that a subject who violates a precept imposed under censure while he is outside the diocese incurs the censure, though St Alphonsus admits that the opposite is probable. The jurisdiction of superiors over regulars is personal, and these certainly incur censures imposed on them wherever they may be at the time when it is imposed. Regulars belonging to mendicant orders and members of the Society of Jesus have a special privilege granted by the Holy See, by which they cannot be put under censure by any bishop, even when they do wrong in matters in which their general exemption is of no avail, and in which they are subject to the bishop. In three cases, however, these religious may be punished by episcopal censure, notwithstanding their special privilege. Gregory XV permitted this in case they preach in churches not their own without the bishop's licence, or in their own without asking for his blessing, or against his command; Innocent X added to this the case of disobedience with reference to hearing confessions; and Urban VIII added the case of hanging sacred pictures painted in an unusual or scandalous manner.

5. In order to incur a censure, the delinquent must be subject to the authority which imposes it. Strangers, therefore, do not incur the particular censures which bind in the place where they are staying for a short time. If strangers, however, violate some provision of the common law which for such violation imposes a censure *ferendae sententiae*, the bishop of the place may inflict this on them. Even when they offend in other matters, the local ordinary may punish them by other penalties, and if they prove contumacious, they may be put under censure by him.

A censure *latae sententiae* is multiplied:

(1) If different crimes of which each is punished by censure are committed by the same or distinct actions.

(2) If the same crime punished by censure is often repeated so that there are several distinct crimes.

(3) If a crime punished by different censures by distinct superiors is committed once or several times (Can. 2244).

6. Grave fear and ignorance prevent contumacy, and therefore hinder one who commits a crime under their influence from incurring any censure by which such crime is punished. Grave fear, however, does not excuse from censures inflicted for crimes which produce contempt for the faith, or for ecclesiastical authority, or public harm to souls (Can. 2229, sec. 3, iii). If, however, the ignorance be crass or supine, it will not excuse from grave sin or contumacy, and so the censure will be incurred. But if the censure is inflicted on those who *knowingly, rashly, with rash daring*, or *presumption*, commit a crime, full knowledge is required in order to incur the censure, but merely affected ignorance will not prevent its being incurred (Can. 2229).

CHAPTER II

ABSOLUTION OF CENSURES

1. WHEN a censure has been incurred, it does not cease as a rule merely by lapse of time or on the correction and amendment of the delinquent. The delinquent must obtain absolution of the censure from one who is competent to give it. In some cases, however, a censure is imposed as long as certain conditions last, and then on the termination of those conditions the censure lapses without absolution.

Any confessor in the tribunal of Penance may absolve from censures inflicted by law and not reserved to the Holy See or to the bishop. Censures, too, which are imposed *ab homine* but by a general precept or ordinance are in the same category, and may be absolved by any confessor unless they are reserved (Can. 2253, i).

Absolution for a reserved censure must be sought from him to whom it is reserved, or from his delegate. Similarly, absolution from a censure inflicted *ab homine* by a particular precept must be obtained from him who inflicted it, or from his superior, or successor in office, or from some one delegated by one of these to grant absolution (Can. 2253, ii).

If a confessor in ignorance of the reservation absolves a penitent from a censure and from sin, the absolution of the censure is valid provided that it is not a censure *ab homine* or a censure most specially reserved to the Holy See (Can. 2247, sec. 3).

If there is question of a censure which does not prevent the reception of the sacraments if he who is under censure is rightly disposed and has ceased to be contumacious, he can be absolved from his sins, while the censure remains unabsolved.

But if there is question of a censure which prevents the reception of the sacraments he who is under censure cannot be absolved from his sins unless he has previously been absolved from the censure.

The absolution of a censure in the sacramental forum is contained in the usual form of absolution for sins prescribed in the Ritual; in the non-sacramental forum it may be given in any way, but for the absolution of excommunication it is ordinarily advisable to use the form given in the Ritual (Can. 2250).

If absolution for a censure is given in the external forum it avails also for the internal forum; if it is given in the internal forum he who is absolved if there is no scandal can act as absolved also in the external forum; but unless the grant of absolution is proved or at least can be lawfully presumed in the external forum, the censure can be urged by the superiors of the external forum and the guilty party should obey them until absolution is obtained in the same forum (Can. 2251).

When treating of the sacrament of Penance in the chapter on reserved cases we saw that any priest has unrestricted faculties to absolve any penitent in danger of death, and that a simple confessor has very large powers in more urgent cases by Canon 2254.

Part II
DIFFERENT KINDS OF CENSURES
CHAPTER I
EXCOMMUNICATION

1. OF all the penalties which the Church can inflict, excommunication is the most severe, and it virtually contains the others. It deprives the delinquent of all the advantages which he possessed as a member of the Church, and puts him outside the communion of the faithful. According to the ancient discipline of the Church, no excommunicated person could hold any intercourse with the faithful, nor could the faithful hold intercourse with him, but at the close of the Middle Ages, when heresy became more common, it grew to be impossible to maintain the ancient rigour, and Martin V introduced an important mitigation in the law. By the decree *Ad evitanda*, he distinguished between those under censure who were still to be avoided and those who were to be tolerated. All who were excommunicated by name, and at the same time specially denounced by name, together with all who notoriously violated the privilege of the canon by striking clerics, were still to be avoided; all others were to be tolerated. By this concession Catholics might without scruple, as far as concerned the censure, henceforth have intercourse with persons under censure who were tolerated. The concession was not, indeed, made directly in favour of those under censure, but these could not fail to benefit indirectly by the relaxation in the law that had been granted to the faithful. The tolerated as well as those to be avoided were still theoretically subject to the former disabilities, but custom made a distinction between them in several important respects.

The Code retains the distinction between excommunicates who are to be avoided and those who are tolerated; no one is to be avoided as excommunicated unless he has been excommunicated by name by the Holy See, publicly denounced as such, and in the sentence it is expressly said that he is to be avoided (Can. 2258).

By the ancient discipline one of the faithful who held unlawful intercourse with one who was under excommunication himself incurred the minor excommunication, but this penalty has ceased to exist since the promulgation of the constitution of Pius IX, *Apostolicae Sedis*, where no mention is made of it.

2. The effects of excommunication, according to the Code, may be enumerated as follows:

(*a*) An excommunicated person has no right to assist at divine offices—that is, functions of the power of order which are ordained to the worship of God by the institution of Christ or of the Church, and which can be exercised by clerics alone.

(*b*) An excommunicated person cannot receive the sacraments, and after a declaratory or condemnatory sentence, not even the sacramentals.

(*c*) As a general rule the lawful administration of the sacraments and sacramentals is forbidden to excommunicated persons. However, especially if other ministers are not to be had, the faithful may ask for the sacraments and sacramentals from an excommunicated priest, and then the latter can administer the same without asking the reason for the request.

But from one who is to be avoided and from others after a condemnatory or declaratory sentence, only in danger of death can the faithful ask for sacramental absolution, and then also the other sacraments and sacramentals if other ministers are not to be had.

(*d*) An excommunicated person does not share in the indulgences, suffrages, and public prayers of the Church.

The faithful, however, are not forbidden to pray for him privately. Priests are not forbidden privately and with the avoidance of scandal to offer Mass for him, but only for his conversion, if he is to be avoided.

(*e*) An excommunicated person is removed from the exercise of ecclesiastical offices in law within the limits laid down under the proper heads.

(*f*) An act of jurisdiction, both of the external and internal forum, when exercised by an excommunicated person is unlawful, and also invalid after a condemnatory or declaratory sentence, with the exceptions mentioned above.

(*g*) An excommunicated person is debarred from the right of electing, presenting, nominating, he cannot acquire dignities, offices, benefices, ecclesiastical pensions, or other posts in the Church; nor can he be promoted to orders.

(*h*) After a condemnatory or declaratory sentence of excommunication he is deprived of the emoluments of office if he had one in the Church, and if he is to be avoided, of the office itself.

(*k*) The faithful ought to avoid communicating in secular matters with one who is to be avoided, unless there is question of a spouse, of parents, children, servants, subjects, and generally unless a reasonable cause excuses it (Can. 2259-2267).

Beside the foregoing effects immediately produced by excommunication, there are others more remote. If the person under excommunication violates the censure by unlawfully and solemnly exercising sacred Orders, he incurs irregularity, and if after due admonitions he takes no steps to be released from the censure but remains in it for a whole year, he becomes suspect of heresy (Can. 985, vii; 2340).

CHAPTER II

SUSPENSION

1. SUSPENSION is a censure by which a cleric is deprived of the use of some ecclesiastical power which he has by reason of his orders, office, or benefice, or, in the words of the Code, it is a censure by which a cleric is debarred from office, or benefice, or both.

This censure, then, differs from the rest in that it is inflicted only on clerics, whom it deprives of the lawful exercise of some portion or of the whole of the ecclesiastical power which they possess. A suspended priest may hear Mass and receive the sacraments, and he retains the order or office from which he is suspended, but he cannot lawfully exercise that order or office as long as he is under censure.

Suspension may be partial, as when it deprives the delinquent of the exercise of some sacred order, or office, or of the administration and fruits of his benefice; or it may be total and embrace all those ecclesiastical powers. When a cleric is simply suspended without any special limitation he is understood to be totally suspended from all sacred orders, the exercise of his office, and the fruits of his benefice.

Suspension *ab homine*, inflicted for the perpetration of a crime, should ordinarily be imposed after the crime has been proved judicially. However, the Council of Trent[1] permitted prelates to suspend their clerics on account of a secret crime and without judicial process. If they use this right, they are said to suspend the delinquent *ex informata conscientia;* if it is inflicted as a censure they are bound to make known the grounds of their action to the delinquent himself, and they should be prepared to submit them to the Sacred Congregation if he have recourse to Rome, as he has a right to do, though he has no right to a strict appeal.[2]

Suspension inflicted for life, or for a crime which is altogether past and done with, or at the will and good pleasure of the superior, is not a censure in the strict sense, but a mere penalty inflicted in punishment for crime.

---

[1] Sess. xiv, c. 1, de Ref.; can. 2186 *ff*.
[2] Instruct. S.C. de P.F., October 20, 1884.

2. A suspended person who exercises an act prohibited him by the censure commits grave sin, and if he solemnly exercises sacred orders after being suspended from them he incurs the penalty of irregularity in addition (Can. 985). An act of jurisdiction on the part of one who is publicly suspended after a condemnatory or declaratory sentence, or if the jurisdiction were expressly revoked by the superior, would be invalid; otherwise it would always be valid, and even lawful if it were exercised at the request of the faithful who have the right to ask it of him.

CHAPTER III

INTERDICT

1. INTERDICT is a censure which prohibits the use of liturgical offices, some sacraments, and ecclesiastical burial. It differs from excommunication and suspension, even when the effects are similar, in that excommunication deprives the delinquent of the use of the sacraments, for example, inasmuch as that use is a communication with the faithful, and suspension deprives the delinquent of the exercise of ecclesiastical power in the administration of the sacraments, while interdict forbids their use inasmuch as they are sacred actions and objects of which for just reasons the delinquent is deprived.

An interdict is local, personal, or mixed, as the prohibition immediately affects the place, certain persons, or both.

It is general or special as it affects the whole of some country or body; or only some particular place or person, physical or moral.

A local interdict, whether general or special, does not forbid the administration of the sacraments and sacramentals to the dying under proper conditions, but it forbids in the place any divine office or sacred rite with the following exceptions:

On the feasts of Christmas, Easter, Whit Sunday, Corpus Christi and the Assumption of the Blessed Virgin, a local interdict is suspended, and the conferring of orders and the solemn nuptial blessing are alone forbidden.

If the interdict was local and general and the decree of interdict did not expressly state otherwise:

(1) Provided that they are not personally interdicted, clerics are allowed in private to exercise all divine offices and sacred rites in any church or oratory, with closed doors, in a low voice and without the ringing of bells.

(2) Moreover, in the cathedral, in parish churches, and in the only church in the place, and in these places alone, the celebration of one Mass, the reservation of the Blessed Sacrament, the administration of Baptism, the Eucharist, Penance, assisting at marriage, with the exclusion of the nuptial blessing, funerals excluding all pomp, the blessing of baptismal water, and of the holy oils, and preaching the word of God are per-

mitted. Moreover, in these sacred functions singing is forbidden and pomp in the sacred furniture, the ringing of bells, the playing of the organ and of other musical instruments; and Holy Viaticum should be carried to the sick privately.

Even if a cemetery is specially interdicted the bodies of the faithful may be buried there, but without any ecclesiastical rite (Can. 2270-2272).

2. The violation of an interdict by doing what it forbids is a grave sin, and a cleric who violates a personal interdict by the exercise of an action belonging to sacred orders or who performs such an action in a place which is interdicted by name incurs irregularity (Can. 985, vii).

CHAPTER IV

ECCLESIASTICAL PENALTIES

1. CERTAIN ecclesiastical penalties resemble censures in some respects, and it will be convenient to say a word about them here. Deposition is an ecclesiastical penalty by which a cleric as a punishment for grave crime is for ever suspended from his office and rendered incapable of holding any office, dignity, benefice, pension, or post in the Church, and deprived of those which he has, even though he was ordained on their title (Can. 2303). It differs from a censure in that it is vindictive, not remedial, and it does not endure merely until correction, amendment, and absolution; but of itself it is perpetual. The deposed cleric retains the privileges of the forum and of the canon.

2. Degradation is a more severe penalty than deposition, inasmuch as it reduces the cleric to the state of a layman as far as it is in the power of the Church so to do, and deprives him of all clerical offices, rights, and privileges. Degradation is inflicted by the bishop in punishment of grave crimes committed by clerics who are incorrigible, by depriving them solemnly of their vestments and insignia of office, and handing them over to be dealt with by the secular arm.

3. By ecclesiastical burial is meant interment in consecrated ground with the rites of the Church. All Catholics who die in communion with the faithful have a right to ecclesiastical burial. If there is no consecrated ground in which they can be buried, the grave in which they are placed is blessed at the time of interment. As far as possible Catholics should have a special cemetery of their own or a portion at least of the common cemetery assigned to them exclusively. In this a part should be left unblessed for the reception of the bodies of unbaptized infants and of those to whom Christian burial is to be denied. These are either such as are deprived of ecclesiastical burial because they died out of communion with the faithful, or those to whom it is denied in punishment of crime.

To the first category belong all who are not baptized, open and public heretics, schismatics, apostates, and those under excommunication, for " with those with whom we have not communicated when alive we do not communicate when dead."[1]

To the second class belong suicides, unless they killed themselves while out of their mind, and this the Church readily presumes, those who have been killed in a duel, those who did not make their Easter duties, and open and public sinners. No Catholic, however, should be refused ecclesiastical burial without the sentence of the bishop.

Those also, who of their own free will chose to be cremated and persevered in this choice till death, are denied ecclesiastical burial. The Church's rites may be performed at the house and in the Church in favour of those who are to be cremated by the wish of another, but no sacred rites are permitted at the crematorium.[2]

Although cremation in itself is not intrinsically wrong, yet the Church for good reasons forbids it, and it is gravely sinful for a Catholic to take a formal part in the cremation of the body of a Catholic.

[1] C. 12, de Sepulturis.
[2] S.O., December 15, 1886; can. 1203, 1240, 2339.

Part III

SPECIAL CENSURES

The special censures which are now in force in the Western Church are contained in Book V, Part III, of the Code—*On the Penalties of Particular Crimes*. Of the excommunications some are reserved to the Holy See in a very special manner, others in a special manner, and others simply reserved; others are reserved to bishops, and others are not reserved but may be absolved on proper conditions by any confessor. Special faculties are required in order to absolve from cases reserved to the Holy See, except in certain circumstances described in the chapter on reserved cases. Faculties for cases simply reserved will not avail for cases specially reserved, and faculties for cases specially reserved will not avail for cases very specially reserved. Censures very specially reserved to the Holy See have other characteristics besides requiring very special faculties for their absolution. Canon 2247, sec. 3, provides that where a confessor in ignorance of the reservation absolves a penitent from a censure and from a sin, the absolution is valid except in the case of a censure *ab homine*, or of a censure very specially reserved to the Holy See. Canon 2237, sec. 2, grants power to bishops to remit penalties *latae sententiae* of the common law in occult cases, but censures very specially and those specially reserved are excepted. Canon 2252 provides that when a penitent has been absolved when in danger of death by a simple confessor from a censure *ab homine* or one very specially reserved to the Holy See, if he recovers he is bound to present himself to the person who censured him or to the Sacred Penitentiary, and submit to their requirements. This is not necessary in the case of one who has been absolved in danger of death from other censures.

We shall give a list of the censures contained in the Code with brief comments where they seem to be called for.

CHAPTER I

SPECIAL EXCOMMUNICATIONS

A.—Excommunications very Specially Reserved to the Holy See

Canon 2320

I. Qui species consecratas abjecerit vel ad malum finem abduxerit aut retinuerit, est suspectus de haeresi, incurrit in excommunicationem latae sententiae specialissimo modo Sedi Apostolicae reservatam, est ipso facto infamis, et clericus praeterea est deponendus.

Abjecerit.—Spit them out, throw them away.
Abduxerit.—Take them away for superstitious purposes, to treat them irreverently.
Retinuerit.—Keep them for show, out of curiosity to see what would happen to them.

Canon 2343

II. Qui violentas manus in personam Romani Pontificis injecerit excommunicationem contrahit latae sententiae Sedi Apostolicae specialissimo modo reservatam, et est ipso facto vitandus; est ipso jure infamis; clericus est degradandus.

It is a censure which safeguards the personal immunity of the Roman Pontiff by a special form of the privilege of the canon.

Canon 2367

III. Absolvens sive fingens absolvere complicem in peccato turpi incurrit ipso facto in excommunicationem specialissimo modo Sedi Apostolicae reservatam; idque etiam in mortis articulo si alius sacerdos, licet non approbatus ad confessiones, sine gravi aliqua exoritura infamia et scandalo, possit excipere morientis confessionem, excepto casu quo moribundus recuset alii confiteri.

Eamdem excommunicationem non effugit absolvens vel fingens absolvere complicem qui peccatum quidem complicitatis a quo nondum est absolutus non confitetur, sed ideo ita se gerit, quia ad id a complice confessario sive directe sive indirecte inductus est.

See the comments on this censure above, Penance, Chapter XI.

Canon 2369

IV. Confessarium qui sigillum sacramentale directe violare praesumpserit, manet excommunicatio specialissimo modo Sedi Apostolicae reservata; qui vero indirecte tantum, obnoxius est poenis [suspensionis a celebratione Missae, et ab audiendis sacramentalibus confessionibus vel etiam pro delicti gravitate inhabilis ad ipsas excipiendas declaretur, privetur omnibus beneficiis, dignitatibus, voce activa et passiva, et inhabilis ad ea omnia declaretur, et in casibus gravioribus degradationi quoque subjiciatur.]

Only a confessor who with full knowledge of the crime which he is committing, and of its penalty, directly violates the seal of confession and incurs *ipso facto* excommunication very specially reserved to the Holy See. The penalties assigned by the Code in punishment of others besides confessors, and of confessors who presume to violate the seal indirectly, are *ferendae sententiae*.

B.—Excommunications Specially Reserved to the Holy See

Canon 2314

I. Omnes a Christiana fide apostatae et omnes et singuli haeretici aut schismatici incurrunt ipso facto excommunicationem; nisi moniti resipuerint priventur beneficio, etc.

The absolution from the above excommunication to be given in the forum of conscience is specially reserved to the Holy See. If, however, the crime of apostasy, heresy, or schism has been brought before the external tribunal of the local Ordinary in any way, even by voluntary confession, the same Ordinary, but not the Vicar-General without a special mandate, can absolve the penitent by his ordinary authority in the external forum, when abjuration has previously been made, according to law and other conditions to be complied with have been fulfilled; but one so absolved can afterwards be absolved from his sin in the forum of conscience by any confessor. But the abjuration is held to have been lawfully made when it is made before the local Ordinary or his delegate and two witnesses at least (Can. 2314, sec. 2).

Canon 1325, sec. 2, defines the terms used in this censure. " If anyone, after having received baptism, while retaining the name of Christian pertinaciously denies any of the doctrines which are to be believed by divine and Catholic faith or doubts about it, he is a heretic; if he wholly abandons the Christian faith, he is an apostate; finally, if he refuses to be subject to the Roman Pontiff or to communicate with the members of the Church subject to him, he is a schismatic."

Canon 2318

II. In excommunicationem Sedi Apostolicae speciali modo reservatam ipso facto incurrunt, opere publici juris facto, editores librorum apostatarum, haereticorum et schismaticorum, qui apostasiam, haeresim, schisma propugnant, itemque eosdem libros aliosve per apostolicas litteras nominatim prohibitos defendentes aut scienter sine debita licentia legentes vel retinentes.

Editores.—The publishers of books defending apostasy, heresy, and schism, written by apostates, heretics, and schismatics, incur this censure when the book is published.

Defendentes.—Also those who defend those same books or others prohibited by name by apostolic letters, such as Fénelon's *Explication des Maximes des Saints.*

Legentes.—Those who read them without leave knowing that they are forbidden under censure.

Retinentes.—Retaining for any purpose whatever without leave.

Canon 2322

III. Ad ordinem sacerdotalem non promotus si Missae celebrationem simulaverit aut sacramentalem confessionem exceperit, excommunicationem ipso facto contrahit, speciali modo Sedi Apostolicae reservatam; et insuper laicus quidem privetur pensione aut munere, si quod habeat in Ecclesia, aliisque poenis pro gravitate culpae puniatur; clericus vero deponatur.

Simulaverit.—So that onlookers think he is saying Mass.

Confessionem.—So that the penitent makes his confession with a view to absolution.

Canon 2332

IV. Omnes et singuli cujuscumque status, gradus seu conditionis etiam regalis, episcopalis vel cardinalitiae fuerint, a legibus, decretis, mandatis Romani Pontificis pro tempore existentis ad Universale Concilium appellantes, sunt suspecti de haeresi et ipso facto contrahunt excommunicationem Sedi Apostolicae speciali modo reservatam.

Appellantes.—Physical persons who appeal from the Pope to an Oecumenical Council, not to a future Pope or to the reigning Pope better informed.

Canon 2333

V. Recurrentes ad laicam potestatem ad impediendas litteras vel acta quaelibet a Sede Apostolica vel ab ejusdem Legatis profecta, eorumve promulgationem vel executionem directe vel indirecte prohibentes, aut eorum causa sive eos ad quos pertinent litterae vel acta sive alios laedentes vel perterrefacientes, ipso facto subjaceant excommunicationi Sedi Apostolicae speciali modo reservatae.

Recurrentes.—Those incur this censure who with effect have recourse to the civil authority to impede any letters or acts of any kind issued by the Holy See, the Roman Congregations, Offices, Legates, Nuncios, Apostolic Delegates.

Prohibentes.—Preventing in any way their promulgation and execution.

Laedentes.—Injuring and frightening with effect those to whom the letters belong or others concerned in their promulgation and execution.

Canon 2334

VI. Excommunicatione latae sententiae speciali modo Sedi Apostolicae reservata plectuntur:

(1) Qui leges, mandata, vel decreta contra libertatem aut jura Ecclesiae edunt.

(2) Qui impediunt directe vel indirecte exercitium jurisdictionis ecclesiasticae sive interni sive externi fori, ad hoc recurrentes ad quamlibet laicalem potestatem.

Edunt.—Public authorities who make laws, issue mandates and decrees against the liberty and rights of the Church, incur this censure.

Impediunt.—As also do those who hinder with effect in any way the exercise of ecclesiastical jurisdiction by having recourse to any sort of lay authority.

Canon 2341

VII. Si quis contra praescriptum [privilegii fori] ausus fuerit ad judicem laicum trahere aliquem ex S.R.E. Cardinalibus, vel Legatis Sedis Apostolicae, vel officialibus majoribus Romanae Curiae, ob negotia ad eorum munus pertinentia, vel Ordinarium proprium, contrahit ipso facto excommunicationem Sedi Apostolicae speciali modo reservatam.

Trahere.—Those who without leave of the Holy See summon as defendants, not as witnesses, Cardinals, Nuncios, Delegates Apostolic, or their own Ordinary before a lay judge in a civil or criminal action incur this censure.

Ausus.—Full knowledge and deliberation are required to incur the censure.

Canon 2343

VIII. Qui violentas manus injecerit in personam S.R.E. Cardinalis vel Legati Romani Pontificis . . . Patriarchae, Archiepiscopi, Episcopi etiam titularis tantum, incurrit in excommunicationem latae sententiae Sedi Apostolicae speciali modo reservatam.

Violentas.—One who inflicts an injury which amounts to a grievous sin on the body, liberty, or dignity of any of the Prelates mentioned incurs this censure. The injury must be personal and by deed, not by word.

Canon 2345

IX. Usurpantes vel detinentes per se vel per alios bona aut jura ad Ecclesiam Romanam pertinentia, subjaceant excommunicationi latae sententiae speciali modo Sedi Apostolicae reservatae.

Usurpantes.—Seizing and holding as one's own what belongs to another.

Detinentes.—Keeping what belongs to the Roman Church though it might have been bought from another who seized it.

Jura.—Rights of all sorts, but here the rights of the Temporal Power of the Pope are specially intended.

Canon 2360

X. Omnes fabricatores vel falsarii litterarum decretorum vel rescriptorum Sedis Apostolicae vel iisdem litteris, decretis vel rescriptis scienter utentes incurrunt ipso facto in excommunicationem speciali modo Sedi Apostolicae reservatam.

Fabricatores.—Forgers and falsifiers of letters, decrees, and rescripts of the Holy See are all subject to this censure.

Utentes.—Those who make use of letters, decrees, and rescripts forged or falsified by others. They must know that the documents which they use are forged or falsified.

Canon 2363

XI. Si quis per seipsum vel per alios confessarium de sollicitationis crimine apud Superiores falso denunciaverit, ipso facto incurrit in excommunicationem speciali modo Sedi Apostolicae reservatam, a qua nequit ullo in casu absolvi, nisi falsam denuntiationem formaliter retractaverit, et damna, si qua inde secuta sint, pro viribus reparaverit, imposita insuper gravi ac diuturna poenitentia, firmo praescripto Can. 894. By Canon 894 the sin, apart from the censure, is reserved to the Holy See.

On this matter, see above, Penance, Chapter XI.

C.—Excommunications Simply Reserved to the Holy See

Canon 2237, sec. 2, provides that in occult cases the Ordinary can remit, himself or through another, penalties *latae sententiae* imposed by common law, except censures very specially or only specially reserved to the Apostolic See.

Canon 2327

I. Quaestum facientes ex indulgentiis plectuntur ipso facto excommunicatione Sedi Apostolicae simpliciter reservata.

Quaestum.—Granting or publishing indulgences for money.

Canon 2335

II. Nomen dantes sectae massonicae aliisve ejusdem generis associationibus quae contra Ecclesiam vel legitimas civiles potestates machinantur, contrahunt ipso facto excommunicationem Sedi Apostolicae simpliciter reservatam.

Nomen dantes.—Becoming a member of the society.

Sectae massonicae.—The society of Freemasons.

Aliisve.—Other societies which are like the Freemasons in that they plot against the Catholic Church or against lawful civil authority, or against both. It is immaterial whether they plot openly or secretly, whether they take a secret oath or an oath of secrecy or not. The only conditions which this canon requires are that the members should form an organized society, a body corporate, and that the society should plot, work by action, speech, writing, against the Church or against lawful civil authority.

Canon 2338

III. Sec. i. Absolvere praesumentes sine debita facultate ab excommunicatione latae sententiae specialissimo vel speciali modo Sedi Apostolicae reservata, incurrunt ipso facto in excommunicationem Sedi Apostolicae simpliciter reservatam.

Praesumentes.—With knowledge of the fact and of the circumstances.

Specialissimo vel speciali.—Not simply reserved cases.

Sec. ii. Impendentes quodvis auxilium vel favorem excommunicato vitando in delicto propter quod excommunicatus fuit; itemque clerici scienter et sponte in divinis cum eodem communicantes et ipsum in divinis officiis recipientes, ipso facto incurrunt in excommunicationem Sedi Apostolicae simpliciter reservatam.

Impendentes.—Giving any sort of material assistance, help, support, or moral encouragement and support.

Vitando.—To an excommunicate who is to be avoided.

Delicto.—Precisely in the crime on account of which he is excommunicated.

Clerici recipientes.—The rector of a church allowing him to say Mass, etc., not others who assist at it.

Scienter et sponte.—Crass ignorance and fear excuse from the censure.

In divinis.—In divine worship, not in secular matters.

Canon 2341

IV. Si quis contra praescriptum [privilegii fori] ausus fuerit ad judicem laicum trahere . . . alium Episcopum etiam mere titularem, aut Abbatem vel Praelatum *nullius*, vel aliquem ex supremis religionum juris pontificii Superioribus excommunicationem latae sententiae Sedi Apostolicae simpliciter reservatam incurrit.

See above, p. 272 *f.*

Canon 2342

V. Plectuntur ipso facto excommunicatione Sedi Apostolicae simpliciter reservata:

(1) Clausuram monialium violantes, cujuscumque generis aut conditionis vel sexus sint, in earum monasteria sine legitima licentia ingrediendo, pariterque eos introducentes vel admit-

tentes; quod si clerici sint, praeterea suspendantur per tempus pro gravitate culpae ab Ordinario definiendum.

(3) Moniales e clausura illegitime exeuntes contra praescriptum Can. 601.

Clausuram monialium.—The papal enclosure of nuns with solemn vows. The enclosure comprises the whole convent except the church and adjoining sacristy and the parlour near the door.

Violantes.—By going into the enclosure without leave of the Holy See. Canon 600 gives the exceptions, which are: The local Ordinary and regular superior with companions on visitation, the confessor, civil rulers with their wives and attendants, Cardinals; with the permission of the abbess and the approbation of the local Ordinary, the doctor, surgeon, workmen for necessary repairs.

Cujuscumque.—Clerics, laymen, women, children under the age of puberty.

Introducentes.—Those who conduct them inside, open the door for them.

Admittentes.—Superioresses, porteresses, whose duty it is to keep them out.

The law of enclosure for nuns not only forbids externs to enter the convent enclosure without leave, but it also prohibits the nuns from leaving it without special leave of the Holy See except in imminent danger of death or other very serious evil (Can. 601).

(2) Mulieres violantes regularium virorum clausuram et Superiores aliique, quicumque ii sint, eas cujuscumque aetatis introducentes vel admittentes; et praeterea religiosi introducentes vel admittentes priventur officio, si quod habeant, et voce activa ac passiva.

Mulieres.—Not, therefore, men, who may enter the enclosure of regular orders of men.

Regularium.—Who take solemn vows.

Superiores.—Higher and lower, porters and others.

The rest is clear from what has been said above.

Canon 2346

VI. Si quis bona ecclesiastica cujuslibet generis sive mobilia sive immobilia, sive corporalia sive incorporalia, per se vel per alios in proprios usus convertere et usurpare praesumpserit aut impedire ne eorumdem fructus seu reditus ab iis ad quos jure pertinent percipiantur, excommunicationi tamdiu subjaciat quamdiu bona ipsa integre restituerit, praedictum impedimentum removerit, ac deinde a Sede Apostolica absolutionem impetraverit.

One who, with full knowledge of the crime and its penalty, converts ecclesiastical property of any sort to his own use, or prevents its revenues going to the persons to whom they belong, cannot obtain absolution, which must be asked of the Holy See, until he has made full restitution and removed the obstacle in the way of the revenues going to those who have a right to them.

Canon 2351

VII. [Mortui ex duello aut ex vulnere inde relato privantur ecclesiastica sepultura nisi ante mortem aliqua dederint poenitentiae signa, ac praeterea] duellum perpetrantes aut simpliciter ad illud provocantes vel ipsum acceptantes vel quamlibet operam aut favorem praebentes, nec non de industria spectantes illudque permittentes vel quantum in ipsis est non prohibentes, cujuscumque dignitatis sint, subsunt ipso facto excommunicationi Sedi Apostolicae simpliciter reservatae.

Duellum.—A single combat with deadly weapons undertaken by agreement. Those who actually fight or challenge, or accept a duel, or afford any assistance or favour to those who do, incur this censure. Spectators of set purpose, those who permit it or do not stop it as far as they can, though they be kings or generals of armies, also incur it.

Canon 2388

VIII. Clerici in sacris constituti vel regulares aut moniales post votum sollemne castitatis, itemque omnes cum aliqua ex praedictis personis matrimonium etiam civiliter tantum contrahere praesumentes, incurrunt in excommunicationem latae sententiae Sedi Apostolicae simpliciter reservatam.

All who have taken a solemn vow of chastity and who presume to attempt marriage, as well as all who knowingly contract marriage with any of them, incur this censure.

Canon 2392

IX. Delictum perpetrantes simoniae in quibuslibet officiis, beneficiis aut dignitatibus ecclesiasticis incurrunt in excommunicationem latae sententiae Sedi Apostolicae simpliciter reservatam.

Delictum simoniae.—Not merely internal but external simony. Canon 728 provides that " when there is question of simony buying and selling, exchange, etc., are to be taken in a wide sense for any convention or agreement although not put into effect, even tacit, in which a simoniacal intention is not manifested expressly but may be gathered from the circumstances." Simony, then, whether of divine or ecclesiastical law, which is committed externally in election, presentation, or collation of ecclesiastical offices, benefices, or dignities, is punished by this censure and by other penalties here and in Canon 729.

Canon 2405

X. Vicarius Capitularis aliive omnes tam de Capitulo quam extranei, qui documentum quodlibet ad Curiam episcopalem pertinens sive per se sive per alium subtraxerint vel destruxerint vel celaverint vel substantialiter immutaverint, incurrunt ipso facto in excommunicationem Sedi Apostolicae simpliciter reservatam.

The terms of the censure are wide and clear. The document, whether public or private, must be of some importance, and must belong to the episcopal Curia as such.

D.—Excommunications Reserved to the Ordinary

Canon 2319

I. Subsunt excommunicationi latae sententiae Ordinario reservatae catholici:

(1) Qui matrimonium ineunt coram ministro acatholico contra praescriptum Can. 1063, sec. 1.

(2) Qui matrimonio uniuntur cum pacto explicito vel implicito ut omnis vel aliqua proles educetur extra catholicam Ecclesiam.

(3) Qui scienter liberos suos acatholicis ministris baptizandos offerre praesumunt.

(4) Parentes vel parentum locum tenentes qui liberos in religione acatholica educandos vel instituendos scienter tradunt.

Four classes of persons are punished by this censure reserved to the Ordinary:

(1) Catholics who contract marriage before a non-Catholic minister, not acting as a civil officer but as a minister of religion, whether only one or both of the parties are Catholics, whether or not a Catholic marriage is also contemplated before or after. Canon 1063 is as follows: " Etsi ab Ecclesia obtenta

sit dispensatio super impedimento mixtae religionis, conjuges nequeunt, vel ante vel post matrimonium cöram Ecclesia initum, adire quoque sive per se sive per procuratorem ministrum acatholicum uti sacris addictum, ad matrimonialem consensum praestandum vel renovandum." Section 2 of this Canon forbids the parish priest to assist at a marriage if he knows that the parties have transgressed or are going to transgress this law. Section 3 allows the exception when the non-Catholic minister acts as a civil officer, and the law requires it.

(2) Catholics who marry with an explicit or implicit agreement that all or any one of the offspring of the marriage are to be brought up outside the Church. The censure would not be incurred if the agreement were made after the marriage had been contracted.

(3) Catholics who knowingly presume to offer their children to non-Catholic ministers for Baptism. Ignorance of the law or only of the censure, or of the fact that those to whom the children are offered are non-Catholic ministers, will excuse from the censure, though it be crass and supine.

(4) Parents or those who hold the place of parents who knowingly give their children to be educated or trained in a non-Catholic religion. Again, even crass ignorance excuses from the censure. *Educated* means taught and brought up in general, *trained* means taught in some special branch or branches when the general education has been completed.

Canon 2326

II. Qui falsas reliquias conficit, aut scienter vendit, distribuit, vel publicae fidelium venerationi exponit, ipso facto excommunicationem Ordinario reservatam contrahit.

Scienter affects only those who sell, distribute, or expose false relics to the public veneration of the faithful, not those who make them.

Canon 2343

III. Qui violentas manus injecerit in personam aliorum clericorum vel utriusque sexus religiosorum, subjaceat ipso facto excommunicationi Ordinario proprio reservatae.

Clericorum.—The inferior clergy, comprising all who have received the first tonsure up to bishops.

Religiosorum.—Religious of both sexes, whether under solemn or simple vows, perpetual or temporary, lay brothers and lay sisters, and also novices, but not postulants. Members of communities living together in common under the rule of superiors according to approved constitutions, but without vows, enjoy the privileges of clerics, according to Canon 680, and this among the rest. Tertiaries who satisfy this condition enjoy the privilege, but not otherwise.

Canon 2350

IV. Procurantes abortum, matre non excepta, incurrunt, effectu secuto, in excommunicationem latae sententiae Ordinario reservatam.

Procurantes.—Using physical or moral means with the intention of prematurely causing the ejection of the fœtus— *i.e*, before the seventh month of gestation.

Matre.—Before the Code some authors excepted the mother.

Effectu.—For the censure to be incurred, it must be certain that abortion followed from the means used.

Canon 2385

V. Religiosus, apostata a religione, ipso jure incurrit in excommunicationem proprio Superiori majori, vel, si religio sit laicalis aut non exempta, Ordinario loci in quo commoratur, reservatam.

Apostata a religione dicitur professus a votis perpetuis sive sollemnibus sive simplicibus, qui e domo religiosa illegitime egreditur cum animo non redeundi vel qui etsi legitime egressus, non redit, eo animo ut religiosae obedientiae sese subtrahat. Malitiosus animus jure praesumitur si religiosus intra mensem nec reversus fuerit, nec Superiori animum redeundi manifestaverit (Can. 644, secs. 1, 2).

Canon 2388

VI. Professi votorum simplicium perpetuorum tam in Ordinibus quam in Congregationibus religiosis [matrimonium etiam civiliter tantum itemque cum aliqua ex praedictis personis contrahere praesumentes] omnes excommunicatio tenet latae sententiae Ordinario reservata.

See above, p. 277.

E.—Excommunications Reserved to No One

From a censure which is not reserved any confessor in the tribunal of Penance, and outside the tribunal of Penance anyone who has jurisdiction over the culprit in the external forum can give absolution (Can. 2253).

Canon 2318

I. Auctores et editores qui sine debita licentia sacrarum Scripturarum libros vel eorum adnotationes aut commentarios imprimi curant, incidunt ipso facto in excommunicationem nemini reservatam.

Auctores.—Authors of notes and commentaries on Holy Scripture.

Licentia.—Leave of the Ordinary of the author, or of the place where the notes, etc., are printed or published.

Imprimi.—Having the books or notes or commentaries printed is what is forbidden under censure without leave.

Canon 2339

II. Qui ausi fuerint mandare seu cogere tradi ecclesiasticae sepulturae infideles, apostatas a fide, vel haereticos, schismaticos, aliosve sive excommunicatos sive interdictos, contra praescriptum Can. 1240, sec. 1 contrahunt excommunicationem latae sententiae nemini reservatam.

Ausi.—Crass ignorance excuses from the censure.

Mandare.—Public authority is to be understood.

Sepulturae.—Which consists not only of burial in consecrated ground, but in transferring the corpse to the church and therein holding a funeral service (Can. 1204). So that mere burial would not incur the censure.

Canon 2347

III. Quod si beneplacitum apostolicum in memoratis Canonibus 534, sec. 1, 1532 praescriptum [ad alienanda bona ecclesiastica] fuerit scienter praetermissum omnes quovis modo reos sive dando sive recipiendo sive consensum praebendo manet excommunicatio latae sententiae nemini reservata.

Scienter.—Full knowledge that there is question of ecclesiastical property, that leave of the Holy See is required for its alienation, and this under censure.

Omnes.—Not only the giver and the receiver, but all whose consent is required for the transaction, and who gave it.

Canon 2352

IV. Excommunicatione nemini reservata ipso facto plectuntur omnes, qualibet etiam dignitate fulgentes, qui quoquo modo cogant sive virum ad statum clericalem amplectendum, sive virum aut mulierem ad religionem ingrediendam vel ad emittendam religiosam professionem tam sollemnem quam simplicem, tam perpetuam quam temporariam.

Cogant.—By violence, threats, instilling grave fear.

Emittendam.—Compelling them after they have entered freely to make their profession against their will.

Canon 2368

V. Fidelis qui scienter omiserit eum a quo sollicitatus fuerit, intra mensem denunciare contra praescriptum Can. 904 incurrit in excommunicationem latae sententiae nemini reservatam, non absolvendus nisi postquam obligationi satisfecerit, aut se satisfacturum serio promiserit.

Fidelis.—He who has been solicited and who refuses to denounce the culprit is subject to this censure, not someone else who knows of the crime.

See above on Penance, Chapter XI.

CHAPTER II

SPECIAL SUSPENSIONS

I. Si clericus, non obtenta ab Ordinario loci licentia, aliam personam [infra Praelatum] privilegio fori fruentem ausus fuerit ad judicem laicum trahere, incurrit ipso facto in suspensionem ab Officio reservatam Ordinario (Can. 2341).

II. Sacerdos qui sine necessaria jurisdictione praesumpserit sacramentales confessiones audire, est ipso facto suspensus a divinis; qui vero a peccatis reservatis absolvere, ipso facto suspensus est ab audiendis confessionibus (Can. 2366).

III. Episcopus aliquem consecrans in Episcopum, Episcopi, vel loco Episcoporum, presbyteri assistentes, et qui consecrationem recipit sine apostolico mandato, contra praescriptum Can. 953, ipso jure suspensi sunt, donec Sedes Apostolica eos dispensaverit (Can. 2370).

IV. Omnes, etiam episcopali dignitate aucti, qui per simoniam ad ordines scienter promoverint, vel promoti fuerint, aut alia sacramenta ministraverint vel receperint, sunt suspecti de haeresi; clerici praeterea suspensionem incurrunt Sedi Apostolicae reservatam (Can. 2371).

V. Suspensionem a divinis Sedi Apostolicae reservatam, ipso facto contrahunt, qui recipere ordines praesumunt ab excommunicato vel suspenso vel interdicto post sententiam declaratoriam vel condemnatoriam; aut a notorio apostata, haeretico, schismatico; qui vero bona fide a quopiam eorum sit ordinatus, exercitio careat ordinis sic recepti donec dispensetur (Can. 2372).

VI. In suspensionem per annum ab ordinum collatione Sedi Apostolicae reservatam ipso facto incurrunt:

(1) Qui contra praescriptum Can. 955 alienum subditum sine Ordinarii proprii litteris dimissoriis ordinaverint.

(2) Qui subditum proprium qui alibi tanto tempore moratus sit ut canonicum impedimentum contrahere ibi potuerit, ordinaverint contra praescriptum Can. 993, n. 4; 994.

(3) Qui aliquem ad ordines majores sine titulo canonico promoverint contra praescriptum Can. 974, sec. 1, n. 57.

(4) Qui salvo legitimo privilegio, religiosum, ad familiam pertinentem quae sit extra territorium ipsius ordinantis, pro-

moverint, etiam cum litteris dimissorialibus proprii Superioris, nisi legitime probatum fuerit aliquem e casibus occurrere de quibus in Can. 966 (Can. 2373).

VII. Qui sine litteris vel cum falsis dimissoriis litteris, vel ante canonicam aetatem, vel per saltum, ad ordines malitiose accesserit, est ipso facto a recepto ordine suspensus (Can. 2374).

VIII. Religiosus fugitivus ipso facto incurrit in privationem officii si quod in religione habeat, et in suspensionem proprio Superiori majori reservatam, si sit in sacris (Can. 2386).

IX. Religiosus clericus cujus professio ob admissum ab ipso dolum nulla fuerit declarata, si sit in minoribus ordinibus constitutus, e statu clericali abjiciatur; si in majoribus, ipso facto suspensus manet, donec Sedi Apostolicae aliter visum fuerit (Can. 2387).

X. Professus votorum perpetuorum ordinatus in sacris dimissus ob delicta minora iis de quibus in Can. 670, ipso facto suspensus manet, donec a Sancta Sede absolutionem obtinuerit (Can. 671).

XI. Clericus qui in manus laicorum officium, beneficium, aut dignitatem ecclesiasticam resignare praesumpserit, ipso facto in suspensionem a divinis incurrit (Can. 2400).

XII. Abbas vel Praelatus *nullius* qui contra praescriptum Can. 322, sec. 2, benedictionem non receperit, est ipso facto a jurisdictione suspensus (Can. 2402).

XIII. Vicarius Capitularis concedens litteras dimissorias pro ordinatione contra praescriptum Can. 958, sec. 1, n. 3, ipso facto subjacet suspensioni a divinis (Can. 2409).

XIV. Superiores religiosi qui contra praescriptum Can. 965-967 subditos suos ad Episcopum alienum ordinandos remittere praesumpserint ipso facto suspensi sunt per mensem a Missae celebratione (Can. 2410).

CHAPTER III
SPECIAL INTERDICTS

I. Universitates, Collegia, Capitula, aliaeve personae morales, quocunque nomine nuncupentur [a legibus, decretis, mandatis, Romani Pontificis pro tempore exsistentis ad Universale Concilium appellantia] interdictum speciali modo Sedi Apostolicae reservatum incurrunt (Can. 2332).

II. Scienter celebrantes vel celebrari facientes divina in locis interdictis vel admittentes ad celebranda officia divina per censuram vetita clericos excommunicatos, interdictos, suspensos, post sententiam declaratoriam vel condemnatoriam, interdictum ab ingressu ecclesiae ipso jure contrahunt, donec arbitrio ejus cujus sententiam contempserunt congruenter satisfecerint (Can. 2338, sec. 3).

III. Qui causam dederunt interdicto locali aut interdicto in communitatem seu collegium, sunt ipso facto personaliter interdicti (Can. 2338, sec. 4).

IV. Sponte sepulturam [ecclesiasticam infidelibus, apostatis, a fide, vel haereticis, schismaticis aliisve sive excommunicatis sive interdictis, contra praescriptum Can. 1240, sec. 1] donantes, interdictum ab ingressu ecclesiae Ordinario reservatum contrahunt (Can. 2339).

V. Catholici qui matrimonium mixtum etsi validum sine Ecclesiae dispensatione inire ausi fuerint, ipso facto ab actibus legitimis ecclesiasticis et sacramentalibus exclusi manent, donec ab Ordinario dispensationem obtinuerint (Can. 2375).

BOOK XI
IRREGULARITIES

CHAPTER I
IRREGULARITY IN GENERAL

1. SOME men are incapable of performing the duties attached to Orders, or, if not altogether incapable, they cannot perform them with that decency and edification which their sacred character and the Church require. A blind man cannot administer the sacraments, and one who has been guilty of great and notorious crimes is not a suitable person to exercise such holy offices and guide others in the way of virtue. Certain defects, then, and crimes, partly from the nature of things, partly because the Church has so ordained, constitute a bar to the reception of Orders. These are called irregularities, and an irregularity is commonly defined to be a canonical impediment which primarily prevents the reception of Orders, and, secondarily, the lawful exercise of the duties and rights annexed to them. It is an impediment constituted by law, though it has its foundation in the nature of things, and so there can be no irregularity unless it is expressly sanctioned by law (Can. 983). It does not make the reception of Orders or their exercise invalid; it only makes these acts gravely sinful in one who is under irregularity, and forbids under pain of grave sin the admission of such a one to the clerical state or the conferring of Orders on him. When Orders have been already received, an irregularity can only produce its secondary effect and hinder their lawful exercise (Can. 968, sec. 2). Even this effect has place only in respect of sacred Orders, for, according to present discipline, laymen may lawfully exercise the functions of the minor Orders, with the exception of those of the exorcist.

2. Irregularities are said to be *from defect* when they arise from an incapability of exercising the functions of Orders or from the indecency there would be in exercising them. They are said to be *from crime* when the Church has expressly laid down that the commission of such a crime shall entail irregularity in the delinquent.

Irregularity is perpetual and lasts for life unless it is removed by dispensation, and no dispensation can be granted for some irregularities arising from defect (Can. 983).

Irregularity which prevents the reception of Orders, and consequently the exercise of them, is said to be *total;* that which supervenes on the reception of Orders and only prevents their lawful exercise is *partial*.

3. As only males and those who are baptized can be validly ordained, the same two conditions are required in order to be subject to irregularity. There is nothing to prevent the same person from being subject to several different irregularities arising from different defects or crimes, nor from being subject to several irregularities of the same species arising from several crimes committed against different people, as from several homicides; but otherwise only one irregularity is contracted from one and the same cause though several times repeated, and so a priest who while under suspension celebrates Mass several times only incurs one irregularity (Can. 989).

Whenever there is a doubt either of law or of fact as to whether an irregularity has been incurred, almost all authorities agree that in practice it must be held not to have been incurred.

Irregularities are incurred even by those who are ignorant of them (Can. 988).

Besides irregularities which of themselves are perpetual impediments to the reception of Orders, the Code enumerates certain simple impediments which cease to exist on certain conditions. They are: (1) The sons of non-Catholics as long as their parents remain in error; (2) husbands who have wives; (3) those who hold an office forbidden to clerics; (4) slaves; (5) those bound to military service; (6) neophytes; (7) those who labour under infamy of fact (Can. 987).

CHAPTER II

IRREGULARITIES FROM DEFECT

THE illegitimate are irregular from defect of birth (Can. 984).

1. Defect of birth arises from illegitimacy, when the parents are either not married at all, or their marriage in the eyes of the Church is null and void on account of some diriment impediment known to both parties. If the impediment was unknown to at least one of the parents, the marriage is called putative, and the offspring is legitimate. When there is a doubt concerning legitimacy, as in the case of foundlings, legitimacy may be presumed until the contrary is proved.

This irregularity ceases by legitimation, dispensation, and solemn religious profession. If the parents at the time of conception or birth of the child could have been married, the child is by ecclesiastical law legitimized by subsequent marriage (Can. 1116); otherwise it can only be legitimized by the rescript of the Pope. A dispensation from this irregularity may be granted by the Pope, and by delegated authority by bishops, regular prelates, and others. Solemn religious profession takes away the irregularity as far as it is a bar to the reception of Orders, but not so as to enable the party to accept prelacies in the Order without dispensation.

2. Any bodily defect which makes it impossible to say Mass and fulfil the other functions of Orders, or prevents the person afflicted from exercising the sacred ministry with decency and edification, constitutes an irregularity. Thus the blind, deaf, mute, lame, crippled or maimed in limb or even necessary fingers, notably deformed, and those who cannot drink wine, are irregular.

In case of doubt the bishop may decide as to whether a person is irregular, and in such a case he may dispense as far as is necessary. If the irregularity is certain, only the Pope or his delegate can dispense. A dispensation from this impediment is more easily granted after ordination than before, to enable a priest to exercise his functions.

3. Marriage as a sacrament symbolizes the union of Christ with his Church, but to represent that union perfectly it should be a marriage of one man with one woman. In a

second marriage the representation is less perfect, and such a bigamous marriage gives rise to the irregularity from defect of the sacrament.

A man becomes irregular from bigamy when he has contracted two or more valid marriages in succession.

4. Defect of lenity may cause irregularity in two ways:

(1) In the case of a judge who has passed sentence of death.

(2) In those who have undertaken the office of executioners of a death sentence and their voluntary and immediate assistants.

5. Loss of reputation, or infamy, is a cause of irregularity. Those who are guilty of certain grave crimes are declared by canon law to be *ipso facto* infamous, and become irregular.

6. Those who are or who have been epileptics, insane, or possessed by the devil are irregular; if they became such after being ordained and are now certainly free, the Ordinary can permit his subjects to exercise again the Orders which they have received.

CHAPTER III

IRREGULARITIES ARISING FROM CRIME

According to Canon 985, the following are irregular from crime. These crimes, however, do not cause irregularity unless they were grave, external sins, whether public or occult, and committed after Baptism, except in the case of receiving Baptism from non-Catholics (Can. 986).

(1) Apostates from the faith, heretics, schismatics.

(2) Those who have allowed themselves to be baptized by non-Catholics in any way except in case of extreme necessity.

(3) Those who have dared to attempt marriage or to go through the form of a civil marriage, when either they themselves are bound by the bond of marriage or of a sacred Order or religious vows though only simple and temporary, or with a woman bound by the same vows or united in a valid marriage.

(4) Those who have committed voluntary homicide, or procured with effect the abortion of a human fœtus, and all who co-operate in these crimes.

(5) Those who have mutilated themselves or others or have attempted to take away their own life.

(6) Clerics who practise medicine or surgery forbidden to them, if death follows therefrom.

(7) Those who exercise an act of Orders reserved to clerics constituted in a sacred Order, when either they do not possess that Order, or have been forbidden its exercise by a canonical penalty, whether personal or local, medicinal or vindictive.

CHAPTER IV

REMOVAL OF IRREGULARITIES

As a general rule irregularities cease only by dispensation granted by the Holy See through the Sacred Congregation on the Discipline of the Sacraments for the external forum, and through the Sacred Penitentiary for the internal forum.

Ordinaries personally or through another have power to dispense their subjects from all irregularities arising from occult crimes, except from voluntary homicide or the procuring of abortion with effect, and others brought before their judicial forum.

All confessors have the same power in more urgent occult cases in which not even the Ordinary can be approached, and there is danger of serious harm or loss of reputation, but only to enable a penitent to exercise lawfully the Orders which he has already received (Can. 990).

When there is a doubt of fact about an irregularity an Ordinary can dispense if the Holy See is accustomed to dispense in such cases (Can. 15).

The simple impediments cease on the total cessation of the cause or fact from which they arise, and by dispensation.

In the petition for a dispensation from irregularities and simple impediments all the irregularities and impediments in the case should be mentioned. A general dispensation will not avail for those not mentioned in bad faith.

If there is question of a dispensation from voluntary homicide, the number of crimes must be mentioned under pain of invalidity of the dispensation (Can. 991).

BOOK XII

INDULGENCES

CHAPTER I

THE NATURE OF AN INDULGENCE

1. IN every sin the teaching of the Catholic Church distinguishes two elements: the *guilt* and the *penalty* which it incurs. The guilt is the injury committed against God by the sinner and the displeasure with which God views the sinful act. If the sin is mortal, it deprives the soul of sanctifying grace and of God's friendship, so that a state of enmity exists between God and the sinner. A venial sin is an injury against God; it is the object of his displeasure, and is a stain on the soul, but it does not rob the soul of sanctifying grace or deprive it of the friendship of God. Besides this guilt a sin deserves and ordinarily receives punishment at the hands of God. It is a law of God's justice that wrongdoing entails suffering either in this world or in the world to come. It is the sanction which in the nature of things is annexed to the great moral law. The penalty for mortal sin, as befits the unrepenting and obstinate enemies of God, is eternal separation from him and punishment in the fires of hell; the penalty for venial sin is temporary punishment in this world or in purgatory. These two elements in sin are not only distinct from each other in thought; they may be, and frequently are, separated in reality. When God pardons mortal sin, the eternal penalty which it deserves in hell is also remitted, but we know from revelation that he frequently exacts from the sinner some temporary punishment for the serious offence which has been committed against him and right order. The guilt of David's adultery was forgiven on his repentance, but he had to endure the loss of the child and other punishments. This is only in keeping with what we might expect at the hands of a wise Providence and with what observation of the order of nature teaches us. A man may truly repent of his sin, and he may have the fullest confidence that God has pardoned it, but he knows that he will have to bear the sad effects of it till his dying day.

This distinction between the guilt of sin and the penalty

due to it is necessary for the understanding of what is meant by an indulgence. An indulgence is not the forgiveness of the guilt of sin; much less is it a permission to commit sin. It is the remission of the temporal punishment which often remains due to sin after its guilt has been forgiven. An indulgence, then, cannot be gained for unrepented sin, nor for sin of which the guilt still stains the soul. If, however, the guilt has been forgiven, any temporal punishment which remains to be suffered in consequence of it may be remitted by indulgences and by other means.

2. As the Catholic Church claims that her divine Founder empowered her ministers to forgive sin, provided that the sinner has the requisite dispositions, so she also lays claim to the power of remitting the temporal punishment due to sin both by the ministration of the sacraments and by granting indulgences. From the first centuries of the Christian era her bishops have used the power to condone temporal punishment due to sin outside sacramental confession, and they have understood that this power was contained in the general power to bind and loose granted to the Apostles and their successors by our Lord. As the Pope has jurisdiction over the whole world, he can grant indulgences to all the faithful; a bishop can only grant indulgences to those who are within his diocese, and up to the limits imposed on him by the supreme authority of the Roman Pontiff (Can. 349, sec. 2, ii).

The doctrine of indulgences is intimately connected with other dogmas of the Catholic faith. When the Church remits temporal punishment due to sin, she does not simply condone it outright in the name of God, but she pays the debt due to sin out of the treasure of the Church. This treasure of the Church is made up of the satisfactions of our Lord and of his saints. Christ and all the members of his Church form one mystical body: "For as in one body we have many members, but all the members have not the same office: so we being many, are one body in Christ, and every one members one of another."[1] "One body and one Spirit: as you are called in one hope of your calling. One Lord, one Faith, one Baptism. One God and Father of all, who is above all, and through all, and in us all."[2] By virtue of this oneness in Christ, there is among the faithful what is called the communion of saints. Not only do all get the benefit of the same sacrifice and sacraments, but the good works of each benefit to some extent all the rest. The merit, indeed, which every good action possesses

[1] Rom. xii 4.   [2] Eph. iv 4-6.

with God, with a view to an eternal reward, is personal and belongs exclusively to the doer of it; but besides meriting, every good action has also a power of placating God and satisfying for sin, as well as a power of impetrating his graces and blessings. The satisfactory part of the good actions of Christ and his saints was not required to satisfy for their own offences, and it is available to satisfy for the sins of those who form with them one mystical body. It needs, however, application to the individual soul, and one of the ways in which this is done is through indulgences. The dispensing of the mysteries of God belongs to the prelates of his Church, and inasmuch as they have jurisdiction over the faithful in this life, indulgences are applied to them directly by the power of the keys.

Over the faithful departed who are suffering for their sins in purgatory the Church has no jurisdiction, but as we can pray for them, and they are helped thereby, so if the Church permits it we can gain indulgences and apply them to the souls of the faithful departed by way of suffrage, asking God to accept the satisfaction offered for the holy souls (Can. 911).

3. A plenary indulgence is one by which all the debt of temporal punishment due to a person for his sins is remitted, while a partial indulgence, of say, forty days, remits the same amount of temporal punishment as would have been remitted by undergoing canonical penance for forty days according to the ancient discipline of the Church.

Indulgences are local, if they can only be gained in a particular place, as by visiting some particular church; they are personal, if they are attached to certain persons who fulfil certain conditions; they are real, if they are attached to a particular object, as to a crucifix or a rosary.

Again, they are temporary if they can only be gained within a specified time; if granted without any time limit, they are perpetual.

CHAPTER II
CONDITIONS REQUIRED FOR GAINING INDULGENCES

1. THERE must always be a just cause for granting an indulgence, otherwise the grantor would not be a faithful dispenser of the mysteries of God, and he would fail in the trust committed to him by God. In practice, however, this does not concern the faithful to whom indulgences are granted; they may rest assured that there is always a just cause for the indulgences which the Church offers for their acceptance.

2. No one can gain an indulgence unless he is a member of the Catholic Church, and, moreover, he must have the requisite intention, he must be in the state of grace, and he must fulfil all the conditions prescribed for gaining the indulgence.

It is not necessary that the intention be actual; it is sufficient if it be virtual, so that there was the wish to gain the indulgence, and it continues to influence the actions whose performance is required for the purpose of gaining the indulgence. It will be sufficient to form an intention in the morning of gaining all the indulgences which may be annexed to any of the good works done during the following day. Some authorities hold that such a virtual intention is not necessary, but that an habitual, or even an interpretative intention, will suffice. An habitual intention is one which was formed and which has not been retracted, but which does not influence the performance of one's actions any longer. An interpretative intention does not exist in reality, but it would be elicited if the agent thought of the matter. Inasmuch as an indulgence is a grant made by the Church to all who fulfil certain conditions, these authors maintain that all pious Catholics who value indulgences gain such as are annexed to their prayers and other good deeds without any special intention. This opinion, however, though probable, is not certain, and so it is safer in practice to follow the other, which requires at least a virtual intention, especially as it is doubtful whether probabilism can be used in this matter. Canon 925, sec. 2, says that a *general* intention is requisite, which many interpret as signifying an habitual intention.

3. The person who gains an indulgence must also be in the state of grace, for one who is in mortal sin, at enmity with

God, and liable to eternal punishment, is not a fit subject for the remission of temporal punishment due to his sins. The Church, too, requires that those who wish to gain the indulgences which she offers to her children should be contrite in heart, or, in other words, in the state of grace, recovered, if they had fallen, by means of sacramental confession, or at least by an act of perfect contrition. When several actions, such as visiting a church, prayer for the Pope, confession, etc., are prescribed for gaining an indulgence, it is not absolutely necessary that all such actions be performed while the agent is in the state of grace; it will be sufficient if the soul be in the state of grace when the last condition is fulfilled and when the indulgence is applied.

4. Finally, all the conditions laid down by him who granted the indulgence must be faithfully fulfilled by anyone who wishes to gain it. If the indulgence be annexed to the saying of a prayer, the prayer must be said with the lips; it is not sufficient to repeat it mentally. Deaf-mutes satisfy the condition by raising their minds to God in the place where public prayers are said by others (Can. 936), and if one of the conditions for gaining an indulgence is visiting a church and praying therein for the intentions of the Holy Father, they may fulfil this condition by visiting the church and praying mentally or reading the prayers from a book.

The ordinary conditions prescribed for gaining a plenary indulgence are: prayer for the intentions of the Sovereign Pontiff, visit to a church, and confession and Holy Communion.

To satisfy the condition of prayer for the intentions of the Pope, any form of prayer which is not already of obligation will suffice. A priest, therefore, could not satisfy this condition by saying his breviary, to which he is already bound by the law of the Church, but it has been decided that when indulgenced prayers are prescribed by a confessor for sacramental penance, the penitent may say his penance and gain the indulgence at the same time. The length of prayer for the Pope's intention is not ordinarily defined, but authors are agreed that five Our Fathers and five Hail Marys will suffice. The Pope's intentions are: the common good of the Church, the propagation of the Faith, the conversion of sinners, heretics, and schismatics, and peace and concord among Christian peoples. To gain the indulgence it is not necessary to have these intentions distinctly in mind; it will be sufficient to pray for the Pope's intentions in general.

The prayers may be said alone or with others alternately, and they may be said anywhere, unless it is specially prescribed that they are to be said while visiting the church.

Unless some special church is mentioned for the visit, any church or public oratory to which the public have free access may be selected. Semi-public oratories of religious and other communities will suffice (Can. 929), but private chapels will not suffice, unless by special indult.

5. Canon 931 specially provides that for the gaining of any indulgences whatever, when confession is required, it may be made within the eight days which immediately precede the day to which the indulgence is annexed, and the Communion may be made on the eve of the same day; and, moreover, both may also be made within the whole of the following octave.

The faithful who are accustomed, unless they are lawfully prevented, to go to sacramental confession at least twice a month, or to receive Holy Communion daily with a right intention and piously, in the state of grace, though they may abstain from it once or twice in the week, can gain all indulgences, even without actual confession, which otherwise would be necessary to gain them, except the indulgences of an ordinary or extraordinary jubilee or one granted after the manner (*ad instar*) of a jubilee.

If a visit to a church or oratory is required for gaining an indulgence annexed to a certain day, the visit may be made at any time between midday on the previous day and midnight which terminates the day itself (Can. 923).

Canon 935 grants power to confessors to commute the good works enjoined for gaining indulgences into other good works in favour of those who are hindered from fulfilling them by any lawful impediment.

The conditions enjoined may be fulfilled in any order.

6. According to the general rule, an indulgence can only be gained once on the day designated, but not infrequently an indulgence is granted *toties quoties*, and then it may be gained as often as the conditions are fulfilled. In this case if confession and Communion, or in general any good work which is not capable of being repeated on the same day, be among the conditions prescribed, such conditions are only fulfilled once, and the others are repeated as often as it is desired to gain the indulgence. When several indulgences are attached to the same action, and this cannot be repeated, as is the case with Holy Communion, all the indulgences may be gained by

the one action. If, however, the action enriched by several sets of indulgences be capable of being repeated on the same day, such as saying the rosary, as a general rule only one set of indulgences determined by him who wishes to gain them can be gained by performing the action once. Pius X, however, by a decree dated June 12, 1907, made an exception to this rule in favour of rosaries enriched with the Croisiers' indulgences, which may now be gained in reciting the rosary cumulatively, together with other indulgences already granted to the same rosaries.

It must frequently happen that plenary indulgences cannot be gained in full on account of some obstacle in the way, such as unforgiven venial sin. In such a case Canon 926 makes it clear that according to the intention of the Church the indulgence takes its effect as far as possible, and becomes in fact a partial indulgence.

7. Almost all indulgences are now applicable to the souls in purgatory (Can. 930). In order that they may be applied to them in fact, the person who fulfils the conditions should form his intention of offering them to God for the benefit of certain souls, or for the benefit of the souls in purgatory in general. It is a controverted point among the theologians whether such application is infallible in its effect or not. The difficulty is about the divine promise to accept such offerings, some theologians holding that such a promise is implicitly contained in the words of our Lord: " Whatsoever you shall loose on earth shall be loosed also in heaven "; others denying this. The negative opinion seems to be more in accordance with the mind and practice of the Church.

Similarly, it is a disputed question among theologians whether one who gains an indulgence for the souls in purgatory must himself be in the state of grace. Many hold that he must be, as he must gain the indulgence himself before he can apply it to the holy souls. Others do not see the necessity of this, for such a one only fulfils the conditions, and on the fulfilment of these the Church offers to God the corresponding satisfactions. Both opinions are probable, but the former is safer in practice.

8. Objects to be indulgenced should be solid and not easily breakable. Hence pictures on paper, and hollow glass beads, may not be indulgenced; but beads made of solid glass, or of iron, or wood, may be.

Objects do not lose their indulgences as long as they remain morally the same. In a rosary the indulgences are attached to the beads, not to the string, so that even though the string be changed, or a few beads be lost and others substituted for them, the indulgences are not lost. When a crucifix is indulgenced, the indulgence is attached to the image, not to the cross.

To prevent the danger of simony, indulgences attached to a movable object are lost if it is sold, or if it is completely destroyed (Can. 924, sec. 2).

CHAPTER III
THE JUBILEE

1. A JUBILEE is a plenary indulgence granted by the Pope with greater solemnity than usual for a definite time, together with special faculties for confessors. The first jubilee was granted by Boniface VIII in the year 1300 with the intention that it should be held thereafter every hundred years, but subsequent Popes changed the period into fifty, thirty-three, and finally into twenty-five years. This is called a greater or ordinary jubilee, to distinguish it from the less or extraordinary jubilee, which the Pope grants on some special occasion, as, to celebrate his election to the papacy. A general jubilee is granted to all the faithful, usually in the first place at Rome, and afterward it is extended to the rest of the world; a particular jubilee is granted to a particular province or religious order.

2. The conditions prescribed for gaining an ordinary jubilee are: confession, Communion, and prayer for the Pope's intentions in churches to be visited for the purpose a certain number of times.

Confession is necessary for those who wish to gain the jubilee even if they are not conscious of mortal sin, and the annual confession which is prescribed by ecclesiastical law will not suffice. If a grievous sin is inadvertently omitted from the jubilee confession, this is nevertheless sufficient for gaining the indulgence, but of course the sin which was forgotten must be mentioned in the next confession. If, after going to confession and before fulfilling the other conditions for gaining the jubilee, mortal sin is committed, the person should go again to confession to gain the indulgence.

A good Communion distinct from the ordinary Easter Communion is another of the conditions to be fulfilled.

At Rome the four basilicas, St Peter's, St Paul's outside the Walls, St John Lateran, and St Mary Major, are usually designated to be visited a certain number of times, and during the visits prayer is to be offered up for the Pope's intention. Outside Rome the churches to be visited are usually left to be determined by the bishop. The visits must be made in one day according to either the civil or the ecclesiastical method of reckoning, or, in other words, reckoning either from midnight to midnight, or from the hour of vespers.

For an extraordinary jubilee, besides the above conditions, fasting and almsgiving are also prescribed.

The fast is a strict one. A day which is not a fasting day by ecclesiastical law must be chosen, unless the contrary is specially conceded in the bull of indiction of the jubilee, and then the strict fast must be observed, nor can advantage be taken of any indult. Even those who are not bound by the ecclesiastical law of fasting must fulfil this condition if they wish to gain the jubilee.

The amount to be given in alms is not generally specified, and any amount will suffice provided that it is not so small as not to deserve the name. Religious, wives, children, and servants, may have their obligation fulfilled for them by superiors, husbands, parents, and masters.

Bishops and confessors receive faculties to commute all the above conditions for ordinary and extraordinary jubilees except prayer, confession, and sometimes Holy Communion. For the lawful and valid use of this faculty there should always be a just cause, and some good work of more or less equal merit should be enjoined in place of that commuted.

3. Regulars who desire to gain the jubilee may choose a confessor from among those, whether secular or regular, who are approved by the bishop, or they may confess to one approved by their superiors. Nuns are sometimes empowered to choose a confessor for the purpose of gaining the jubilee from any priests approved by the bishop; sometimes it is prescribed that the confessor chosen must be one of those who are approved for the confessions of nuns. Confession may be made to the priest thus chosen as often as the penitent desires before the fulfilment of the last condition for gaining the jubilee, but not afterward.

The confessor chosen for the jubilee confession has special faculties given to him by the bull of indiction. This should always be carefully studied in order that the confessor may know the extent of his powers. Ordinarily, he is empowered to absolve penitents from all censures and sins, even those that are reserved. The cases of attempted absolution of an accomplice and a false charge of solicitation are generally excepted, or power to absolve them is only granted under restriction. The absolution would be valid if the penitent who came to confession with the intention of gaining the jubilee afterwards changed his mind and gave up the attempt; and probably the reservation would be removed if a reserved sin were confessed by such a penitent, though the confession were sacrilegious, or inculpably null and void.

Jubilee confessors have also ample faculties granted them for dispensing from vows or commuting them, though vows of perpetual chastity, of entering a religious order with solemn vows, and those which have been accepted by third parties, are usually excepted.

While the greater jubilee is being celebrated at Rome, the special faculties granted to bishops and priests for the internal forum are ordinarily suspended, at least with respect to penitents who can make the journey to Rome.

In the same way during this time other indulgences granted by the Pope in favour of the faithful who are living are suspended, though they may all be gained for the faithful departed. Certain special indulgences, as those for the saying of the Angelus, those granted to the dying, and for the solemn exposition of the Blessed Sacrament, are excepted.

APPENDIX

A SHORT HISTORY OF MORAL THEOLOGY

ETHICS has a special place in the Christian religion. Lactantius, writing under the Emperor Constantine, points out this fundamental difference between paganism and the true religion. Pagan religion, he says, is concerned only with external rites and ceremonies performed in honour of the gods; it gives no precepts of righteousness and virtue; it does not form and cultivate men's characters.[1] On the other hand, ethics forms an essential part of the Christian religion. Christ was called Jesus because he came among us to save us from our sins. This he did not only by atoning for them, but by his example, his teaching, and his grace he showed us how to lead good lives and enabled us to do it. He came to do and to teach, so that not only his words but his actions, too, were lessons to us in conduct. He proposed himself to us as the Way by which we should walk; he bade us follow his example; he taught us to learn of him meekness, humility, and all virtues. In him God, our Creator and Lord, was revealed to us; he is our first beginning and last end. To him we must refer and order our whole lives and our every action. We are his stewards, and when life comes to an end each of us will be called upon to render a strict account to him, as our judge, of every thought, word, and action of our lives. Heaven will be the reward of the faithful servant, eternal suffering in hell will be the just punishment of the wicked.

Before finally quitting the earth our Lord founded his Church, a hierarchical society of men, to continue the work which he had begun for the sanctification and salvation of the whole human race. His last solemn commission to his Apostles was a command to teach men to observe all that he had commanded; certain truths had been revealed to them concerning God, as well as moral rules for their guidance, but even the truths concerning God were not merely speculative; they, too, were revealed for the sanctification and salvation of men. A duty of submission of the intellect, under pain of eternal

---
[1] *De Divinis Instit.*, iv, c. 3.

damnation, was laid on all who heard the Gospel preached. The basis of Christian morality thus rests firmly established on the word of God, requiring unwavering faith, not on the uncertain and shifting sands of human opinion. That Gospel contained not only moral precepts which are obligatory on all, but counsels also of great perfection which those who had the moral strength were encouraged to adopt as rules for the conduct of their lives. The perfect holiness of God himself was held up as the model which they were to imitate and the lofty ideal at which they were ever to aim.

This revelation of Christ was committed to the Church as a sacred deposit to be faithfully kept, guarded from all admixture of error, and diligently preached to men for their instruction, guidance, sanctification, and salvation. The Catholic Church has always understood that this was the object of her foundation by Jesus Christ. That was her mission, to preach the Gospel, to keep the deposit of faith, to teach what Christ had revealed, and not to allow it to be changed or corrupted even by an angel from heaven. It is the boast of the Catholic Church that by the assistance which Christ promised her, through the constant guidance of the indwelling Spirit of Truth which he sent down upon her, she has faithfully accomplished her task. In spite of enemies within and without, in defiance of the hostile powers of hell and of the unbelieving world, she has persisted through the ages in preaching in season and out of season the divine revelation which was committed to her faithful keeping. At first sight it might seem that no history of such a system of doctrine is possible. History is the scientific narration of the varying fortunes and changes which befall the subject of it. What history can there be of a system of doctrine which has always been the same?

The Christian revelation as taught by the Catholic Church does indeed always remain the same in itself, objectively, as it was completed when the last of the Apostles died. This revelation, and nothing else, the Church was commissioned to keep and to preach to the end of time for the salvation of men. It is the Church's greatest boast, as it is her highest claim to our gratitude, that she has ever preserved unsullied through the ages the divine teaching of Jesus of Nazareth. No man ever taught like him. The moral doctrine which he inculcated by word and by deed is the loftiest ideal of conduct which has ever been manifested to the world. It cannot be improved upon, and it is impious to attempt to change it. The

Catholic denies that it has been changed in the Catholic Church. Non-Catholic historians of Christian morals profess to discover instances of change, but this is due to their own philosophical or religious presuppositions. Thus when the Lutheran Dr. Luthardt discovers in the *Didaché*, written, as he acknowledges, at the end of the first century, " the beginnings of a false view of works,"[1] we reply that the same view of works appears in the documents that make up the New Testament, and that it is not false. Lecky discovered a change of view as to the lawfulness of taking human life when Christianity became the official religion of the Roman Empire.[2] In proof of this he quotes Lactantius and one or two other Fathers who held that it is never lawful to take human life. It would not be difficult to quote instances of Christian writers up to our own days who have held the same doctrine, and one might deduce therefrom an argument to show either that Christian morality had progressed, or deteriorated, or had remained stagnant for nineteen centuries, according to the exigencies of one's philosophical system. Harnack discovers the sources of Catholic monachism in the writings of St Methodius.[3] The Catholic sees them writ large in the Gospel of St Matthew.

These instances will show why the Catholic cannot accept the accounts of growth, change, and decay which are given in many so-called histories of Christian morals. Nevertheless, he allows that there is a progress and development which admits of being traced historically. The Catholic Church has always been explicit on this point. After teaching that the revealed doctrines of the Faith were not proposed by God to man's intellect to be improved upon like some philosophical system, but were committed to the Church as a divine deposit to be faithfully kept and infallibly explained, the Council of the Vatican could find no better terms in which to describe true development of that doctrine than those which had been used by St Vincent of Lerins in the fifth century.

" Therefore," it says, " let the understanding, knowledge, and wisdom of each and of all, of individuals as well as of the whole Church, increase and make much and great progress through the ages and the centuries; but only in its own line, that is, in the same truth, in the same sense, and in the same thought."[4] Change in Christian dogma and morals we refuse

[1] *History of Christian Ethics*, p. 117.
[2] *History of European Morals*, ii, p. 42.
[3] *History of Dogma*, iii, p. 110.
[4] Vatican, sess. iii, c. 4.

to accept or to acknowledge; we readily admit that there has been and ought to be development. The precepts of Christian morality have not always been equally well understood; what was obscure and uncertain has been made more clear and certain. The existence of different conditions, circumstances, and wants, in different ages and countries, necessitated some change in the adjustment of the teaching to the varying surroundings. New duties arose from new positive legislation. Besides, the science of Christian morals is not a mere exposition of the moral precepts of the Gospel and of the positive legislation of the Church. Books have been written containing such an exposition in the very words of Scripture, like the *Speculum* of St Augustine, and the *Scintillæ* attributed to Venerable Bede,[1] but such as these are not works of moral theology. The science of moral theology arranges its subject-matter in an orderly and logical way; it shows the grounds and the reasons of the doctrine, it harmonizes part with part so as to form a compact and systematic body of doctrine. All this is the work of time and of many minds, and it admits of historical treatment. In the brief space at our disposal we propose to trace at any rate the chief stages in the development of Catholic moral theology. Our history may conveniently be divided into three periods; the first will embrace the age of the Fathers, the second that of the scholastics, the third will be the modern period.

Section I

The Patristic Period

The end for which Jesus Christ established his Church was the sanctification and salvation of souls. This end the Church was to obtain chiefly by preaching the Gospel which her Founder had revealed and by administering the sacraments which he had instituted.[2] Men were to be sanctified and prepared for eternity by holy living through the grace of God communicated to them principally by means of the sacraments. The Gospels contain a short summary of the general teaching of Jesus Christ; this is developed somewhat in certain directions in the other writings of the New Testament, but the preachers of the Word soon found it convenient to have by them brief summaries of the moral teaching of our Lord by itself. This need was met by such works as the *Didaché*,

[1] Migne, P.L. 88, 598.   [2] Matt. xxviii 19, 20.

or *Teaching of the Twelve Apostles*, composed about the end of the first century, and the *Pastor* of Hermas, written a little later. It would be utterly impossible to give even an outline of the ethical works of all the Fathers of the Church. Together they form a very voluminous and complete course of moral theology, and more than one such course has been put together by simply printing a consecutive selection of their works. Thus in 1791 an Italian priest, Angelo Cigheri, published at Florence his *Veterum Patrum Theologia Universa*, in thirteen volumes quarto, of which the three last are devoted to morals. A fairly complete catalogue of ethical works by the Fathers will be found in the indices of Migne's *Patrology*, arranged under the separate headings which figure in our modern manuals of moral theology. All that we can do here is to select a few typical works which exhibit the gradual development of the science of Christian ethics. The *Didaché* may be looked upon as the first handbook of morals which has come down to us, and it will be worth while to give a short analysis of its contents.

This first handbook of moral theology begins with the first general principle of ethics. All righteousness is summed up in the general precept to avoid evil and do good. The doing of good consists in the observance of the two great commandments of love for our God and for our neighbour. The golden rule is added to the statement of the general first principles of morality. "There are two ways," we read, "one of life and one of death; and there is much difference between the two ways. Now the way of life is this: First thou shalt love God that made thee; secondly, thy neighbour as thyself; and all things whatsoever thou wouldest should not happen to thee, neither do thou to another." The rest of the first chapter is occupied with a development of the precept of love for our neighbour, expressed for the most part in the language of the Sermon on the Mount. The second chapter enumerates some of the principal negative duties toward our neighbour. A similar enumeration occupies the third chapter, but here there is an attempt to give the reason for the different prohibitions, as, for example: "Be not prone to anger, for anger leads to murder; neither a zealot, nor contentious, nor passionate, for from all these things murders are begotten." In the fourth chapter are set down the duties towards preachers of the Gospel, of making peace, of judging righteously, of almsgiving; duties toward parents, children, servants; of avoiding hypocrisy, and not adding to or taking away from the precepts of the Lord which they had been taught. The chapter concludes with, " This is the way of life."

The fifth chapter consists of a long enumeration of sins, and ends with the prayer, " May ye be delivered, children, from all these."

In the sixth chapter there is a warning against being led away from this teaching by anyone, for such a one would not teach according to God. A distinction is drawn between what is required for perfection and what is morally possible. The faithful are bidden specially to beware of what has been sacrificed to idols.

A brief instruction on Baptism occupies the seventh chapter, and in the eighth Christians are taught to fast on Wednesdays and Fridays, so that their fasting-days may be different from those of the Jews, who fasted on Mondays and Thursdays. They are told to say the Our Father three times a day. The ninth and tenth chapters give instructions on the celebration of the Eucharist, while the two following deal with the way in which prophets and strangers should be received. The thirteenth chapter prescribes the offering of firstfruits. In the next chapter the faithful are instructed to meet together on every Lord's Day, to offer the eucharistic sacrifice, after confessing their sins, so that their sacrifice may be pure. Enemies, too, should be reconciled lest the sacrifice be defiled. It was of this sacrifice that Malachias prophesied. The fifteenth chapter deals with the election of bishops and deacons and the respect which is due to them. The duties of fraternal correction, of prayer and almsdeeds, are enjoined as they are contained in the Gospel of our Lord. The last chapter contains an exhortation to watch, and inculcates the necessity of faith and perseverance, for Antichrist will appear and seduce many. The treatise concludes with a short description of the signs of the last day.

The whole of the second book of the *Pastor* of Hermas is a document of early Christian moral teaching very similar to the *Didaché*, but more attempt may be observed in it to show the connection between one prohibition and another, and to give reasons and motives for their observance.

A great advance is observable in the catechetical works of Clement of Alexandria. They are almost exclusively devoted to moral teaching, which their learned author illustrates and confirms by constant quotations from the Greek classical authors. With an enthusiastic and personal love for Jesus Christ, and faith in his teaching as a divine and full revelation of the truth to men, he combines a high esteem for reason and philosophy. According to Clement, philosophy was the pedagogue of the pagan world, preparing it for Christ and leading it to him, as the law did the Jews. Philosophy is the handmaid of theology, he says, and the dictates of reason are but the promptings of the Word which illuminates every man that cometh into the world. This, of course, is but a development of ideas which we find in the Scriptures of the Old and New Testament, and it is a natural consequence of Christian teaching concerning God and his relation to man and to the world. It is a very superficial view which regards the action of Clement and other Fathers in the use they made of reason and philosophy as a corrupting influence in Christian teaching. With them, as with the scholastics in the Middle Ages, that action was the necessary result of a firm faith in the Gospel message, and the natural desire to understand it and penetrate its full meaning as far as possible. It was *Fides quaerens intellectum*, the moving spirit of Catholic theology from the beginning. Better than any lengthy exposition, an extract or two from Clement will show how far the science of moral theology had progressed at the end of the second century. The following extract is taken from an apologetic work entitled *An Exhortation to the Heathen*.

"Wherefore, since the Word himself has come to us from heaven, we need not, I reckon, go any more in search of human learning to Athens and the rest of Greece, and to Ionia. For if we have as our teacher him that filled the universe with his holy energies in creation, salvation, beneficence, legislation, prophecy, teaching, we have the Teacher from whom all instruction comes; and the whole world, with Athens and Greece, has already become the domain of the Word. For you, who believed the poetical fable which designated Minos the Cretan as the bosom friend of Zeus, will not refuse to believe that we who have become the disciples of God have received the only true wisdom; and that which the chiefs of philosophy only guessed at, the disciples of Christ have both apprehended and proclaimed."[1]

The next extract, from the *Pædagogus*, a work containing instructions for recent converts, shows the place which reason or conscience holds in Christian ethics.

"Everything that is contrary to right reason is sin. Accordingly, therefore, the philosophers think fit to define the most generic passions thus: lust, as desire disobedient to reason;

[1] *Exhortation to the Heathen*, c. 11.

fear, as weakness disobedient to reason; pleasure, as an elation of the spirit disobedient to reason. If, then, disobedience in reference to reason is the generating cause of sin, how shall we escape the conclusion that obedience to reason—the Word—which we call Faith, will of necessity be the efficacious cause of duty? For virtue itself is a state of the soul rendered harmonious by reason in respect to the whole life. Nay, to crown all, philosophy itself is pronounced to be the cultivation of right reason; so that, necessarily, whatever is done through error of reason is transgression, and is rightly called sin."[1]

The *Stromata*, or *Miscellanies*, are a collection of materials for the ethical instruction and training of the Christian theologian. The philosophical and theological detail to which Clement descends in the treatment of his subject may be illustrated by an extract from the fourteenth chapter of the second book of the *Stromata*, on the different ways in which an act may be involuntary. The matter, of course, belongs to the treatise on Human Acts, sometimes said to be the last treatise which was added to our manuals of morals.

"What is iunvoluntary is not matter for judgement. But this is twofold—what is done in ignorance, and what is done through necessity. For how will you judge concerning those who are said to sin in involuntary modes? For either one knew not himself, as Cleomenes and Athamas, who were mad; or the thing which he does, as Aeschylus, who divulged the mysteries on the stage, who being tried in the Areopagus was absolved on his showing that he had never been initiated. Or one knows not what is done, as he who has let off his antagonist, and slain his domestic instead of his enemy; or that by which it is done as he who in exercising with spears having buttons on them, has killed someone in consequence of the spear throwing off the button; or knows not the manner how, as he who has killed his antagonist in the stadium, for it was not for his death but for victory that he contended; or knows not the reason why it is done, as the physician who gave a salutary antidote and killed, for it was not for this purpose that he gave it, but to save."[2]

As yet no attempt had been made in the Church to write a systematic treatise of morals by reducing the various virtues and vices to logical order under appropriate general principles. This step was taken by St Ambrose at the end of the fourth century. This great Father and Doctor of the Church com-

---

[1] *Pædagogus*, i, c. 13.   [2] *Stromata*, ii, c. 14.

posed his work *De Officiis* for the instruction of the clergy of his church of Milan. He expressly tells us that he followed Cicero's work with the same title as his pattern. Cicero wrote his book for the instruction of his son; St Ambrose desired to write for the instruction of his spiritual children. Although he followed Cicero closely in the arrangement and treatment of the matter, yet he never loses sight of what appears to have been the chief motive that he had in view in the composition of his work—namely, to demonstrate the superiority of Christian over pagan ethics.

The work is divided, like Cicero's, into three Books. In the first he treats of what is honourable and dishonourable. He points out that the philosophic distinction between ordinary and perfect virtue has its counterpart in the Gospel, which distinguishes between what is matter of strict precept and of counsel. Certain elementary duties, as those toward parents and elders, are touched on, and then follows a discussion on the four cardinal virtues. The second Book treats of what is expedient with reference to eternal life. The third Book treats of what is honourable and expedient in conjunction, and the author has no difficulty in reconciling these conflicting principles according to Christian teaching. "For," he writes, "I said that nothing can be virtuous but what is useful, and nothing can be useful but what is virtuous. For we do not follow the wisdom of the flesh, whereby the usefulness that consists in an abundance of money is held to be of most value, but we follow the wisdom which is of God, whereby those things which are greatly valued in this world are counted but as loss. For this $\kappa\alpha\tau\acute{o}\rho\theta\omega\mu\alpha$, which is duty carried out entirely and in perfection, starts from the true source of virtue. On this follows another or ordinary duty. This shows by its name that no hard or extraordinary practice of virtue is involved, for it can be common to very many."[1] This principle of perfection is then applied to the pursuit of gain and other questions.

A very famous book on morals, somewhat more restricted in scope than the *De Officiis* of St Ambrose, is the *Pastoral Care* of St Gregory the Great. This, together with the same author's *Morals* on Job, was a favourite textbook in the Middle Ages. It lays down the qualities required in those who have the cure of souls, how they themselves should live, how they should instruct and admonish those subject to their authority. The book was brought to England by St Augustine and trans-

[1] *De Officiis*, iii, c. 2.

lated into English by King Alfred for the benefit of the bishops and priests of his kingdom.

A word must here be said on Christian asceticism, which has been so utterly misunderstood and misrepresented by such writers as Lecky and Harnack, and whose true relation to Christian morals is so seldom perceived by non-Catholic authors.

Christ our Lord expressly taught that renunciation of self, of the world with its riches and pleasures, was in a certain sense a necessary condition of discipleship. This renunciation, however, admitted of different degrees, as is also plain from the Gospels. Some were called only to spiritual poverty and detachment, and these hoped to save their souls by remaining in the world without being of it. Outwardly they lived much like other people, but their affections were detached from this world and centred on God and eternity. They went to heaven by the way of the commandments. Others, on the contrary, voluntarily embraced the counsels of poverty, chastity, and obedience, given by our Lord to those who were called, and who felt that they had the spiritual strength to follow the call. They made a special profession of following the counsels, and were assigned a place of honour in the Christian assemblies, but at first they seem to have lived in the bosom of their families. They soon, however, began to find it very difficult to persevere in their adopted form of life while exposed to the distractions and temptations of the world, and this, together with the violence of the persecutions, drove them into the desert. There they lived at first solitary lives as hermits, but before long they began to come together and put themselves under the authority of some ancient Father of the desert renowned for his prudence and sanctity. Their aim was to subdue their passions and ascend the heights of Christian perfection. The task is notoriously difficult both in theory and in practice, and many mistakes were made. The Church had not yet drawn up her minute code of laws for the regulation of religious life. Those writers, however, who industriously pick out the mistakes and the exaggerations of indiscreet fervour, and piece them together to produce a picture of Christian monachism and asceticism, only succeed in producing a caricature. To convince one's self of this it is sufficient to dip into the *Institutes of Monasteries* and the *Conferences* of Cassian, who was in the middle of a long life in the year 400. In the twelve Books of his *Institutes* Cassian describes the dress of the monks, their method of singing the divine office, the training of postulants and novices, and then he devotes the last eight Books to a minute account of the nature, causes, and remedies of the eight principal vices which bar the way to the summit of Christian perfection. He maps out every portion of the pilgrim's progress to his heavenly country, and shows what dangers and obstacles he will meet by the way. In brief, he says, progress toward perfection begins with the fear of God, from which arises a salutary sorrow for sin, which leads to renunciation and contempt of the world; this begets humility, from which springs mortification of the will, and by this all vices are subdued and extirpated. Then all virtues begin to flourish in the soul, which thus arrives at purity of heart and the perfection of apostolic charity.[1]

The vices to be overcome are classed under eight different heads by Cassian, and he says that the classification was admitted by all.[2] These principal or capital vices are typified by the seven people, whom the Israelites were commanded by God to extirpate when they came into the land of promise. Egypt makes the eighth, from which they had been delivered, and which, Cassian says, typifies gluttony. From this vice the monk is indeed delivered by his abandoning the world for the desert, but he may not extirpate it altogether; he should aim only at curbing its excesses. Gregory the Great adopted in substance the teaching of Cassian on the capital vices, but by making pride the queen of all the rest, and placing it in a category by itself, the other seven became the seven deadly sins which with their daughter vices were so famous in the literature of the Middle Ages, and figure in the books of morals and in the catechisms of Christian doctrine to the present day.

To show how conservative the Catholic tradition has been, even in the expression of doctrine, I will give the following passage in St Gregory's own words:

" Ipsa namque vitiorum regina superbia cum devictum plene cor ceperit, mox illud septem principalibus vitiis, quasi quibusdam suis ducibus devastandum tradit. Quos videlicet duces exercitus sequitur, quia ex eis proculdubio importunae vitiorum multitudines oriuntur. Quod melius ostendimus, si ipsos duces atque exercitum specialiter, ut possumus, enumerando proferamus. Radix quippe cuncti mali superbia est, de qua, Scriptura attestante, dicitur: Initium omnis peccati est superbia (*Ecclus.* x 15). Primae autem ejus soboles, septem nimirum principalia vitia, de hac virulenta radice proferuntur,

[1] *De Cœnobiorum Institutis*, lib. iv, c. 43.
[2] *Collatio* v, c. 18.

scilicet inanis gloria, invidia, ira, tristitia, avaritia, ventris ingluvies, luxuria. Nam quia his septem superbiae vitiis nos captos doluit, idcirco Redemptor noster ad spirituale liberationis proelium spiritu sepitformis gratiae plenus venit.

"Sed habent contra nos haec singula exercitum suum. Nam de inani gloria inobedientia, jactantia, hypocrisis, contentiones, pertinaciae, discordiae, et novitatum praesumptiones oriuntur. De invidia, odium, susurratio, detractio, exsultatio in adversis proximi, afflictio autem in prosperis nascitur. De ira, rixae, tumor mentis, contumeliae, clamor, indignatio, blasphemiae proferuntur. De tristitia, malitia, rancor, pusillanimitas, desperatio, torpor circa praecepta, vagatio mentis erga illicita nascitur. De avaritia, proditio, fraus, fallacia, perjuria, inquietudo, violentiae, et contra misericordiam obdurationes cordis oriuntur. De ventris ingluvie, inepta laetitia, scurrilitas, immunditia, multiloquium, hebetudo sensus circa intelligentiam propagantur. De luxuria, caecitas mentis, inconsideratio, inconstantia, praecipitatio, amor sui, odium Dei, affectus praesentis seculi, horror autem vel desperatio futuri generantur. Quia ergo septem principalia vitia tantam de se vitiorum multitudinem proferunt, cum ad cor veniunt, quasi subsequentis exercitus catervas trahunt. Ex quibus videlicet septem quinque spiritalia, duoque carnalia sunt."[1]

The *Conferences* of Cassian are represented by him as the teachings of celebrated abbots on various questions of the spiritual life. They are partly speculative, partly practical. There are twenty-four in all, each being divided into a greater or less number of chapters. These two works have provided an ample store of moral and ascetical doctrine for all subsequent Catholic writers on the subjects treated in them.

A large portion of moral theology is taken up with the duties arising from the positive legislation of the Church. In this legislation we have the practical application of Christian moral principles to the varying requirements of time and place, and change and variety are here conspicuous. With the establishment of the Christian religion the positive precepts of the Mosaic law ceased to be binding, but the Church received from her divine Founder authority to make new laws for the sanctification and salvation of her children. The Apostles used this legislative authority, as we see from the Epistles of St Paul, especially from those to Timothy and Titus, and within twenty years after the Ascension we find them legis-

[1] *Moralium*, lib. xxxi, c. 45.

lating in the Council of Jerusalem on the disputed question of legal observances. The decree which we have in the Acts[1] was a true positive law imposing a new obligation on the faithful concerned, as long as the peculiar circumstances of the time rendered its observance desirable and necessary.[2] This council of the Apostles formed the type and pattern for the oecumenical and provincial councils of the Church which were to be held in the future. Innumerable laws and regulations have been enacted by these, affecting Catholic life, discipline, and worship. The bishops, too, as successors of the Apostles, have continued in all ages to exercise the legislative authority committed by them to God and the Church. The Roman Pontiffs, especially, in the exercise of their jurisdiction over the whole Church in succession to Blessed Peter, have in all ages made wise laws for the peace and prosperity of the Christian people. As instances of this action of the Popes in the early centuries may be mentioned St Clement's first epistle to the Corinthians in the first century, St Victor's decision about the observance of Easter in the second century, St Stephen's about the baptism of heretics in the third, and similar action on the part of Popes Liberius, Damasus, and Siricius. Subsequently papal decisions became frequent and notorious. Collections of the decisions issuing from all these sources of positive law began to be made in very early times. Of these some have survived the ravages of time. The *Didascalia of the Apostles* may, in the judgement of the learned, be ascribed to the first half of the third century, and the so-called *Constitutions of the Apostles*, together with the *Canons of the Apostles*, to the early part of the fifth century. The materials of which these collections are composed are, of course, still more ancient. At the beginning of the fourth century the decrees of the councils were collected and arranged at first in chronological order in the East. At the beginning of the sixth century systematic collections arranged under suitable titles began to appear. Of these early collections of canons the most celebrated is that of John the Scholastic. In the West, Dionysius Exiguus made his translation of Greek canons into Latin about the year 500. A copy of this collection was presented by the Pope to Charlemagne when he was in Rome, and he caused it to be received and approved by the clergy of his empire in 802 at the great Council of Aix la Chapelle. Collections of Church laws continued to grow in number and

[1] Acts xv 28, 29.
[2] It ceased to bind in the Latin Church about the ninth century.

in bulk until in the twelfth century the monk Gratian issued his *Decretum*, which became the most famous of them all, and still forms the first volume of the *Corpus Juris Canonici*. It contains some 4,000 decisions on law and morals taken from the decrees of Popes, the canons of councils both general and particular, the opinions of the Fathers, and even from the civil law.

No attempt, of course, can be made in this short sketch to trace the varying phases through which the innumerable positive laws of the Church have passed. It will be sufficient for our purpose to trace in outline those chief precepts which bind all Catholics and which are specially known as the precepts of the Church. They are usually reckoned six in number: the due observance of Sundays and feast-days, the days of fasting and abstinence, confession and Communion, the support of pastors, and the prohibition of marriage within certain degrees of kindred and of its solemnization at certain times of the year.

The observance of the Sunday and its substitution for the Sabbath appears to be due to apostolic institution. There are traces of it in the New Testament; in the *Didaché* the faithful are bidden to come together on the Lord's Day, as it was called even then in honour of the Resurrection, and offer the eucharistic sacrifice after confessing their sins. In the second century the custom of observing the Lord's Day was universal throughout the Church. The chief duty to be performed on that day was to hear Mass. Very soon particular provincial laws began to be enacted urging the obligation and imposing penalties on transgressors. At the beginning of the fourth century the Council of Illiberis in Spain decreed that anyone who might be absent from Mass on three successive Sundays should be deprived of Communion. The Council of Agde at the beginning of the sixth century prescribed that all were to hear an entire Mass on Sunday and not leave until after the blessing of the priest on pain of a public reprehension by the bishop.

It was natural that when Sunday became the Christian Sabbath it should be kept much in the same way as the Jews kept their Sabbath. While knowing from the teaching of our Lord himself that pharisaic exaggeration was to be avoided in this matter, and from St Paul that the sabbatical rest was no longer of obligation, still St Caesarius of Arles in the sixth century expressly says that the Doctors of the Church decreed to transfer all the honour of the Sabbath to the Lord's Day.

The very necessity of hearing Mass on that day made a certain abstention from work also necessary. Tertullian testifies to the Christian custom of his day in this respect. Constantine prescribed that judges and artisans in towns should abstain from work on the Sunday, but that agriculture should be allowed on account of necessity. The strictness with which the Sunday repose was observed varied somewhat according to time and place in the period with which we are dealing.

Besides the Sunday other feast-days began gradually to be observed in the same manner by hearing Mass and abstaining from servile work. Easter and Pentecost were assigned to movable Sundays, but the days on which renowned martyrs suffered for the Faith, those on which churches were dedicated, Ascension Day, Christmas Day, and the Epiphany, were soon added to the list. The letter of the Church of Smyrna concerning the martyrdom of St Polycarp in the middle of the second century expresses the intention of celebrating the anniversary of the day of martyrdom with joy, both in memory of those who had suffered and as a preparation for those who survived.[1]

As the Christian Church took over the Jewish Sabbath but changed the day on which it was observed and rejected the exaggerations of the Pharisees in its observance, so, too, it adopted the Jewish practice of fasting at stated times. As we have seen from the *Didaché*, the fast of Monday and Thursday was changed into one on Wednesday and Friday. The obligation of fasting on all Wednesdays and Fridays ceased almost entirely about the tenth century, but the fixing of those days by ecclesiastical authority for fasting, and the desire to substitute a Christian observance at Rome for certain pagan rites celebrated in connection with the seasons of the year, seem to have given rise to our Ember Days. In the time of St Leo, in the middle of the fifth century, the Ember Days were a settled institution, though the time at which they fell varied somewhat at different times and in different places.

The earliest indication that we have of the fast of Lent is contained in a short extract from Irenaeus which has been preserved for us by Eusebius.[2] Writing to Pope Victor about the middle of the second century, St Irenaeus says that the controversy in the East was not merely about the proper time of celebrating Easter but also about the manner of fasting. "For some think," he says, "that they ought to fast only one

[1] *Cf.* A. Villien, *Histoire des Commandements de l'Église*, 1909.
[2] *Historia Ecclesiastica*, v, c. 24.

day, some two, some more days; some compute their day as consisting of forty hours night and day; and this diversity existing among those that observe it is not a matter that has just sprung up in our times, but long ago among those before us, who, perhaps not having ruled with sufficient strictness, established the practice that arose from their simplicity and inexperience, and yet with all these maintained peace, and we have maintained peace with one another; and the very difference in our fasting establishes the unanimity of our faith." At the time this was written the Lenten fast was obviously very short, and there was no uniformity even in its duration. Tertullian, fifty years later, refers to the Lenten observance as the fulfilment of the words of our Lord: " But the days will come when the bridegroom shall be taken away from them; then shall they fast in those days."

The first allusion to a period of forty days' fast occurs in the fifth canon of the Council of Nicaea (325). In the time of St Leo in the fifth century the period was sufficiently well established to be referred by him to apostolic institution. The period was six weeks, but omitting Sundays the actual fasting days were only thirty-six in number. The four days before the first Sunday of Lent were added sometime in the seventh century. The fasts assigned to certain vigils arose from the practice of the early Christians of assembling on the eve of a feast and spending the night in prayer, fasting, and reading the Scriptures. By degrees Matins took the place of the night office, and the vigil office was moved back to the Saturday morning, as we see to this day from the morning office of Holy Saturday. The fast was thus prolonged through the Saturday till after the morning office of the feast of the next day.

The fast which used to be observed on the rogation days took its rise in France at the close of the fifth century, and by degrees spread to other Churches. The interrupted fast of Advent was introduced as a preparation for Christmas toward the end of the fourth century. The manner of fasting has varied greatly at different times and in different places. At first the fast seems to have been absolute and continuous. During the days of the bridegroom's absence the faithful neither ate nor drank anything. When the period was lengthened such a total fast became impossible, but at least in the East food was restricted on fast days to one meal of bread, salt, and water, taken in the evening, or at least not before three in the afternoon. In the time of St Gregory fish was allowed at the single meal in the West. Flesh meat was never allowed on fasting days.

The essence of fasting is still placed by theologians in the single meal, but many relaxations have crept in by degrees. The monks while listening to a *Collatio* of Cassian before going to bed introduced the practice of drinking an acidulated liquor called *posca*. By degrees fruits and lighter kinds of food in limited quantity were added, and when about the thirteenth century the full meal began to be taken at twelve midday, the evening collation became an established practice.

In the thirteenth century it was an accepted principle that liquid does not break the fast, and this became the source of another relaxation. A little wine, or coffee, or chocolate, was taken sometimes in the morning, with candied fruits (*electuaria*) on occasion. The practice was not condemned when the Sacred Penitentiary was asked about it in 1843, provided that the solid food taken then did not exceed two ounces in weight.

At first all seem to have fasted except children and those who were sick. St Thomas's opinion that those who are still growing are not bound to fast, and that in general the period of growth lasts till the completion of the twenty-first year, has prevailed. Exemptions in favour of workmen and others were soon admitted, and toward the close of the Middle Ages dispensations from the law of fasting began to be granted. The Lenten indult was an established custom before the new Code came into force.

The precept of abstinence from flesh meat which is still observed on Fridays is a survival of the obligation of fasting on that day which obtained in the primitive Church. As we have seen, the *Didaché* prescribed fasting on all Wednesdays and Fridays, and to this fast all the faithful except mere children and the sick were formerly bound. About the tenth century the obligation of the Friday fast was reduced to one of abstinence from flesh meat, and the Wednesday fast, after being similarly mitigated, gradually disappeared altogether.

While in the East Saturday was observed as a festival in honour of the creation,[1] at Rome and in other Churches of the West it began in early times to be observed as a fasting day. On account of the difference of discipline on this point great difficulties arose in the fourth century, as we know from the correspondence of St Augustine and St Jerome. St Ambrose said that he kept festival on Saturday when he was at

[1] Apostolic Constitutions, vii, 23.

Milan and a fast when at Rome, and he advised St Augustine to follow the same rule. About the eleventh century the Saturday fast was reduced to an obligation of abstinence, and this was the common law of the Church until the new Code of Canon Law came into force. A dispensation from abstinence on Saturdays, the feast of St Mark, and on Rogation Days was granted for England by a rescript of Propaganda, May 29, 1830.

The Sundays in Lent were never observed as fasting days, but they early became days of abstinence as they remained till the new Code came into force on May 19, 1918.

Annual confession and Communion was first made a positive universal law of the Catholic Church in the Fourth Lateran Council (1215). As we know from the Gospel of St John,[1] both confession and Communion were prescribed by our Lord, but he determined neither precept in detail. The practice of the different Churches in the early ages was various in respect to both precepts. We will first trace in outline the history regarding the precept of annual Communion.

From the earliest times, as we have seen, Mass was celebrated for the assembled faithful on Sundays, and all who were present appear to have received Holy Communion. In some places it was the practice for the faithful to take home with them consecrated particles and communicate themselves therewith out of Mass. Many at Rome, in Spain, and in Africa received Communion daily. This was a common practice at the end of the fourth century, as we learn from the letters of St Jerome and St Augustine. The latter interprets the daily bread for which we ask in the Lord's Prayer as Holy Communion. The Council of Agde (506) decreed that those who did not communicate at least on the feasts of the Nativity, Easter, and Whit-Sunday were not to be reckoned as Catholics. In subsequent centuries this became a general rule in the Western Church; in the East, according to Theodore of Canterbury, the law was much stricter. The Greeks, he says, both laity and clerics, communicate every Sunday, and anyone who omits to do so on three Sundays is excommunicated. A synod held (747) at Cloveshoe in England prescribed that innocent youths and those in whom years had cooled the ardour of passion should be exhorted to communicate very frequently. A synod held under St Patrick in the fifth century decreed that the Eucharist was to be received at all events at Easter, and that anyone who neglected this duty was not a member of the

[1] John vi 54.

Church. Robert Pullen, an Englishman who wrote in the middle of the twelfth century, tells us that in his day some communicated more frequently, others less so, but that even laymen followed the rule of the Fathers and communicated at least three times a year. So that when the Lateran Council established the universal law that all who had come to years of discretion were bound to communicate at least at Easter, it made no new rule; it merely enforced by universal statute the least that was expected of anyone who called himself a Catholic.

The precept of annual confession is intrinsically connected with that of Easter Communion both in the Church's legislation and in its own nature. For, as the Catechism of the Council of Trent teaches,[1] the power of order, although primarily it refers to the consecration of the Eucharist, yet also comprises all that is necessary to dispose the faithful to receive the Eucharist worthily and profitably. It comprises, then, the power to forgive sins, inasmuch as no one who is conscious of mortal sin may receive Holy Communion without previous confession and absolution. The Council of Trent[2] teaches that the words of St Paul, " Let a man prove himself," have always been understood in the Church of the necessity of sacramental confession and absolution before Holy Communion when there is consciousness of mortal sin. The law of the Lateran concerning annual confession and Communion is thus one law, confession being ordinarily a necessary preparation for Holy Communion in those who rarely communicate. That the Church always understood this is witnessed to by Alcuin in the eighth century,[3] by St Leo in the fifth,[4] St Augustine in the fourth,[5] and St Cyprian in the third.[6] We have the same conjunction of confession and Communion in the sentence of the *Didaché:* " But on the Lord's day do ye assemble and break bread, and give thanks, after confessing your transgressions, in order that your sacrifice may be pure."[7] In all probability the confession here spoken of should be interpreted as meaning sacramental confession to a priest. The Council of Trent, then, was justified in saying that before receiving Holy Communion it had always been considered

---

[1] Pt. ii, c. 7, q. 6.   [2] *Supra*, p. 102.
[3] De Psalmorum Usu, P.L., ci, 499.
[4] Epist. 108, P.L., liv, 1011.
[5] Serm. 278, P.L., xxxviii, 2273.
[6] Epist. 10, P.L., iv, 254; Epist. ii, *ib.* 257; De Lapsis, xvi, *ib.* 479.
[7] C. xiv.

a duty to go to confession when there was consciousness of mortal sin. In the fifth or sixth century a practice sprang up which was the forerunner of the Lateran law of annual confession. At the beginning of Lent public penance was imposed on those who had been guilty of great and notorious crimes. In some of the Penitential Books[1] the priest is bidden to invite all who are conscious of mortal sin, and even all who by any sin whatever have soiled their baptismal robe, to make humble confession to their own priest on Ash Wednesday, and accept the penance enjoined according to the canons. If there was any special reason for granting absolution at once, that was done, otherwise absolution was deferred till Maundy Thursday, when, the penance having been performed, the penitent was absolved and admitted to Communion. This was a mitigation of the earlier discipline of some Churches, especially in the East, according to which public penance sometimes lasted for years.[2] The name of Shrove Tuesday and the custom of receiving ashes on the head on Ash Wednesday, still remind us of the old discipline of the Catholic Church. It was natural, then, that when the Church made it obligatory on all to receive Holy Communion at least every Easter, it should also impose the obligation of annual confession. The law indeed does not indicate Easter as necessarily the time for the annual confession, but in practice it follows the time for the annual Communion. Originally the annual confession had by law to be made to the parish priest or to the bishop of the penitent, but for centuries it has been lawful to make it to any priest who has faculties for hearing confessions in the place.

The faithful are bound by natural and divine law according to the teaching of St Paul[3] to contribute to the support of their pastors. For some centuries the revenues of the Church derived from the offerings of the faithful and from other sources constituted one fund, and this was administered by the bishop. The support of the poor, the maintenance of public worship, as well as the support of the clergy and other needs, were all supplied from the common fund. According to a decretal of Pope Gelasius (501) the Church revenues were to be divided into four portions, one for the bishop, another for the clergy, a third for the relief of the poor and strangers, the fourth for the Church fabrics. In his celebrated

[1] Schmitz, *Bussbücher*, i, 775.
[2] Duchesne, *Christian Worship*, p. 435.
[3] 1 Cor. ix; Gal. vi 6.

answers to St Augustine, Gregory the Great tells the first Archbishop of Canterbury that as he was a monk he did not need a separate portion, and should be content to share in common with his clergy. For several centuries no positive law of the Church was needed to compel the faithful to do their duty in this matter. The Fathers who occasionally urge the obligation are content to appeal in support of it to the teaching of St Paul or to the law of tithes under the Mosaic dispensation. The Penitential attributed to St Theodore enjoins that the custom of the province should be observed relative to contributions to the Church, but that the poor were not to be subjected to violence for the sake of tithes or other matters. Positive ecclesiastical laws, however, began to appear both on the Continent and in England in the eighth century. Thus the seventeenth article of the legatine council held in England by the authority of Pope Adrian I (785-787) contained the following provision: " Wherefore also we solemnly lay upon you this precept, that all be careful to give tithes of all that they possess, because that is the special part of the Lord God; and let a man live on the nine parts, and give alms." At first there was some variety in the appropriation of tithes, but when the parochial system was introduced, between the tenth and thirteenth century, the appropriation of tithes to the parish priest became the settled rule. In modern times, at least in English-speaking countries, the offerings of the faithful constitute almost the only source of Church revenues as they did in the early ages of Christianity, and their apportionment and distribution are regulated by special laws.[1]

As marriage was raised to the dignity of a sacrament by Christ our Lord, and the Church alone has jurisdiction over the administration of the sacraments, it follows that Christian marriage is subject exclusively to the laws of God and of the Church. There are several passages in the Epistles of St Paul[2] which show that the Church was conscious of her authority in this matter, and that she used it from the earliest times. St Ignatius in his letter to St Polycarp says that it is proper that Christians should contract marriage according to the judgement of the bishop, and Tertullian asserts that marriages which were contracted without being previously notified to the Church were in danger of being considered as no better than adulteries and fornications. The history of the many laws relating to Christian marriage is too large a subject

[1] Constitution of Leo XIII, *Romanos Pontifices*.
[2] 1 Cor. v, vii; 2 Cor. vi 14.

to be treated here even in outline. We will confine ourselves to the impediments of consanguinity and close time.

The natural and divine law prohibits marriage in the first degree of the direct line, and most probably in all degrees indefinitely in the same line. In the collateral line, also, it most probably forbids marriage at least in the first degree. With respect to further degrees in the collateral line the Church adopted the Mosaic legislation, and there are no traces of her having exercised further the independent power which she certainly possessed to enlarge or restrict the limits of kindred before the fourth or fifth century. The Council of Epaon (517) forbade marriages between second cousins, Gregory II (721) prohibited marriage with relations in general, and from the eighth to the eleventh century the prohibition was extended to the seventh degree according to the canonical mode of reckoning. The Fourth Council of Lateran (1215) restricted the prohibition to the fourth degree, and the new Code restricts it to the third.

As the solemn celebration of marriage is not in keeping with penitential exercises, a council of Laodicea in the fourth century forbade the celebration of marriage during Lent. Subsequently the solemnization of marriage was forbidden from Septuagesima Sunday till the octave of Easter, during three weeks before the feast of St John Baptist, and from Advent till after the Epiphany. There was a dispute as to the three weeks before the feast of St John Baptist, and Clement III, at the end of the twelfth century, decided that the period was to be interpreted as extending from the Rogation Days till the Sunday after Pentecost. The Council of Trent[1] decreed that close time for the solemnization of marriage was to extend from Advent till after the Epiphany, and from Ash Wednesday till after Low Sunday, which the Code has altered as above (p. 212).

We must not leave this first period in the history of moral theology without saying something about the penitential books which began to appear in the sixth century and subsequently became very numerous. They were intended as a help to bishops and priests in their duty of imposing canonical penances on sinners and reconciling them to God and the Church. At first they were little more than lists of sins with the appropriate canonical penance annexed to each sin. The quality and length of penance assigned were derived from the councils or from the canonical letters of St Basil,

[1] Sess. xxiv, c. 10.

St Peter of Alexandria, St Athanasius, and other Fathers of the Church. Afterward chapters were added containing short moral rules on a great variety of subjects, the method of receiving and dealing with penitents, and the method of reconciling them. They are of importance in the history of moral theology as furnishing a standard by which the malice of various transgressions was measured according to a great variety of circumstances. They fell into disuse with the gradual cessation of public penance in the Church.

SECTION II

The Scholastic Period

It is not possible to indicate any particular year when the scholastic period began. We may say that the patristic period closed with the death of St Bernard, the last of the Fathers, in the year 1153. Many of the characteristics of scholasticism, however, and especially the application of philosophy to the exposition and defence of theology, are conspicuous in the works of many of the Fathers. In their work, too, of systematizing theology the schoolmen had many predecessors among the Fathers, and especially St John Damascene and St Isidore of Seville. Nor is the common assertion that the Fathers favoured Platonism while the scholastics adopted Aristotelianism quite warranted by facts. Clement of Alexandria especially, and other Fathers as well, were eclectic as philosophers, and borrowed what they thought was true from any and every source. Still we may for practical purposes say that scholasticism began in the twelfth century. Then it was that the growth and development of theology began afresh. It had been interrupted for seven hundred years by the necessity of civilizing the barbarians who had broken up the Roman Empire and settled in its territories. From this time moral theology has come down to us in two distinct channels. Peter Lombard may be looked upon as the fountain-head of the first stream, and St Raymund of Pennafort of the second.

Peter Lombard wrote his work on the Sentences between the years 1145 and 1150. He therein treats of the whole of theology, both dogmatic and moral. He wished to counteract the rationalizing tendencies which as a pupil of Abelard he had noticed in the schools of Paris. To the various and erroneous views which the spirit of rationalism had introduced, Peter opposed the traditional doctrine handed down in the writings of the Fathers. After much consideration, as he tells us, he found a guiding principle for the distribution and ordering of the subject-matter of theology in a sentence of St Augustine. Christian revelation, contained in the Holy Scriptures, has for its subject-matter either things or signs. Under signs come the sacraments, and things are either such as we have fruition of, or such as we use, or such as we both use and enjoy by fruition. Under the first head comes God, one in nature and three in person. Under the second come all created things, the angels, man, his end, fall, and redeeming grace. Under the third, the incarnation, faith, hope, charity, the seven gifts of the Holy Spirit, the Ten Commandments. The whole matter of theology is thus systematically arranged in four Books. Each Book is divided into Distinctions, devoted to some special point on which the traditional doctrine is laid down by quoting appropriate extracts (*Sententiae*) from the works of the Fathers. Apparent or real differences of opinion are noted and as far as possible reconciled with each other. Although Hugo of St Victor, Robert Pullen, and other theologians had previously composed similar books of Sentences, yet the work of Peter Lombard soon eclipsed them all in the welcome that it received. It remained the recognized textbook of theology until the end of the sixteenth century, when its place was taken by the *Summa* of St Thomas. Nearly all the great scholastics wrote Commentaries on the *Sentences* of Peter Lombard, developing, illustrating, defending, and sometimes correcting the doctrine which they found there, especially from the speculative point of view. In these Commentaries and in the Summas of scholastic theology we have a most abundant and valuable source of the speculative side of Christian ethics.

To meet the more practical and concrete needs of the confessor, St Raymund of Pennafort composed his *Summa de Pœnitentia et Matrimonio* about the year 1235. He, also, merely collected and systematized the abundant material which had been left by his predecessors. He had no more intention of introducing changes into the traditional doctrines of Christianity than had Peter Lombard. But as his aim was not speculative but practical, he drew his material especially from Gratian's *Decretum*, from the decisions of Popes and the councils of the Church, as well as from the Fathers. The work *De Pœnitentia* is divided into three Books. In the first Book sins against God are treated of, in the second sins against one's neighbour, and in the third irregularities, dispensations, purgations, sentences, penances, and remissions. Each Book is divided into Titles, which contain an orderly and logical exposition of some particular subject. Thus, in the first title on *Simony*, the sin is defined, the origin of the name is explained, the different kinds of simony are indicated, with the penalties incurred and the dispensations which may be obtained. Then follows a discussion of doubtful questions and cases. Finally some rules of law on the matter are laid down and explained.

The work of St Raymund was the first of those innumerable handbooks written for the training and use of the confessor especially from the practical and casuistical point of view. Although in the treatment of the different titles the work of St Raymund leaves little to be desired, yet it lacks something in orderly arrangement and in completeness. These defects were soon made good by others. A Friar Minor, of Asti, in the north of Italy, composed the *Summa Astensis* in the year 1317. In the Roman edition of 1728 it fills two volumes folio, and in its aim, in the matter which it contains, and in the method of treatment, it differs little from the handbooks of moral theology which are published at the present day. The matter is divided into eight Books. The first Book treats of divine and human law and contains the doctrine of the Ten Commandments. The second treats of virtues and vices, beginning with several titles devoted to human acts, voluntary and involuntary actions, to expounding in what the goodness or malice of actions consists, and merit. The cardinal and theological virtues and the sins opposed to them are explained in detail. The third Book contains the doctrine on contracts and last wills; the fourth that on the sacraments in general, and on Baptism, Confirmation, and the holy Eucharist. The treatise on Penance and Extreme Unction in the fifth Book contains also the doctrine on prayer, fasting, almsdeeds, restitution, and indulgences. That on Orders in the sixth Book treats also of churches and sacred vestments, ecclesiastical burial, parishes, prebends, tithes, of the various grades of the clergy and of religious and their obligations. Censures and ecclesiastical penalties occupy the seventh, and Matrimony the eighth Book.

The dogmatic treatment of moral theology reached its high-water mark in the second part of the *Summa* of St Thomas Aquinas. That marvellous production of genius has never been surpassed or even equalled as an exposition of the general principles of Christian ethics. Neither has the casuistic treatment of morals in general made much progress since the thirteenth century. Of course, there have been numerous changes in discipline during the last six centuries, and these require to be noted in new moral treatises as they occur. There have also been some changes in theological opinion. As an illustration of such a change we may instance that concerning the use by superiors of knowledge gained from confession. St Thomas and scholastic theologians commonly held that a superior who knew from confession of a dangerous occasion of sin to one of his subjects might use his authority to remove his subject out of the danger, provided that thereby he violated no principle of justice nor made known to others the sin which had been confessed to him. This opinion is now quite obsolete, and it has been virtually condemned by the Holy See.[1] But in spite of some such changes in detail, the general assertion remains true that moral theology to-day is substantially what it was in the thirteenth or at the beginning of the fourteenth century. There is, however, one important exception to this general statement. That exception is due to the express formulation at the end of the sixteenth century of the doctrine of probabilism.

We must, however, be on our guard against exaggerating the importance of probabilism, and confounding it with moral theology in general. After all, probabilism is only concerned with the solution of doubtful questions. There is an immense body of moral doctrine which is certain and where probabilism or other similar theory of morals does not enter. There are also, it must be confessed, many doubtful questions, especially connected with the application of general rules to particular cases, and it is in the solution of these doubtful and disputed questions that probabilism is concerned. All Catholic divines state or take for granted the doctrine that it is sinful to act with a doubtful conscience, without making up one's mind that the action which is contemplated is morally right. This is the teaching of Holy Scripture: "All that is not of faith"—*i.e.*, done with the conscientious conviction that it is right—"is sin," says St Paul.[2] But if this be so, what are we to do in doubtful matters, where perhaps divines themselves disagree, and some teach that an action is right, while others assert that it is wrong? In such cases we can only act, according to the doctrine of St Paul, if we are able to make up our mind that the action is lawful and honest. How can this be done?

Before the close of the sixteenth century, when Bartholomew à Medina published his *Exposition* on St Thomas, there was

[1] *Supra*, p. 232. [2] Rom. xiv 23.

no commonly recognized method for forming one's conscience in doubtful matters. The *Summa Astensis* devotes the last title of the second Book to the subject of "Perplexities of Conscience." The author distinguishes perplexities of law from perplexities of fact. The former, he says, occur when there are two apparently contrary opinions about the lawfulness of an action, the latter when a man believes that in avoiding one sin he must perforce commit another. He has much to say about perplexities of fact, but about perplexities of law, which alone concern us here, he simply observes that they can be removed in whatever state a man may be, but he does not tell us how this may be done. He refers, indeed, to Alexander of Hales, who wrote before St Raymund of Pennafort, and who in the article of his *Summa* devoted to the subject of "Conscience" tells us that a perplexity of law is to be removed by the unction of the Holy Spirit, who teaches concerning all things.[1] St Raymund gives a more satisfactory rule and says shortly that a perplexity arising from a difference among Doctors is to be solved by reducing the contrary opinions to agreement, for there is no real but only apparent contradiction in law. This puts us on the right track; it tells us that for the solution of doubtful cases the theologians of the time followed the ordinary rules of legal interpretation, the chief among which was the rule of law which guided Gratian in the composition of the *Decretum* and Peter Lombard in his work on the Sentences, and which the Roman lawyers had expressed by saying that it is meet to make one law agree with another— *Conveniens est jura juribus concordare.*[2]

Although this was the chief rule of law to be followed when authorities differed, it was by no means the only one. Later authors, such as Angelus de Clavasio (1480), Sylvester Prierias (1516), and Navarrus (1560), give lists of the different rules of law to be applied to the solution of doubtful cases in different circumstances. We may take them from Navarrus, as they are substantially the same in all the authorities of the time. When there are different opinions among Doctors, says Navarrus in effect, that opinion should be preferred which is confirmed by custom, or grounded on a text of law, or which rests on an invincible argument. If none of these rules serves, then the common opinion should be followed, and that may be called a common opinion which six or seven approved authors adopt, though there may be fifty others who blindly follow each other

---

[1] *Summa*, ii, q. 120.
[2] L. unica, C., de inofficiosis dotibus.

like sheep against it, for weight and not number is mainly to be considered in such questions. If that rule does not suit the case, then the opinion should be chosen which is backed by more numerous authorities and reasons; then that which is more lenient, or which favours marriage, a last will and testament, liberty, a private individual against the State, the validity of an act, or the defendant in an action at law. If in none of these ways one opinion is better than the other, then that should be adopted which the greater number of theologians follow if the matter belong to theology, or canonists if it belong to canon law, or civilians if it belong to civil law. To these rules Navarrus adds the note that in the forum of conscience it is sufficient to choose as true the opinion of a man of virtue and learning.[1]

Sylvester Prierias tells us that all were agreed that when Doctors differed, a man might follow the opinion of one Doctor even though he was drawn to follow him by affection without subtle investigation into the grounds on which his opinion rested.

While the Fathers of the Church, such as Gregory Nazianzen, and the schoolmen with St Thomas solved particular cases of doubt in favour of liberty by applying the rule of probabilism that a doubtful law cannot impose a certain obligation, yet up to the time of Medina it was commonly held that in doubtful cases a man was bound to follow the opinion which seemed to him the better grounded or the more probable. The Dominican Bartholomew à Medina (1577) was the first to show that if it were a question of obligation, not of mere counsel, this was illogical. The more probable opinion may be the safer and better opinion, but we are not usually bound to take the safer or better way; we are at least allowed to take that which is good and safe. And a probable opinion is safe, for good and wise men see no sin nor danger of sin in it, else it would not be probable. So that a probable opinion may be followed even by one who knows and holds that the contrary opinion is more probable.

By these and other arguments Medina put probabilism on a firm basis, and the doctrine was at once received on all hands. It was the logical deduction from principles which all admitted, and so theologians of all schools accepted it at once, though some of them do not seem at first to have realized its far-reaching consequences. Dr. Hall, who published his work *De Quinquepartita Conscientia* in 1598, accepted and defended

[1] *Manuale Confessariorum*, c. 27, n. 288.

the new principle, but he placed it side by side with the older methods of forming one's conscience which he copied from Navarrus. Of these methods he remarks that they are so many different ways of forming a probable opinion. He did not fully realize, as it seems, that the new principle was universal, and rendered the use of the old rules to a great extent unnecessary in the forum of conscience. The same may be said of Azor, who published the first volume of his *Institutiones Morales* in the year 1600. Other theologians, however, such as Vasquez, Suarez, Salon, Laymann, soon realized the significance of the new method, and proceeded to explain, develop, and on certain points to limit its application. It was seen that it can only be applied where the sole question is whether an act is sinful or not; it may not be applied where an end must be attained and may not be placed in jeopardy, or where the validity of an act is in question, or where there is question of the certain right of another.

Section III
The Modern Period

Almost the whole modern period from the opening of the seventeenth century is occupied with the controversy about the right system of moral theology. Modern research has confirmed the historical accuracy of the account of the origin of this dispute which Fr. Antony Terill or Bonville prefixed to his work *Regula Morum*, published in 1676. Fr. Terill, S.J., was a learned and acute theologian who taught theology at the English College of the Society at Liège, now represented by Stonyhurst and St Beuno's. Besides his *Regula Morum* he published another work, *De Conscientia Probabili*, in 1668. He was a good and conscientious man, and had ample means of knowing the facts to which he testifies. According to Fr. Terill, until about the year 1638 practically all Catholic theologians of all schools accepted and taught probabilism. The only exception was the not very notable Italian Jesuit Comitolus, who published his *Responsa Moralia* in 1608. Comitolus taught probabiliorism and attributed the doctrine of probabilism quite falsely to what he calls the shameful lapse of Armilla. The opinion of Comitolus passed almost unheeded, and there was peace and comparative harmony in the schools of morals. This peace began to be broken when the friends of Jansen were planning the publication of his famous book *Augustinus*. The first of the five propositions which were extracted from that book and condemned by Innocent X in 1653 asserted that there were some laws of God which could not be observed even by the just, do what they would, and that God did not give grace to enable them to observe these laws. This heretical and blasphemous proposition, which made God a tyrant who gave orders which he knew could not be obeyed, was altogether out of harmony with the prevailing system of moral theology, and its Jansenist supporters began to attack probabilism in order to make an opening for their own rigoristic doctrine. According to Caramuel, who was at Louvain at the time and who wrote a book against them in 1639, they began to teach covertly that the use of probabilism was something new; that he who leaves the safe way and follows probabilism cannot but be condemned by God; that opinions which are styled probable among us are not probable with God. The war between probabilism and antiprobabilism had broken out, a war conducted with the greatest heat and passion for two hundred years, and not even yet quite ended. The Louvain Doctors, after the condemnation of *Augustinus* by the Holy See, retaliated by issuing their propositions against probabilism in 1655. The strategy was the same as led Döllinger and Reusch to publish their work on *Moralstreitigkeiten*, after the definition of Papal Infallibility. The war, however, was soon carried into France, where Jansenism had won the support of a few proud spirits of the highest intellectual gifts. Among these Pascal was pre-eminent, and he struck the hardest blow which probabilism has ever sustained by publishing his *Lettres Provinciales* in 1656. The book is unfair and misrepresents the doctrines which it attacks, but its wit and style gave it at once a place in the classical literature of the world. It was condemned by Alexander VII at Rome in 1657, but by non-Catholics it is still regarded as the last word on the subject of Catholic, and especially Jesuit, moral theology.

Although the rise of Jansenism was the occasion of the outbreak of war, there were other causes also which contributed to the heat of the combat. Fr. Terill laments the disastrous laxity of opinion on moral questions which was conspicuous in many of the probabilist authors of the day. Many of these wrote books, not to expound the truth, but to attract attention to themselves and acquire notoriety. The means they employed for this purpose was the ventilation of new opinions in morals. By making use of the weak argument from similar cases they broached hitherto unheard-of doctrines which were industriously collected by the casuists. The fact that somebody or other had said in his book that an opinion was probable and that it had not been condemned by the Holy See was held sufficient to merit for it a place among probable opinions in moral theology. Fr. Terill, himself a strenuous defender of probabilism, raised his voice against the inrush of laxity. He did much by his writings to improve the theory by stating and explaining it more accurately than had been done hitherto. He insisted that in order to be accepted as a rule of conduct it was not sufficient that an opinion should have some slight degree of probability, or should only be probably probable; it should be well grounded, seriously and solidly probable in the judgement of experts, of men of virtue and learning. The common method of proving probabilism by saying that one who acts on a probable opinion acts prudently was objectionable on the theoretical side, and Terill improved it by making use of reflex principles, such as, " A doubtful law is not promulgated and cannot bind." This eminent English Jesuit thus tried to stem the tide of laxity in an age of immorality by stating the theory of probabilism more accurately and limiting its use to its proper sphere. Other theologians with the same laudable end in view threw probabilism overboard altogether. This was especially the case with the theologians of the great Order of St Dominic. A member of this Order had first formulated probabilism, as we have seen, and, as Salon testifies, other Dominicans were conspicuous as being the first to accept and teach it. The most famous Dominican theologians of the time, Ledesma, Bañez, Alvarez, Ildephonsus, and others were all probabilists. No anti-probabilist Dominican was heard of till the year 1656. In that year a general Chapter of the Order was held at Rome, and all the members were urged to adopt the stricter opinion in morals. From that time onward the chief Dominican theologians have almost without exception been probabiliorists. Among others are the well-known names of Mercorus, Gonet, Contenson, Natalis Alexander, Concina, Billuart, and Patuzzi, the adversary of St Alphonsus Liguori.

From the strife of parties different moral systems began to emerge. Jansenist rigorism, which required direct moral certainty against the law to justify a departure from its observance, and which was not satisfied even with a most probable opinion in favour of the lawfulness of an action, was condemned by Alexander VIII in 1690. Laxism, which was satisfied with even a slightly probable opinion as a rule of conduct, had been condemned by Innocent XI in 1679. Probabiliorism and probabilism together held possession of the field. At the beginning of the eighteenth century a few theologians such as Amort, Rassler, and Mayr, defended equiprobabilism. This system required an opinion in favour of liberty to be equally probable with that in favour of the law before allowing it to be used as a rule of morals. It would not allow anyone to follow an opinion in favour of liberty which was distinctly less probable than that which favoured the law.

These three systems still have their defenders, and the last has acquired strength from the adhesion to it of St Alphonsus in the later portion of his life. St Alphonsus Liguori is recognized as the Doctor of moral theology as St Thomas is of dogmatic. By his writings he drove out of the Church the last remnants of rigorism, and firmly established that common doctrine in moral theology which it has been the aim of the author to expound in these volumes. In spite, however, of general agreement, there are some points of detail which are still matter of controversy among moral theologians.

St Alphonsus was ordained priest in 1726 when he was thirty years of age. He had been taught the probabiliorist system of morals, but in the course of fifteen years of study and experience in the confessional he came to the conclusion that the system was false and harmful to souls. He then adopted probabilism, and mainly using recognized probabilist authorities, especially of the Society of Jesus, whom he acknowledged to be his masters in this branch of learning, he composed his chief work, the *Theologia Moralis*. The first edition appeared in 1748, and a second and much enlarged edition was issued in 1753. In 1755 St Alphonsus published an elaborate dissertation on probabilism in which he proved the doctrine and refuted the objections commonly brought against it. He became Bishop of St Agatha of the Goths in 1762, and published another dissertation in which he appeared to adopt a new system of moral theology. While admitting that it is lawful to follow a solidly probable opinion, he denied that when in favour of the law there is an opinion which is certainly and notably more probable than its opposite, this latter can be really and solidly probable. The question is one of fact. If this proposition be considered from the practical and concrete point of view, its practical truth may be admitted, and St Alphonsus probably understood it in this sense. Furthermore, it may be admitted that the doctrine has its value in deciding when an opinion is solidly probable or not, and this was what St Alphonsus intended. He wished to exclude laxism from his system, and he invented this formula for the purpose. Moderate probabilists secure the same end by stressing *solidly* when they require a *solidly* probable opinion for a lawful rule of action. Considered theoretically and logically, the formula of St Alphonsus is open to attack, as it is not true that a greater probability, even if notable and certain, does necessarily deprive the opposite opinion of all solid probability. On this point there is still some difference of opinion between simple probabilists and equiprobabilists, but the dispute has little to do with practical morals. The dissertation of St Alphonsus was not inserted in the *Moral Theology* of the saint till it reached its sixth edition, and his change of formula made little change in the doctrine of his work. It remained substantially what it always had been—a great work on moral theology written by a moderate probabilist.

Moral theology is still what St Alphonsus left it. There is general agreement in the schools, a common doctrine which all accept; it only remains to apply this to the social and political conditions which we see growing up around us.

In this modern period of moral theology the sufficiency of attrition without any strictly so-called initial charity on the part of the penitent as a proximate disposition for the remission of sin in the sacrament of Penance may be considered as established. The changed conditions in our modern capitalist society have had their effect on moral questions, for morality must always take account of altered circumstances. Perhaps the chief result in this direction is that a practical solution has been attained of the long controversy about the lawfulness of taking interest for a loan of money. The lawfulness of the practice is now admitted; the only moral question is concerning the amount which may be exacted. The doctrine of the just price is applicable here; money, like other commodities, has in our modern capitalist society its just price.

The new Code of Canon Law came into force on Whit Sunday, May 19, 1918, and made many and important changes in the discipline of the Church, and thus indirectly in many ways affected moral theology.

BIBLIOGRAPHY

Patristic Period

TRANSLATIONS OF THE FATHERS have been published in the Library of the Fathers, Oxford, 1839.
ANTE-NICENE CHRISTIAN LIBRARY, T. and T. Clark, Edinburgh.
NICENE AND POST-NICENE FATHERS, Oxford and New York, 1890.

ALCUIN, Migne, P. L., 100, 101.
AMBROSE (S), Migne, P. L., 14, 16, 17.
ATHANASIUS (S), Migne, P. G., 25-28.
AUGUSTINE (S) of Hippo, Migne, P. L., 32-45.
BARDENHEWER, O., *Patrology*, transl. T. J. Shahan, St Louis, 1908.
BASIL (S), Migne, P. G., 29-32.
BEDE, Migne, P. L., 94.
BENEDICT (S), Migne, P. L., 66.
BERNARD (S), Migne, P. L., 182, 183.
CAESARIUS (S), Migne, P. L., 67.
CASSIAN, Migne, P. L., 49.
CLEMENT OF ALEXANDRIA, Migne, P. G., 8; 9.
COUNCILS OF THE CHURCH, Mansi, *Amplissima Collectio Conciliorum*, Paris, 1901; Hefele, *Conciliengeschichte*, Freiburg, 1873.
CYPRIAN (S), Migne, P. L., 4.
DIDACHÉ, or TEACHING OF THE TWELVE APOSTLES, ed. R. D. Hitchcock, London, 1895.
DIONYSIUS EXIGUUS, Migne, P. L., 77.
DUCHESNE, Mgr. L., *Christian Worship*, London, 1904.
GREGORY THE GREAT, Migne, P. L., 75-77.
ISIDORE (S), Migne, P. L., 83.
JEROME (S), Migne, P. L., 22, 26.
JOHN CHRYSOSTOM (S), Migne, P. G., 47-64.
JOHN DAMASCENE (S), Migne, P. G., 94-96.
LACTANTIUS, Migne, P. L., 6, 7.
LEO THE GREAT, Migne, P. L., 55.
PALLADIUS, *Lausiac History*, ed. Dom Butler, Cambridge, 1898.
PATRICK (S), Migne, P. L., 53.
REGINO, Migne, P. L., 132.
SCHMITZ, H. J., *Die Bussbücher*, Mainz, 1883.
TERTULLIAN, Migne, P. L., 1, 2.
VILLIEN, A., *Histoire des Commandements de l'Église*, Paris, 1909.
WERNZ, F. X., *Jus Decretalium*, Rome, 1905.

Scholastic Period

ALBERTUS MAGNUS, Opera, Vives, Paris.
ANGELUS DE CLAVASIO, (1495), *Summa angelica*.
ANTONINUS (S), (1459), *Summa theologica*.
AQUINAS, ST THOMAS, Opera, Parma.
ASTENSIS, *Summa Astesana*.
AZPILCUETA (Navarrus), (1586), *Manuale confessariorum*.
BONAVENTURA (S), Opera, Vives, Paris.
DIONYSIUS CARTHUSIANUS, (1471), Opera.
FUMUS, B., (1545), *Armilla*.
GERSON, J., (1429), Opera, Anvers, 1706.
HALES, ALEXANDER OF, (1245), *Commentaria in IV libros sententiarum*.
PALUDANUS, (1342), *Commentarii in libros sententiarum*.
PANORMITANUS, (1443), *Commentaria in libros decretalium*.
PETRUS LOMBARDUS, (1164), *Quatuor libri sententiarum*.
RAYMUNDUS (S), (1275), *Summa de Poenitentia et Matrimonio*.
SCOTUS, DUNS, (1308), Opera, Vives, Paris.
SYLVESTER (Prierias), (1523), *Summa silvestrina*.
TABIENA, (1525), *Summa summarum*.

Modern Period

ALPHONSUS DE LIGORIO (S), (1787), Opera, Turin.
AMORT, E., (1775), *Theologia eclectica; Ethica Christiana*.
D'ANNIBALE, Card., (1892), *Summula theologiae moralis*.
AZOR, J., (1607), *Institutiones morales*.
BALLERINI, A., (1881), *Opus theologicum morale*, Prato.
BAÑEZ, D., (1604), *Commentarii in S Thomam*.
BILLUART, C., (1757), *Commentarii in S Thomam*.
BUCCERONI, J., *Institutiones theologiae moralis*, Rome.
BUSEMBAUM, H., (1668), *Medulla theologiae moralis*.
CAJETAN, Card., (1534), *Summula casuum; in Summam S Thomae*.
CARAMUEL, (1682), Opera.
CARDENAS, J. DE, (1684), *Crisis theologica*.
COMITOLUS, P., (1626), *Responsa moralia*.
CONCINA, D., (1756), *Theologia Christiana*.
DIANA, A., (1663), *Resolutiones morales*.
ESCOBAR, A., (1669), *Universa theologia moralis*.
FERRARIS, L., (1670), *Prompta bibliotheca*.
GONZALEZ, T., (1705), *Tractatus theologicus*.
GURY, P., (1866), *Compendium theologiae moralis*.
ILDEPHONSUS, J. B., (1639), *Commentarii in I-II S Thomae*.
LACROIX, C., (1704), *Theologia moralis*.
LAYMANN, P., (1625), *Theologia moralis*.
LEDESMA, B., (1604), *Summa casuum conscientiae*.

BIBLIOGRAPHY

Lessius, L., (1623), *De Justitia et Jure.*
Lugo, J. de, Card., (1660), *De Justitia; de Poenitentia.*
Lupus, C., (1681), *De antiquitate sententiae probabilis.*
Mayr, A., (1749), *Theologia scholastica.*
Medina, B., (1581), *Expositio in I-II S Thomae.*
Mercorus, J., (1669), *Basis totius theologiae moralis.*
Molina, L., (1600), *De Justitia et Jure.*
Nicole, P., (1695), *Notes to Lettres provinciales; Essais.*
Patuzzi, V., (1769), *Theologia Moralis.*
Rassler, C., (1730), *Norma recti.*
Reginaldus, V., (1623), *Praxis fori poenitentialis.*
Reuter, J., (1762), *Theologia moralis.*
Salmanticenses, *Cursus theologiae moralis.*
Salon, M., (1620), *De Justitia.*
Sanchez, T., (1610), *Disputationes de matrimonio.*
Sayrus, G., (1602), *Clavis regia.*
Suarez, F., (1617), Opera, Vives, Paris.
Tamburini, T., (1675), *Theologia moralis.*
Terillus, A., (1676), *De conscientia probabili; regula morum.*
Vasquez, G., (1604), *Commentarii in S Thomam.*
Villien, A., *Histoire des Commandements de l'Église*, Paris, 1909.
Viva, D., (1710), *Trutina theologica.*
Wernz, F. X., *Jus Decretalium*, Rome.
Zech, F. X., *Rigor moderatus circa usuras.*

INDEX

ABDUCTION, impediment of marriage, ii, 231
Abortion, i, 201; penalty, ii, 280
Absolution, of sin, ii, 147; of reserved cases, 159; in urgent cases, *ib.*; of censures, 257
Abstinence, i, 360; who bound to, *ib.*; dispensation from, 361
Acceptation or respect of persons, i, 250
Accession, i, 244
Act, human, i, 1; elicited, 3; commanded, *ib.*; external, *ib.*, 20; ii, 140
Acta Apostolicæ Sedis, i, 48
Actions, good, i, 1, 26; bad, *ib.*; indifferent, 1, 20, 52; valid and invalid, 1; voluntary, 5; meritorious, 26
A cunctis (prayer), i, 358
Administrator of will, i, 320
Adoption, impediment of marriage, ii, 221; in English law, *ib.*
Adult and Baptism, ii, 79
Adultery, sin, i, 212; impediment of marriage, ii, 226
Advocate, ii, 5; and client, *ib.*; and matrimonial causes in civil court, *ib.*; fees of, 6; and poor, *ib.*
Affinity, ii, 220; multiplied, *ib.*
Age and marriage, ii, 216; in English law, *ib.*
Agency, i, 344; duties in, *ib.*; liability in, 345; determined, 346; and clerics, ii, 22
Agents provocateurs, i, 131
Alienation of Church property, i, 235; ii, 281
Alluvion, i, 245
Almsgiving, i, 123; how much to be given, 124; gravity of obligation, 125

Altar, for Mass, ii, 119; portable *ib.*; when desecrated, 120
Altum dominium of Church property, i, 235
Ambition, i, 98
Amendment, purpose of, ii, 136; qualities of, *ib.*
Anger, i, 100
Animals, property in, i, 241
Antonelli, i, 202
Apostasy, i, 112; penalty, ii, 270; from religion, 280
Approbation for confessors, ii, 153, 154
Arbitrators, ii, 4; and civil law, cf. Can. 1930
Astrology, *see* Divination
Attention, in Mass, i, 172; in divine Office, ii, 20; in minister of sacraments, 61
Attrition, i, 16; ii, 132
Auction, i, 336
Augury, *see* Divination
Austin and legal obligation, i, 80
Avarice, *see* Covetousness

Backbiting, i, 284
Bailment, i, 341
Bankrupt and debts, i, 277; and discharge, 282
Banns of marriage, ii, 197; obligation imposed by, 198; dispensation from, *ib.*; impediment discovered by, *ib.*; and mixed marriage, 199
Baptism, ii, 75; effects of, *ib.*; necessity of, *ib.*; of desire and of blood, 76; matter and form of, 77; minister of, 78; ceremonies in, *ib.*; place of, 79; and adults, *ib.*; sponsors in, 81; subject of, 83; of fœtus, 84; of convert. *ib.*

Benefice, fruits of, i, 236; what, ii, 25
Bequest to pious causes, i, 317
Bestialitas, i, 218
Bet, i, 354
Betrothal, ii, 189; form of, *ib.*; conditional, 191; effects of, 192; consent of parents to, *ib.*; dissolved, 194; no action for breach of, in ecclesiastical court, 196
Bigamy and irregularity, ii, 290
Bishops, legislators, i, 51; and papal law, 58; can dispense, 71, 156; ii, 238; special duties of, ii, 27
Blackstone and legal obligation, i, 80
Blasphemy, i, 155
Boasting, i, 99
Bona vacantia, i, 243
Books, forbidden, i, 133, ii, 271
Booty in war, i, 208
Breviary, ii, 17; obligation of, *ib.*; Roman, 18; and calendar, *ib.*; order in, *ib.*; vocal prayer, 19; intention and attention in, 20; what excuses from, 21
Bulla cruciata, i, 72
Burial, ecclesiastical, ii, 266; who refused, *ib.*

Cabalistic signs, i, 144
Caesarian section, i, 202; ii, 85
Calumny, i, 286
Candles for Mass, ii, 121
Canons, duties of, ii, 29; in England, *ib.*
Capellman, i, 201
Capital and money, i, 323
Capital punishment, i, 196; belongs to State, 197
Carriers, i, 342
Cassel, Dr. G., i, 322, 325
Catholics, duties of, to ecclesiastical superiors, i, 192
Celibacy of clergy, ii, 13
Censures, ii, 253; conditions for incurring, 254; who inflicts, 255; when multiplied, 256; and ignorance, *ib.*; absolution of, 257; kinds of, 259; special, 268
Ceremonies in administering sacraments, ii, 68; in Baptism, 78

Chalice for Mass, ii, 121
Character in sacraments, ii, 55; in Baptism, 75; in Confirmation, 87; in Orders, 183
Charity, i, 115; when of obligation, 116; well ordered, 117; order of, 119; due to enemies, 120
Charms, i, 144
Chastity, ii, 49; vow of, *ib.*
Children, duties of, i, 176; when bound to support parents, 177; when emancipated, *ib.*; brought up as Protestants, ii, 278
Chiromancy, *see* Divination
Choice, 2
Chrism, in Baptism, ii, 78; in Confirmation, 87
Church (corporation), right to own property, i, 234
Church, (building), pollution of, ii, 119; reconciliation of, 120; desecration of, *ib.*
Circumstances, source of morality, i, 25; aggravating, 26; in confession, ii, 139
Clandestinity and marriage, ii, 232; present law of, 233; who subject to law of, 234
Clerics, property of, i, 236; special duties of, ii, 11; sanctity of, *ib.*; celibacy of, 13; dress of, 15; what forbidden to, 22; women servants of, *ib.*; and theatres, 23; and trading, *ib.*; incardination of, 34; and secret sin, 35; conditions for reception into seminary, 36; presuming to marry, 277
Codicil, i, 316
Collectivism, i, 229
Communicatio in sacris, i, 109
Communion, Easter, i, 365; refused to whom, ii, 68, 102; before marriage, 69; age for, 101; frequent, *ib.*; fasting, 103
Complicis absolutio, ii, 163; quis complex, 164; in articulo mortis, *ib.*
Conception, preventing, i, 201
Concupiscence, i, 13; antecedent and consequent, 14; neutrality under assaults of, 15

INDEX

Confession, annual, i, 363; before Communion, ii, 102; in Penance, 138; integrity of, 139; general, 142; seal of, 174
Confessor, in state of sin, ii, 65; of religious, 153; of nuns, 154; as spiritual father, 165; physician, 166; counsellor, 168; judge, 170; mistakes of, 172
Confirmation, matter and form of, ii, 87; minister of, 89; subject of, 90; sponsor in, *ib.*; may not be neglected, *ib.*
Congregations, Roman, power of, i, 51; of Sacred Rites, *ib.*
Consanguinity, ii, 218; in English law, 219; multiplied, *ib.*
Conscience, i, 29; divisions, *ib.*; binds in name of God, 32; doubtful, 34; probable, 37; and civil law, 79
Consent, i, 3; to injustice, 270; in contracts, 300; in marriage, ii, 201
Conspiracy in injustice, i, 271
Contract, and law of place, i, 57; nature of, 297; divisions, *ib.*; formal, 298; in canon and civil law, 299; and consent, 300; and mistake, 301; and misrepresentation, 302; and duress, *ib.*; undue influence, *ib.*; capacity of parties, 303; matter of, 305; consideration in, 308; discharge of, 309; of marriage, ii, 200
Contrition, ii, 132; qualities of, 133
Contumacy and censures, ii, 254
Contumely, i, 101, 289
Convert, and Baptism, ii, 84; and confession, 128
Convict and contracts, i, 304
Co-operation, in another's sin, i, 132; in injustice, 269; by counsel, *ib.*; by command, 270; by consent, *ib.*; by provocation, praise, or flattery, 271; as partner, *ib.*; by silence or defence, 272
Copyright, i, 227
"Corners," i, 339
Corporations, right to form, i, 231; to own property, *ib.*; contracts of, 304
Corpus juris, i, 75
Covetousness, i, 99
Craniotomy, i, 202
Creditor, secured, i, 278; preferred, *ib.*
Cremation and will, i, 319; forbidden by Church, *ib.*, ii, 267
Crime, impediment of marriage, ii, 226; adultery, *ib.*; murder, 227; adultery and murder, 228; and ignorance, *ib.*
Criminal assault, i, 213
Criminal, obligations of, ii, 7
Crystal-gazing, i, 143
Cunningham, Dr. W., i, 324
Curates, ii, 33; duties of, *ib.*
Cursing, i, 157
Custom, i, 67; qualities of, 68; abrogation of, *ib.*

Damnification, i, 255, 262
Dancing, i, 134
Debt, barred by time, i, 79; priority, 277; of deceased, 277; in marriage, ii, 248
Decalogue, i, 135
Defects, in things sold, i, 328; in betrothal, ii, 195
Defendant, ii, 7; when interrogated, *ib.*
Degradation, ii, 266
Denunciation, i, 127
Deposit, i, 341; and religious poverty, ii, 48
Deposition, ii, 266
Desire, i, 94
Despair, i, 113
Detraction, i, 286; making known secret sin of another not always wrong, 287; listening to, 288
Difference of religion, ii, 223, 225; and baptized non-Catholics, 226
Discharge of bankrupt, i, 282
Disparitas cultus, see Difference of religion
Dispensation, i, 70; who can dispense, *ib.*; interpretation of, 72; ceases, *ib.*; from abstinence, 361; from fasting, 362; from banns, ii, 198; from impediments of marriage, 238;

canonical reasons for, 241 ff.; petition for, 243; *in forma commissoria*, 244; *in forma gratiosa*, 245; how executed, *ib.*
Divine Office, *see* Breviary
Divine right, i, 59
Divining-rod, i, 143
Divorce, ii, 206; and civil courts, 208
Doctor, duties of, ii, 9; and safe remedies, *ib.*; and Baptism, 10
Domicile and quasi-domicile, i, 56
Doubt, i, 34; sin to act in, *ib.*; how to act in, 35
Dower, of widow, i, 233; of benefice, ii, 25
Dreams, i, 142
Drunkenness, i, 103; sins committed in, *ib.*
Duelling, i, 204; penalty of, *ib.*; illegal, 205; censure on, ii, 277
Duress, i, 17; in contracts, 302

Earnest to bind contract, i, 327
Education of child, i, 179; in Catholic school, 180; ii, 278
Effect of sin and confession, ii, 140
Emancipation of minor, i, 178, 232
Embryotomy, i, 202
Employers' liability, i, 188
Enclosure, religious, ii, 50, 275
End, of man, i, 1; does not justify bad means, 8, 24, 202; source of morality, 22
Enemies, to be loved, i, 120; reconciliation of, 121
Engagement, *see* Betrothal
Envy, i, 101
Epieikeia, i, 63
Equity, *see Epieikeia*
Error, distinguished from ignorance, i, 11; in contract, 301; in marriage, ii, 228
Estate, i, 225
Eucharist, ii, 91; as sacrament, effects of, 92; matter and form of, 93; minister of, 96; reservation of, 98; necessity of, 100; dispositions for receiving, 102; penalty for abusing, ii, 269. *See* Mass

Euthanasia, i, 104
Evil effect when imputed, i, 6, 8; gravity of malice, 9
Excommunicates tolerated or not, ii, 259
Excommunication, ii, 259; of those to be avoided or tolerated, *ib.*; effects of, 260; irregularity from violating, 261; special, 269 ff.
Executor of will, i, 319; duties of, *ib.*
Exemption of Regulars, i, 57, 82
Extreme Unction, ii, 179; effects of, *ib.*; matter and form of, 180; minister of, 181; recipient of, 182; obligation to administer, *ib.*

Faith, i, 105; necessity of, *ib.*; when of obligation, 107; external profession of, 108
Fare on railway, i, 252
Fasting, i, 361; who bound to, 362; who excused, *ib.*; before Communion, ii, 103
Fault, theological and juridical, i, 262 f.
Fear, i, 16; divisions, *ib.*; effect of, on voluntary actions, *ib.*; on positive law, 17; impediment of marriage, ii, 229; how purged, 230
Finding, title to property, i, 243
Firm, i, 347; liability of, *ib.*
Fixtures, i, 350
Flattery, i, 271
Form, in sacraments, ii, 57; change in, 58. *See* under name of each sacrament
Fornication intrinsically wrong, i, 212
Fraternal correction, i, 126; when of obligation, *ib.*; order in, 127; and paternal correction, *ib.*; of material sin, 128
Fraudulent preference in bankruptcy, i, 278, 279
Freemasons excommunicated, ii, 274
Freewill, i, 2
Fruition, i, 3
Fruits, natural, industrial, civil, i, 245; whose property, 256

INDEX

Fungible, i, 321; and money, 322
"Futures," i, 355

Gambling or gaming, i, 353; forbidden to clerics, *ib.*, ii, 22
Gift, i, 314; *inter vivos* and *mortis causa*, *ib.*
Gluttony, i, 102
God's name, irreverent use of, i, 154
Grace, *ex opere operato*, ii, 54; sacramental, 55
Guardians of minors, i, 183

Hatred of abomination and enmity, i, 121
Hereditary taint, i, 14
Heresy, i, 111; a crime, 112; penalty of, ii, 270
Heretics, subject to Church, i, 55; disputes with, 109; communication in rites of, *ib.*; formal and material, 112; reception into Church, *ib.*; excommunicated, ii, 270
Hiring, i, 342
Holidays of obligation, i, 357
Homicide, when justifiable, i, 198; in defence of another, 199; and irregularity, ii, 291
Honestas publica, *see* Public Propriety
Hope, i, 113
Humility, i, 98
Hunting forbidden to clerics, ii, 22
Husband, bound to support wife, i, 185; and step-children, 182, 185
Hypnotism, i, 145
Hypocrisy, i, 99

Idolatry, i, 141
Ignorance, i, 11; divisions, *ib.*; when sinful, 13; excuses from penalty, 77; and reserved cases, ii, 158; and irregularity, 288
Illegitimates, and parents, i, 182; and irregularity, ii, 289
Illusions, i, 14, n.
Imbecility, impediment of marriage, ii, 229
Immunity, *see* Privilege

Impediment, of Orders, ii, 288; of marriage, ii, 210; prohibitory and diriment, *ib.*; who bound by, *ib.*; prohibitory, 212; dispensation from, 213, 238; doubtful, 236; of minor degree, 240. *See* under name of each
Imperfection, i, 83
Impotence, ii, 215
Impurity, nature of, 209; malice of, 210; indirectly voluntary, *ib.*; consummated sins of, 212; non-consummated sins of, 219
Incest, i, 211; and confession, ii, 141
Indulgences, selling, ii, 274; nature of, 293; divisions, 295; conditions for gaining, 296; applicable to holy souls, 299
Infidelity, i, 111
Inheritance, i, 232
Injury, i, 251; divisions, *ib.*; requires restitution, 255
Injustice, i, 250; modes of co-operation in, 269
Innocent, killing of, i, 200
Insurance, i, 351; kinds of, *ib.*
Intention, i, 3; does not change nature of external action, 24, 264; of God's glory, 27; in saying Breviary, ii, 20; in minister of sacraments, 62; in reception of sacraments, 72; in applying Mass, 108; for indulgences, 296
Interdict, ii, 264; violation of, entails irregularity, 265; special, 285
Interest, i, 324
Interpretation of law, i, 62
Interstices in Orders, ii, 187
Intestacy, i, 319
Irregularity, ii, 287; divisions, *ib.*; and ignorance, 288; from defect, 289; from crime, 291; removal of, 292

Jesuits deny that end justifies means, i, 24, 202, 291
Jubilee, ii, 301
Judge, and bribe, i, 306; ii, 2; duties of, *ib.*; may he condemn

the innocent, *ib.*; and unjust law, 3; civil and matrimonial causes, *ib.*; 209
Jurisdiction, ii, 150; ordinary and delegated, *ib.*; ceases, 151; when Church supplies, 152, 257
Jury, ii, 4
Justice, i, 222; species of, 223, 250; sins against, 250

Kissing, i, 220; malice of, *ib.*

Landlord, i, 350
Law, i, 47; promulgation of, *ib.*; differs from precept, 48; divisions, 49; power of making, 50; subject-matter of, 52; and heroic acts, 53; and internal acts, *ib.*; subjects of, 55; imbeciles and children, *ib.*; drunken people, *ib.*; heretics and schismatics and law of Church, *ib.*; domicile and quasi-domicile in relation to, 56; strangers, *ib.*; acceptance of, 58; obligation of, 59; moral, penal, mixed, *ib.*; interpretation of, 62; excused from observing, 65; cessation of, 67; useless, 69; dispensation of, 70; natural, 73; positive divine, 74; ecclesiastical, 75; penal and voiding, 76; civil, 78; formally distinct, 89 f.
Lawyer, and fees, ii, 6; and action for divorce, 209
Laxism, i, 38
Lease, i, 349
Legacy, i, 316; to pious causes, 317
Letters requiring secrecy, i, 296
Liberality, i, 99
Life must be preserved, i, 194
Ligamen, see Previous marriage
Limitation Acts, i, 79, 264
Loan for consumption and for use, i, 321, 341
Lots, casting, i, 143
Lottery, i, 353
Lust, i, 100
Lying, i, 290; malice of, 291; not merely against justice, 292

Magic, i, 144
Malice, subjective and objective, i, 88
Mandate, i, 341
Manslaughter, i, 200
Market overt, i, 257
Marriage, and contracts, i, 303; contract of, ii, 200; a sacrament, *ib.*; rights, 201; and consent, *ib.*; under condition, 202; minister of, 204; matter and form of, *ib.*; and State, *ib.*; where contracted, 205; unity and indissolubility of, 206; ratified, dissolved by Pope and religious profession, *ib.*; and Pauline privilege, 207; and parish registers, 234; dispensations for, 238 ff.; revalidation of, 246; *in radice*, 247; *debitum*, 248; before non-Catholic minister, 278
Martyrdom called baptism of blood, ii, 76
Mass, of precept, i, 169; where to be heard, 171; conditions, 171; excuses from hearing, 172; said in sin, ii, 65; nature of, 106; fruits of, 107; for whom offered, 108; application of, 110 ff.; stipends for, 113; time for, 117; place, 119; requisites, 121; rubrics of, 122
Masters and servants, i, 186
Matter of sacraments, ii, 57; change in, *ib.*; probable, 58. *See* under name of each
Members of Parliament and clerics, ii, 22
Menstrua, i, 217
Mental reservation, i, 292
Merit, i, 46
Military service and clerics, ii, 23
Minister of sacraments, ii, 61; attention of, *ib.*; intention of, 62; ignorance of, 63; faith and holiness of, 64; in sin, 65. *See* under name of each
Minors, and property, i, 231; contracts of, 303; marriage of, ii, 199
Mistake in contract, i, 301; in marriage, ii, 228

INDEX

Mixed marriage, ii, 224; promises in, *ib.*; and negligent Catholics, *ib.*; ceremonies in, 225; banns in, *ib.*; not to be repeated before non-Catholic minister, *ib.*
Money, a fungible, i, 322; as capital, 323
Monopoly, i, 338
Morality, i, 19; norm of, *ib.*; in will, 20; sources of, 21
Morose pleasure, i, 95; in past sins, *ib.*; in the unmarried, 96; in evil as cause of good, *ib.*
Morphia, i, 104
Motus primo-primus, i, 3
Murder, i, 200
Mutilation, i, 195
Mutuum, i, 321

Natural acts, i, 4
Necromancy, *see* Divination
Negligence, i, 9; degrees of, 262
Neophyte and Orders, ii, 288
Notary public, ii, 6
Novel-reading, i, 220
Novitiate, who can enter, ii, 41
Nuns, confessor of, ii, 154. *See* Religious
Nuptial blessing, ii, 205

Oath, i, 157; divisions, *ib.*; conditions for, 158; interpretation of, 159; under grave fear, 160; ceases, *ib.*
Obedience, ii, 51; vow of, *ib.*
Object and morality of act, i, 22
Obligation of law, i, 59; kind of, 60; how satisfied, 61
Occasions of sin, i, 60, ii, 168; what to be avoided, *ib.*
Occult compensation, i, 283
Occupation, title to property, i, 242
Offerings of faithful, i, 237; at Easter and Christmas, 240
Oils, kinds of holy, ii, 78, 87
Omission, sin of, i, 9
Onanism, ii, 249
Opinion, i, 38; divisions, *ib.*
"Options," i, 355
Ordeal, i, 146
Orders, ii, 183; minister of, 185; subject of, 186; interstices in, 187; and marriage, 222

Ovaries, removal of, and marriage, ii, 215
Ownership, i, 225; absolute and qualified, *ib.*; objects of, 226; and vow of poverty, ii, 45

Parent, duty of, i, 179; authority over child, 181; and child's property, *ib.*; and illegitimate child, 182; child's Catholic education, ii, 278
Parish priests, not legislators, i, 51; can dispense, 71; who are, ii, 30; duties of, 31; and marriage, 233; marriage dispensations, 239
Parochial system, ii, 30
Partner in injustice, i, 271
Partnership, i, 347; dissolved, 348
Passion and sin, i, 14
Pastors, support of, i, 366
Patriotism, i, 176, 193
Patron saint, i, 358
Pauline privilege, ii, 207
Pawnbrokers, i, 342
Peculium of religious, ii, 48
Penalty, when incurred, i, 77; ecclesiastical, ii, 266
Penance, virtue of, ii, 125; sacrament, 126; necessary, 127; matter of, 128; and doubtful sins, 130; unformed, 135; form of, 147; minister of, 149
Peregrini, *see* Strangers
Perjury, i, 158
Perpetuities, rule against, i, 317
Picketing in strike, i, 275
Planchette, i, 143
Pleasure as motive not sinful, i, 25
Pledge, i, 342
Poaching, i, 244
Policy in insurance, i, 351
Pollutio, i, 215; in somno, 216; apud mulieres, *ib.*; apud impuberes, 217; frequens ex causa levi, *ib.*
Pollution of church, ii, 119
Poor, alms due to, i, 123; spiritual ministrations not to be refused to, 367
Pope, legislator, i, 50; dispensing power of, 70; Constitutions of, 76; supreme administrator of Church property, 235

Porro, operation, i, 203
Possession, principle of, i, 35
Possessor, in good faith, i, 256; in bad faith, 259; in doubtful faith, 260
Poverty, religious, ii, 44; solemn and simple vow of, 45; and canon law, 46; sins against, 47
Prayer, divisions, i, 136; obligatory, *ib.*; conditions for being heard, *ib.*; to whom and for whom made, 137; *A cunctis*, 358
Precept, i, 48; of Church, 357
Premium in insurance, i, 351
Prescription, i, 246; conditions for, *ib.*; good faith in, 247; in canon law, 248
Presumption (conjecture), i, 36; (vice), 98, 114
Previous marriage, ii, 216; second marriage in doubt, 217
Price, just, i, 329; in special cases, 330; in monopolies, 339
Pride, i, 97
Priest without charge, ii, 34; and Mass, 36
Principal and agent, i, 344
Principle of double effect, i, 7, 200
Privilege, i, 80; divisions, 81; how interpreted, *ib.*; ceases, *ib.*; of religious, 82; of forum, ii, 272, 275; of canon, 273, 279
Prize, in war, i, 208; got by unjust means, 264
Probable opinion, i, 38; intrinsic and extrinsic, *ib.*, 41; and sacraments, ii, 64
Probabilism, i, 38; and the Church, 40; not the ideal of Christian life, 41; limitation of, 42
Prodigality, i, 99
Profession of faith, i, 108; religious, ii, 43
Prohibition of marriage, ii, 212
Promise, i, 312; ceases to bind, 313
Property, private, i, 128; who may own, 230; and societies, 231; and minors, *ib.*; and married women, 233; of Church, 234; of clerics, 236; title to, 242; in things found, *ib.*; and wild animals, *ib.*
Prosecution, when to be undertaken, ii, 7
Puberty and reserved cases, ii, 157
Public propriety, ii, 222
Pupil, duties of, i, 191
Pusillanimity, i, 98

Quasi-domicile, i, 56
Quasi-parish priest, ii, 30

Rape, i, 211
Raptus, *see* Abduction
Rash judgements, i, 284
Recidivists, ii, 166; how treated, 167
Referee, ii, 4
Reflex principles for forming conscience, i, 35
Regulars, exemption of, i, 82. *See* Religious
Relatives, duties of, i, 183
Relics, worshipped, i, 139; false, *ib.*; ii, 279
Religion, virtue of, i, 135; who may enter, ii, 40; forcing to enter, 281
Religious, contractual capacity of, i, 303; and laws binding clerics, ii, 16; state, 37; duties of, 38; confessors of, 153; presuming to marry, 277, 280
Religious prelates, legislators, i, 51; dispensing power of, 71
Remedies for sin, ii, 166
Reputation, right to, i, 226
Reserved cases, ii, 156; papal cases, *ib.*; Bishops', 157; of religious, *ib.*; and ignorance, 158; reservation ceases, *ib.*; absolution of, 159; occult papal, 274; presuming to absolve from papal, 275
Residence of Bishops, ii, 27; of parish priests, 31
Restitution, i, 255; roots of, *ib.*; for damage done, 262; for spiritual harm, 265; in another kind, 266; in reputation, *ib.*; for wounding, 267; for fornication, *ib.*; for adultery, 268;

INDEX

made to whom, 273; how much, 274; manner of, 279; time and place of, 280; excuses, 281; obligation of confessor, ii, 172
Revenge, i, 100
"Rigging" market, i, 355
Right, i, 224; *in re* and *ad rem, ib.*; inalienable, 251
Rigorism, i, 38
"Rings," i, 339
Rite in reception of sacraments, ii, 74
Robbery, i, 251
Rubrics of Mass, ii, 122
Rule of religious, ii, 38

Sabbath day, i, 169
Sacrament, ii, 53; number, 54; formed and unformed, 55; reviviscence of, *ib.*; of living and dead, 56; matter and form, 57; under condition, 59; minister of, 61; duty of administering, 66; refused to whom, 67; simulation of, 69; recipient of, 71; dispositions for, *ib.*
Sacramentals, ii, 54
Sacred, objects, i, 147; vessels to be handled by clerics, 150
Sacrifice, ii, 106
Sacrilege, i, 147; personal, local, 148; real, 149, 214
Sadness at good, i, 96
Sale, of dangerous or immoral object, i, 133; of another's property, 257; of goods, 327; defects in goods, 328; price, 329; when property passes, 330; title, 331; execution of, 333; of realty, 334; by auction, 336
Satisfaction, in Penance, ii, 144; of obligation, 145; commutation of, 146
Scandal, i, 129; passive, to be avoided, 131
Scapulars, i, 140
Schismatics, and sacraments, ii, 70, 73; excommunicated, 270
Schoolmasters, i, 191
Schools, non-Catholic, i, 180; ii, 278
Scrupulous conscience, i, 43; causes of, 44; remedies, *ib.*

Seal of confession, ii, 174; penalty for violating, *ib.*, 270; who bound by, 175; broken directly or indirectly, 176
Secret commissions, i, 345
Secrets, i, 294; cease to bind, 295; privileged, 296
Separation *a toro et mensa*, ii, 208; and civil courts, *ib.*
Servants, duty of, i, 186; and master's property, *ib.*; rights of, 187; contract dissolved, 190
Servile work, i, 174; excuses for, 175
Simony, i, 151; divisions, 152; penalties, 153; ii, 277
Simulation of sacraments, ii, 69
Sin, i, 83; divisions, *ib.*; conditions for, 84; gravity of, 85; venial disposes to mortal, 87; species of, 89; number of, 91; of thought, 94; capital or deadly, 97; guilt and penalty, ii, 293
Slander, i, 286
Slavery, i, 228; impediment of marriage, ii, 229
Sloth, i, 102
Smegma, i, 215
Socialism, *see* Collectivism
Sodomia, i, 217
Soldiers and war, i, 207
Solicitation, malice of, i, 130
Sollicitatio ad turpia, ii, 161; munus Ordinarii, 162; munus confessarii, 163; denuncianda, *ib.*; falsa accusatio, *ib.*, 274; omitting to denounce, 282
Specification, i, 245
Spells, i, 144
Spiritism, i, 143
Spiritual relationship, in Baptism, ii, 81; in Confirmation, 90; and Marriage, 221
Sponsors, in Baptism, ii, 81; in Confirmation, 90
State and labour questions, i, 189
Sterility, ii, 215
Stipends for Mass, i, 153; property of priest, 240; origin of, ii, 113; law regarding, *ib.*; manual and funded, 114; registers of, 116

INDEX

Stole fees, not simony, i, 153; whose property, 240
Stolen goods, and sale, i, 157; receiver of, 271
Strangers, and law, i, 56; and Baptism, ii, 78; and reservation, 158
Strikes, i, 189 f.; picketing in, 275
Stuprum, see Criminal assault
Suicide, i, 194; indirect, 195
Sunday to be kept holy, i, 169, 357; servile work, 174; trading on, 175; and English law, *ib.*
Supernatural acts, i, 4
Superstition, i, 140 ff.
" Superstitious uses," i, 317
Surety and clerics, ii, 22
Surgery and medical practice forbidden to clerics, ii, 22, 291
Suspension, ii, 262; *ex informata conscientia*, *ib.*; violated, entails irregularity, 263; special, 283
Suspicion, i, 34, 284

Table-turning, i, 143
Tempting God, i, 146
Tenant's, improvements, i, 245; duties, 350
Ten commandments, see Decalogue
Theatre-going, i, 134; and clerics, ii, 23
Theft, of sacred object, i, 149; in general, 252; grave matter, 253; small thefts, 254; of what is specially valued, *ib.*
Theological virtues, i, 105 ff.
Title to property, i, 242; by occupation, *ib.*; accession, 244; prescription, 246
Tonsure, ii, 15
Trading forbidden to clerics, ii, 23
Treasure of Church in indulgences, ii, 294
Treasure-trove, i, 243
Trusts, and bequests, i, 317; and combines, 340
Truth, right to, i, 292; requirements of, 293

Undue influence, i, 302
University, non-Catholic, i, 180
Use, i, 3; and custom, 67
Usury, i, 322; and Church, 323; and modern times, 324

Vagi, i, 57
Vainglory, i, 99
Value, i, 321
Vendors and purchasers, i, 334
Vengeance belongs to public authority, i, 100, 198
Vestments for Mass, ii, 121
Vicarii co-operatores, see Curates
Violence, i, 17; impediment of marriage, ii, 229
Visitation of diocese, ii, 27
Vocation to priesthood, ii, 35; to religion, 40
Voluntary actions, i, 5; divisions, *ib.*; obstacles to, 11
Vote at elections, i, 193
Vow, violation of, a sacrilege, i, 148; nature of, 161; divisions, *ib.*; mistake in, 162; fear, *ib.*; who bound by, 163; ceases, 164; annulling of, *ib.*; dispensation from, 165; reserved, 166; chastity commuted, 167; commutation of, *ib.*; of religion, ii, 38; of poverty, 44; of chastity, 49; of obedience, 51; and marriage, 213, 222, 277, 280

Wage of workmen, i, 188
Wager, see Bet
War, i, 206; conditions for just, *ib.*; what allowed in, 207; restitution for unjust, 275
Warranty, i, 327
Wife, duties of, i, 185
Will, i, 315; whence power to dispose by, *ib.*; form of, *ib.*; and canon law, 318; who may make, *ib.*; and undue influence, *ib.*; and legitim, *ib.*; when revoked, *ib.*; executor of, 319; probate of, *ib.*
Witchcraft, i, 144
Witness, duties of, ii, 8
Worship, i, 135, 138; kinds of, *ib.*; and Church, *ib.*

Made in the USA
Middletown, DE
18 November 2014